# POLITICAL MONEY
## *Deregulating American Politics*

*The Hoover Institution*
*gratefully acknowledges generous support from*

TAD AND DIANNE TAUBE
TAUBE FAMILY FOUNDATION
KORET FOUNDATION

*Founders of the Program on*
*American Institutions and Economic Performance*

*and Cornerstone gifts from*

SARAH SCAIFE FOUNDATION

# POLITICAL MONEY
## Deregulating American Politics

SELECTED WRITINGS ON CAMPAIGN FINANCE REFORM

*Edited by*
## Annelise Anderson

HOOVER INSTITUTION PRESS
Stanford University   Stanford, California

www.hoover.org

Hoover Institution Press Publication No. 459

First printing, 2000
05   04   03   02   01   00        9   8   7   6   5   4   3   2   1

Manufactured in the United States of America

The paper used in this publication meets the minimum requirements
of American National Standard for Information Sciences—Permanence
of Paper for Printed Library Materials, ANSI Z39.48–1984. ∞

Library of Congress Cataloging-in-Publication Data
Political money : deregulating American politics, selected writings on
campaign finance reform / edited by Annelise Anderson.
        p.      cm.
    Includes bibliographical references and index.
    ISBN 0-8179-9672-9 (alk. paper)
    1. Campaign funds—United States.    2. Campaign funds—Law and
legislation—United States.    I. Anderson, Annelise Graebner.
JK1991 .P59   2000
324.7′8′0973—dc21                                          00-021268

# Contents

# About the Contributors

FLOYD ABRAMS is a partner in a law firm and a contributor to the Democratic Party and its candidates.

MICHAEL PATRICK ALLEN is a professor of sociology at Washington State University.

ANNELISE ANDERSON is a senior research fellow at the Hoover Institution, Stanford University. She has written on a variety of public policy issues and is a former associate director of the federal Office of Management and Budget.

MARTIN ANDERSON is a senior fellow at the Hoover Institution, Stanford University, and the author of books and articles on public policy. He served as assistant to the president for domestic policy in the first Reagan administration.

TOM BETHELL is a journalist, commentator, and the author of several books, the latest of which is *The Noblest Triumph* (St. Martin's Press).

PHILLIP BROYLES is an assistant professor of sociology and a fellow of the Center for Applied Research and Policy Analysis at Shippensburg University. His research focuses on social and political inequality.

BOBBY R. BURCHFIELD is a partner in the law firm of Covington and Burling.

WARREN BURGER is retired chief justice of the Supreme Court.

JOHN T. DOOLITTLE is a Republican from California and a member of the House of Representatives.

PETE DU PONT is a former governor of Delaware and policy chairman of National Center for Policy Analysis.

WILLIAMSON M. EVERS is a research fellow at the Hoover Institution, Stanford University, and teaches political science at Santa Clara University.

RUSSELL D. FEINGOLD is a Democrat from Wisconsin and a member of the Senate.

STEVE FORBES is editor in chief of *Forbes* and was a presidential candidate in the 1996 and 2000 races.

DAVID FRUM is a contributing editor to the *Weekly Standard*.

MEG GREENFIELD edited the *Washington Post* editorial page for twenty years and was a columnist for *Newsweek*. She died May 13, 1999.

CHARLES KRAUTHAMMER is a columnist for the *Washington Post* and a television commentator. He won the Pulitzer Prize for distinguished commentary in 1987.

DAN MANATT is the assistant editor of the new web site Recent Developments in Campaign Finance Reform.

JOHN MCCAIN is a Republican from Arizona and a member of the Senate.

MITCH MCCONNELL is a Republican from Kentucky and a member of the Senate. He chairs the National Republican Senatorial Committee.

THOMAS E. MANN is a partner in a Washington law firm.

DAVID MASON is a former senior fellow at the Heritage Foundation and currently a member of the Federal Election Commission.

TREVOR POTTER is a partner in a Washington law firm and a former member and chairman of the Federal Election Commission.

JONATHAN RAUCH is a senior writer and columnist for *National Journal* magazine, a weekly on politics and government published in Washington, D.C. He is the author of three books—most recently, *Demosclerosis: The Silent Killer of American Government* (1994)—and a graduate of Yale University.

LARRY J. SABATO is a professor of political science at the University of Virginia and the author of several books on the American political process.

ROBERT J. SAMUELSON is a columnist for *Newsweek*.

BRADLEY A. SMITH is an associate professor at Capital University Law School in Columbus, Ohio, and a graduate of Harvard Law School. He has published numerous scholarly articles on campaign finance reform and election law.

FRANK J. SORAUF is a distinguished political scientist recently retired from the University of Minnesota. He has written widely on the U.S. political system and political campaigns.

DAVID STROTHER is a syndicated columnist and television commentator.

# Introduction

Annelise Anderson

Campaign finance reform has been an issue on the American political agenda for several years. Legislation mandating reform failed to pass again in the fall of 1999. This issue will continue to be with us because Americans are concerned about the political system—whether there is too much money in campaigns and whether the need to raise money to run effective campaigns subverts the political process, occupying too much time and effort of candidates and making them beholden to contributors.

At the core of campaign finance reform is the issue of freedom of speech and freedom of association versus censorship of political speech by the government. Censorship is a word proponents of further regulation do not like to use, but all so-called reforms involve additional restrictions on contributions or spending or both. This control of resources is the method of censorship most commonly used by modern governments.

Current law regulates the amounts individuals and the associations in which they participate—political action committees—can donate to federal campaigns. Many states also have such limitations. Spending is limited in presidential elections if candidates choose to accept federal funds. The current morass of rules and regulations is the result of the 1974 Federal Election Campaign Act and various amendments, Supreme Court decisions relating to this act, and efforts to find legitimate ways around specific restrictions, most prominently contributions to political parties for purposes more general than the specific support of a candidate and expenditures made by individuals and organizations independent of the candidate.

The Supreme Court's decisions are central to the debate. The Court rejected all but voluntary spending limitations as a restriction on freedom of speech, including spending by candidates themselves. Thus a wealthy candidate can spend a fortune on his or her own campaign but not contribute those funds in support of a chosen candidate. The Court left in place, however, limits on contributions, on the grounds that the government had a legitimate role in controlling corruption and the appearance of corruption. Contribution limits were upheld with the court's January 2000 decision in a case challenging a state law limiting contributions.

Although Supreme Court decisions have thus far protected freedom of speech and explicitly stated that the people, not the government, must decide how much is appropriate to spend on elections, we cannot indefinitely depend on the Court to protect freedoms that we do not ourselves understand and support. Attempts have been made to amend the Constitution to give the U.S. Congress the power to regulate campaign contributions and spending. The latest attempt failed resoundingly in the Senate; even the senators who wrote the proposed legislation voted against it.

Public opinion polls reflect support for added government control, possibly because both the print and the television media have beaten their drums for so-called reform and claimed that its failure to pass is merely the result of craven self-interest. But the media has its own self-interest: its power would increase if the money candidates could raise and spend to communicate directly with the electorate were limited.

Allowing government to decide how much can be spent by candidates for public office will have important ramifications for our political future. This book is a collection of selected articles and essays that I hope will let readers reach an informed and independent conclusion of the issues involved. It includes articles by experts on the American political process, selections from decisions of the Supreme Court, shorter pieces by a variety of commentators, and speeches and articles by politicians prominently involved in the debate. Several authors support further restrictions—what most call reform—but because the media reporting and editorializing has been so one-sided, the majority of the selections attempt to redress the imbalance.

The alternative to increased control proposed in several of the selections is deregulation—getting rid of restrictions on contributions and spending altogether—coupled with prompt and full disclosure. Internet technology makes prompt disclosure possible and inexpensive. Proponents of regulation object that people are not capable of monitoring contributions, absorbing the information, or making decisions about it, even though the information would be widely available to individuals, organizations, campaign opponents, and the media in an easy-to-analyze form. This view expresses a distrust of the people's ability to make judgments about their government, those they want to elect, and, ultimately, their ability to control their government rather than be controlled by it.

Would deregulation lead to more campaign spending? The amount of money spent in the 1995–96 election cycle on all the primary campaigns and the general election campaigns for federal offices—the U.S. House of Representatives, the Senate, and the presidency—was only about $10 per person of voting age in the country, including the money spent by the national political parties. Another $4 per person was spent independently. The amounts in the 1999–2000 cycle are expected to be a little larger but are still minor, dramatically so when compared with the taxing and expenditures for which our elected officials are responsible. This per-person calculation cuts the ground from under the argument that we spend too much on elections. Under deregulation, direct contributions to candidates would probably increase at the expense of contributions to independent groups and political parties. This shift would increase accountability and make it easier to know where a candidate's money was coming from.

Would deregulation increase the influence of those with money? Supporters of contribution limits argue that the wealthy should have no more influence in the political process than their one-person, one-vote gives them. But the wealthy are diverse in their political preferences.

Although wealth is often considered an advantage of Republicans, private fortunes provided the initial seed money for two Democratic presidential candidates in recent memory, George McGovern and Eugene McCarthy. We might also see fewer campaigns by the very wealthy themselves with their money. Ultimately a candidate's ability to raise money, in small and large amounts, depends on her or his ability to attract the support of the public. Prompt and full disclosure would give us the information essential to making the decision for whom to vote.

# PART ONE

# Articles

These articles are
the work of political
scientists, lawyers,
and economists
analyzing campaign
finance law and its
consequences in the
United States today
and over the past
several decades.

# If It's Not Broken . . . or Is It?

Frank J. Sorauf

This selection was excerpted from *Inside Campaign Finance: Myths and Realities* (New Haven: Yale University Press, 1992). In this article, Frank J. Sorauf, a distinguished political scientist recently retired from the University of Minnesota, looks at the influence of money in campaigns. Does money buy votes in legislatures? Does it determine who gets elected? Are the "smart and savvy" evading regulations? Are candidates spending too much money?

Sorauf decries the tendency of journalists to imply that a legislator's vote is the result of a campaign contribution. It is difficult, he notes, to sort out cause and effect even with sophisticated statistical methods when political money, especially money from political action committees (PACs), is the issue. Was the legislative vote the result of contributions that were better called bribes, or did contributors support the candidate because they knew how he or she would vote?

Sorauf concludes from a review of the academic literature that there is "little if any relationship between the money and the votes" and that work by Janet Frenzke, John Wright, and others demonstrates that the influence of PACs on legislative outcomes is greatly exaggerated. The work of other scholars finds increased congressional efforts on behalf of PAC contributors but not necessarily any change in outcomes and some influence at penultimate stages of the process (e.g., committee actions such as amendments to legislation).

The influence of money in winning elections is a different matter. Incumbents have a great advantage because of the assumption that they are likely to win; therefore they get earlier and larger contributions. Sorauf considers the effects on challengers the greatest problem with the 1974 legislation.

He does not, however, consider campaigns too expensive; rather, what is reasonable to spend can be determined from a stipulated typical campaign costing $500,000 to $600,000. Funds in such amounts are hard to raise, and Sorauf therefore concludes that we may be raising too much and at the same time not spending enough.

On a Sunday edition of the *NBC Nightly News* in April 1991, Garrick Utley, the anchor, segued from a report on the state of banking to the next topic: "And while we're on the subject of money, how about politics. Money buys influence. How do you stop it? We'll find out next. Our

focus this evening, money and politics, efforts to curb widespread corruption in state politics. Consider this. During the past 20 years, convictions of state officeholders on federal corruption charges have increased sevenfold. What kind of corruption is there? How can it be
stopped?"[1] Andrea Mitchell, reporting from Washington, continued the
story: "It's becoming a bigger and bigger problem in state government:
the corrupting influence of special interests using their money to grease
the wheels of politics." She then reported on the alleged bribing of
legislators in South Carolina and Arizona. "In state governments around
the country, corruption is rampant. At a minimum, lobbyists' money
buys access and clout. In the worst cases, state legislators are bought
and sold like trading cards." Mitchell finished the essay on money and
politics with an exploration of public funding and opposition to it by
Republicans and incumbents. The final Utley-Mitchell colloquy
amounted to an enthusiastic endorsement of public funding.

It was only a few minutes of network television on a slow news
day—an inordinate proportion of stories on campaign finance appear
on Sunday television or in Monday morning newspapers—but the story
linked two allegations of bribery of state legislators to perfectly legal
campaign finance practices and then tied the two together with a single
solution: public funding of campaigns. One might pass it by if it were
an isolated linking of campaign finance to bribery and other kinds of
illegality, but it is not. In 1986, *Newsweek*, commenting on the indict-
ment of the Wall Street broker Ivan Boesky for illegalities in the financing of corporate takeovers, observed that the Boesky case "follows what
seems a chronic scandal in the defense industry, where virtually all of
the top contractors have been found cheating the government. Washington is awash in PAC money, and presidential crony Michael Deaver
is only the most conspicuous of the capital's influence peddlers.[2] From
that passage, it would not be easy for even an informed citizen to

---

1. This quotation and the ones that follow are from the network "rush transcript" of
the *NBC Nightly News* for Sunday, April 21, 1991.

2. *Newsweek*, December 1, 1986, p. 49.

conclude that PAC contributions were a legal political activity protected by the First Amendment.

Such an opinion-shaping environment does not encourage much dispassionate analysis of the eight election cycles held under the Federal Election Campaign Act (FECA). Campaign finance becomes an indistinguishable part of broader political and social pathologies. The judgment is clear and in a sense simple: most or all campaign contributions are bribes. If contributions are some form of bribery, it follows that the raising of those contributions by public officials is a form of extortion. The judgment is not only negative, it is absolute as well; there are no hard distinctions to make, no need to separate the positive from the negative, the useful from the destructive, the legal from the illegal in campaign finance.

A parallel, if more systematic, point of view exists within academia. One legal scholar, Daniel H. Lowenstein, argues that all transactions in campaign finance are bribes: "It is a significant and politically relevant fact that under our present system of campaign finance, politicians and interest groups engage routinely not in legalized bribery, as is commonly supposed, but in felonious bribery that goes unprosecuted primarily because the crime is so pervasive."[3] Amitai Etzioni in his survey of the ills and wrongs of American politics refers repeatedly to campaign contributions as "legalized corruption."[4]

Such absolute judgments, if unwarranted, will eventually fall of their own weight. They are certainly at variance with American political tradition and both the norms and the words of the FECA. However much one may disagree with the verdicts of corruption, they and the other unflattering assessments of voluntary campaign finance are an unavoidable part of the politics of reform. Indeed, conventional wisdom

3. "Political Bribery and the Intermediate Theory of Politics," *UCLA Law Review* 32 (April 1985): 848. Philip Stern, in *The Best Congress Money Can Buy*, stops just short of that position, noting that "the line between a campaign contribution and a bribe is only, as one senator put it, 'a hair's breadth'" (p. 18).

4. Amitai Etzioni, *Capital Corruption: The New Attack on American Democracy* (New York: Harcourt, Brace, Jovanovich, 1984). See pages 50–57, for example.

sets the agenda of debate over campaign finance, both among the public
and in legislatures. The diverse and even diffuse complaints about the
post-Watergate regime can be reduced to a relatively small number of
core concerns. Heading the agenda are the twin fears that campaign
money buys excessive influence in legislatures and that it determines
who wins or will win public office. Less well articulated but just as
passionately held are two other convictions: that the smart and savvy
are evading the regulatory system and that candidates are spending too
much money in their campaigns. This chapter is devoted to an examination of those four claims.

Progressive-populist myths about the monied interests have been a
century in the making. They cannot and should not lightly be ignored,
as versions of reality or as shapers of political opinion, or as critiques of
the FECA. All of that, however, does not relieve one of the responsibility
to treat them with a measured skepticism.

## THE PURCHASE OF LEGISLATURES

The question of motive haunts every campaign finance system relying
on voluntary contributions. *Why* do they give? When a disclosure system
discloses as much as the American one does about a visible set of
organized givers representing society's major interests, the question rises
to a salience that campaign finance rarely achieves. The answer to it is
beyond dispute; they give to influence governmental decisions. The hard
questions come next: the nature of the influence the contributors seek,
the ways they go about seeking it, and the extent to which they achieve
it.

The debate over the purchase of legislatures is not about generic
contributors. It is about PAC contributors, whether they appear explicitly or are merely implied in such phrases as "the best Congress money
can buy." Their splendid visibility as the organizations of the "special
interests" links them and their contributions to the ongoing, century-
long debates over the three-way alliance of money, organization, and
interest in American politics. Now that PACs increasingly give to secure

legislative access, a strategy in which their ties both to incumbents and to lobbyists are closer, they underscore all the old concerns. We no longer talk of PAC attempts to penetrate electoral politics but of their part in the traditional struggle of interests in American legislatures. Almost imperceptibly, but fundamentally, the debate has shifted from influence in election outcomes to influence over legislative outcomes.

Thanks to the reporting and publicity the FECA forced on candidates, PACs, and parties, the FEC oversees the largest data archive on any system of campaign finance anywhere in the world. Its data are easily accessible, and the "law of available data" has led to a flowering of research on them, both by the scholarly community and by journalists and public interest organizations. Their industriousness has produced works of many genres, but one of the most common—a veritable industry in itself—is the exploration of the PAC-Congress nexus. The variants on the theme, too, are recognizable: the largest PAC contributors to congressional candidates over a cycle or a decade, the major recipients of PAC money in the Congress, the contributions from PACs of one industry to the members of one committee or to supporters of a particular bill or cause, the mounting flow of PAC money from one sector of the economy as its interests are threatened or challenged. Often the investigations have a current stimulus; they are the campaign finance angle on the broader story, say, of the savings and loan crisis, the rewriting of the federal tax code, or the attempt to pass the Brady Bill's restrictions on the sale of handguns.

Such reports share one limiting defect: they establish correlation, not cause. Yes, PACs do largely give money to candidates who will vote the way they want them to; it would be surprising if that were not the case. Contributors contribute to like-minded candidates, just as voters vote for like-minded candidates. That relationship is easy to document, but the harder question remains: do PACs contribute to candidates because they know how they will vote, or do legislators conform to the wishes of PACS that gave money to their campaigns? Does the money follow the votes, or do the votes follow the money? It is a problem in simultaneous cause that seems to move both ways, between one act and another. Any analysis of campaign finance is repeatedly bedeviled by such problems.

If that were not enough, the journalistic evidence suffers because it is anecdotal, focusing on the limited, often dramatic event. Furthermore, the event and the evidence are often chosen to show a relationship, not because they are representative of the full universe of PAC-incumbent exchanges. So the anecdotes are almost invariably of PAC successes in the legislative process. But what of PACs representing interests on "the losing side"? PACs and their parent organizations suffer frequent, even monumental losses. Many of the savings and loan victories were won over the opposition of the banking industry, and the real estate interests absorbed big losses (for instance, limiting real estate investments as tax shelters) in the 1986 revision of the income tax laws, sometimes even at the hands of legislators who had received contributions from the realtors' PAC.

Beyond these failures of design and method are problems of explanatory assumption. Many of the PAC-Congress studies use money and the whole apparatus of campaign finance to the exclusion of other explanations of legislative behavior. If the PACs do "buy" the Congress, if we are to conclude they are major shapers of legislative decisions, what then of the ability of the parties, the president, the voters, the lobbyists, and Washington representatives to shape those same outcomes? And what of the impact of the personal beliefs and attitudes of the members themselves? The PAC of the National Rifle Association, called the Victory Fund, disburses about $4 million each cycle ($4.2 million in 1988) to candidates for the Congress; the NRA budget for Washington lobbying probably exceeds that figure. The NRA also commands the loyal support of 2.8 million members, who focus intently, even solely, on NRA issues in their voting and grassroots lobbying. Some western members of the House believe that the NRA vote in their districts can shift vote totals by close to 5 percent. One does not easily separate out the effects of the NRA in these various systems of influence, but it should at least be evident that its PAC contributions have not made its other political activities superfluous.

Academic scholars, for their part, attack the same questions in more systematic ways. They cannot, however, escape the need to establish correlations and to infer cause from them, nor can they escape the problem of simultaneity in doing so. Using larger bodies of data—large numbers of roll call votes, for instance—and more sophisticated measures of correlation, they generally find little if any relationship between the money and the votes. In research typifying the best of academic analysis, Janet Grenzke studied the contributions of ten of the largest PACs to 172 long-term members of the House in the 1970s and early 1980s. The PACs were involved in a wide range of policy issues, and all had specified earlier a list of House votes they were interested in during the period. Using a two-stage least squares regression to control for the effect of factors other than the contributions—the political composition of the member's district, for example—she specified the hypothesized direction of cause in the simultaneous correlation: from money to votes. In the subsequent analysis Grenzke found little support for the hypothesis that PAC contributions influence the roll call votes of House members.[5]

How does one explain the gap between popular knowledge and academic conclusion? In part it results from the usual popular overestimation of PAC will and capacity. PACs themselves are more realistic about their bargaining position with incumbents than is the general public. They say over and over that they want to support like-minded men and women in public office and that they seek only "access" to legislators, an opportunity to persuade or make a case. Organizationally they are not adapted to greater political ambitions than that, and they

5. Janet M. Grenzke, "PACS and the Congressional Supermarket: The Currency Is Complex," *American Journal of Political Science* 33 (February 1989): 1–24. For another study coming to a similar conclusion, see William P. Welch, "Campaign Contributions and Legislative Voting: Milk Money and Dairy Price Supports," *Western Political Quarterly* 35 (December 1982): 478–95.

have come slowly to realize it. As John Wright concluded in his study of the contributions of five of the country's most affluent PACs,

> The ability of PACs to use their campaign contributions to influence congressional voting is severely constrained by the organizational arrangements through which money is raised. . . . Because money must be raised at a local, grassroots level, local PAC officials, not Washington lobbyists, are primarily responsible for making allocation decisions. Consequently, congressmen who desire contributions must cultivate favorable relationships with local officials, and this arrangement tends to undercut the value of contributions as a bargaining tool for professional lobbyists."[6]

Behind that conclusion lies Wright's finding that contributions from the five PACs increased only marginally the probability that the recipient House members would vote the position of the contributing PAC—would shift, that is, from an expected vote as measured by the liberal-conservative scale of the Americans for Democratic Action (ADA). Ultimately, Wright comes to the conclusion of many other political scientists: "Of the numerous variables that influence the voting behavior of congressmen, the campaign contributions of PACs appear to take effect only infrequently. Only when other cues, such as party, are weak can PAC contributions be expected to be important."[7] In short, what PACs do is a reflection of what they are able to do. The ability, in turn, stems from their own nature and the bargaining position of incumbents in the exchange.

Such conclusions run counter to the conventional wisdom, and like

6. John R. Wright, "PACs, Contributions, and Roll Calls: An Organizational Perspective," *American Political Science Review* 79 ( June 1985): 411. The five PACs are the American Medical PAC, the PAC of the American Bankers Association (BANKPAC), the Realtors PAC, the Associate General Contractors PAC, and DEAC, the PAC of the National Automobile Dealers Association. It may well be that Wright's conclusions about organization apply more forcefully to PACs of large, federated membership organizations than they would to some other PACs; to say that, however, is not to say that other PACs do not have their own particular kinds of organizational imperatives.

7. Ibid., p. 412.

most academic writing on campaign finance, they fail to disturb or dislodge it. The supporters of the conventional wisdom are tireless, and they have a platform. They also have telling testimony from members of Congress that PACs do indeed change votes (always the votes of other members) with their contributions. To be sure, the testimony is notoriously unspecific; most (but not all) of it comes from liberal Democrats, some of it is ex parte or self-justifying, and some of it is little more than sophisticated scapegoating.[8] Still, congressional observations are not easy to dismiss out of hand. Insiders of any kind are at their strongest in arguments on the nature of influence in the legislative process.

The common sense of the word *access* also makes the case for the conventional wisdom. If access is indeed the goal of PAC contributions, will PACs settle merely for the "opportunity to persuade"? Won't they expect success in a certain number of instances? Will they be satisfied with an invitation to the gaming table if they lose every spin of the wheel? Moreover, the nature of influence in a legislative body involves much more than final roll call votes. PACs exert influence at other points in the legislative process—in initiatives not taken, in committee amendments, or in special rules affecting floor consideration. Some academic political scientists, one should add, have long shared reservations about an exclusive reliance on roll calls.

A side-by-side illustration of studies of the PAC-committee connection, one by a public interest group and one by two political scientists, makes many of those points. In 1991 Congress Watch, the "legislative advocacy arm" of Ralph Nader's Public Citizen, studied votes in a subcommittee of the House Banking Committee on proposals and amendments to proposals that would "substantially deregulate the na-

8. After Senator Alan Cranston was found by the Senate Ethics Committee to have engaged in "improper and repugnant behavior" in soliciting funds from Charles Keating, he defended himself on the floor of the Senate by asserting that, had he been forced to defeat a censure motion, he could have cited "example after example of comparable conduct" on the part of fellow senators to show that he had violated no Senate norms. "Cranston Accepts Panel's Reprimand, Offers Defense," *Minneapolis-St. Paul Star Tribune*, November 21, 1991.

tion's banks." In its summary, Congress Watch reports, "On five key votes, the top five recipients of banking PAC money averaged $190,378 in receipts and voted against banking interests only 24 percent of the time. Conversely, the five lawmakers who received the least bank PAC money averaged $35,521 in receipts and voted with consumers and against the banking industry 76 percent of the time."[9] The data suggest that the bank PACs are clearly mixing their contribution strategies and that by and large they give much more money to committee members sympathetic to them. One has no hint, however, of how to unravel the problem of simultaneous cause. Is there anything more here than decisions by a number of bank PACs to contribute to House members who had proven themselves sympathetic to the banks' interests and policy positions?

Political scientists Richard Hall and Frank Wayman begin the report of their research on PAC money and House committees by reconstructing the logic of what PACs seek with their contributions:

> First, we suggest that in looking for the effects of money in Congress, one must look more to the politics of committee decision making than those of the floor. . . . Second, and more importantly, our account of the member-donor exchange leads us to focus on the *participation* of particular members, not on the votes. . . . If money does not necessarily buy votes or change minds, in other words, it can buy members' time. The intended effect is to mobilize bias in congressional committee decision making.[10]

Hall and Wayman focus, therefore, on three House committees and three different issues before them—and on the effects of PAC contri-

9. Congress Watch, *Banking on Influence: Bank PAC Contributions and Subcommittee Votes on Bank Deregulation*, June 17, 1991, p. 1. The quotations earlier in the paragraph are from the title page and p. 1, respectively, of the same report.

10. Richard L. Hall and Frank W. Wayman, "Buying Time: Moneyed Interests and the Mobilization of Bias in Congressional Committees," *American Political Science Review* 84 (September 1990): 797–820 (emphasis in the original). The article has an especially lucid review of the scholarship on the influence of campaign contributions on legislative decisions.

butions to members of the committees. Instead of using votes in committee as the dependent variable, Hall and Wayman construct a measure of various kinds of participation in the business of committees (such as speaking in committee or offering amendments during markup). In each of the three cases they found that PAC contributions had a moderate but significant degree of influence, explaining more than 55 percent of the variance in participation by individual members. PAC money, therefore, mobilized already like-thinking members to more active support of the PACs' interests in committee. Their conclusion about one of the cases applies to all three:

> The more money a supporter received from the dairy PACs and the stronger the member's support, the more likely he or she was to allocate time and effort on the industry's behalf (e.g., work behind the scenes, speak on the group's behalf, attach amendments to the committee vehicle, as well as show up and vote at committee markups). Alternatively, money may have diminished the intensity of the opposition.[11]

Regardless of why the PACs give, they seem to get heightened activity and support from their congressional sympathizers. We are left, however, to speculate about the ultimate results of such support and activity on congressional decisions.

A consensus about PAC influence is emerging among scholars of campaign finance. It is founded on two central conclusions. First, the influence of PAC contributions tends to be strongest on the narrower, less visible issues before the Congress. Members have long called them "free votes," free in that they are liberated from the usually dominant influences of party, district, leadership, and mass opinion. These are the votes available for less influential constituencies (such as contributors)

---

11. Ibid., p. 810. Hall and Wayman also consider the possibility of simultaneous cause, "that in allocating contributions to committee members during the previous election cycle, a group may attempt to anticipate who the principal players will be on issues it cares about" (p. 809). They deal with the problem by estimating their model of participation using the two-stage least squares procedures.

or even for classic legislative logrolling or horse-trading. Second, the influence of contributions can be directed at all the points of access and influence in the legislative process in the Congress. The kinds of policy refinements and strategic maneuvers crafted in committee may be important for specific interests even though they do not involve great issues of policy. The same can be said of many appointments to the courts and to executive agencies. Contributors do not necessarily seek, or even expect, to score impressive policy victories measured by final roll call votes. In the world of reduced expectations in which PACs are forced to live, the smaller accomplishments have to suffice.

The Hall and Wayman findings narrow the gulf between the academy and conventional wisdom, but the gulf remains. In part it results from major disagreements about evidence and authority, about the credibility of participants and observers in the Congress versus the data-based analyses of scholars, and about fundamental questions of what evidence it takes to come to conclusions. In essence, the gulf reflects different wills to believe. Some scholarship, to be sure, but even more journalistic analysis, begins with deeply set convictions, rooted in the Progressive worldview, about the impact of money on public officials. The line between dispositions to believe and foregone conclusions is very thin.

Most durable are the differences across the gulf on analytical issues. One concerns the credibility of the testimony of participants, and even the weight their words carry, vis-à-vis the detailed data of the scholars. Consider Charles Keating as an authority on the question of the influence of the contributor. Keating, a political pariah now, is nonetheless widely quoted as evidence of the effect of money. When asked by a Senate committee whether his contributions influenced senators to take up his causes, Keating replied, "I want to say in the most forceful way I can: I certainly hope so."[12] The conferral of authority here may reflect

---

12. David J. Jefferson, "Keating of American Continental Corp. Comes Out Fighting," *Wall Street Journal*, April 18, 1989.

only the news media's fondness for campaign finance machismo, but it may reflect, too, a disposition to give great weight to the words of participants. The danger of granting authority status to participants—contributors or recipients—is that authority is conferred even on clearly self-serving conclusions merely because the authority's message is useful or congenial.

Beneath the controversies over the conventional wisdoms, there are also great differences over who carries the burden of proof. Scholars will not readily consent to demands that they accept responsibility for proving or disproving an assertion they do not make: the one about PACs buying influence over the making of policy. Nor will they concede that any assertion is valid until it is disproven. Ultimately, however, the debate comes down to the kinds and weight of evidence that will establish the tie between money and votes or other activity in the Congress. One of the greatest strengths of any conventional wisdom is that by definition it is validated by the sheer number of people who subscribe to it. Such validation does not yield easily to the desiccated numbers and equations of empirical social science.

The conventional wisdom is vulnerable also for its assumption that PACs dominate the exchange between contributor and candidate—an analytical predisposition that comes out of the late 1970s. But we now have abundant evidence that the exchange is bilateral rather than unilateral, that candidates have leverage in it, and that the incumbents among them increased that leverage in the 1980s as their reelection rates soared. As PACs have shifted more and more to the support of incumbents, and to the search for access to them, their freedom of action has diminished. Whereas incumbents have organized with increasing effectiveness, PACs have not. Nor have they maintained their ability to enforce expectations. PAC sanctions depend on the value of withdrawn contributions, and since PACs have continued to disperse their contributions widely, the average PAC contribution amounts to well less than one-half of 1 percent of the average House incumbent's receipts in an electoral cycle. Even a major contribution of $5,000 or more accounts for only a few percent of the average candidate's receipts. Consequently, the PAC position in the 1990s is not what it was in the 1970s.

Finally, the countervailing controls of American pluralism constrain even the most determined PACs. Organizations of interests have greatly proliferated since the 1970s. The larger the number of groups (that is, PACs), the greater the offsetting and limiting effect on the political claims of any one of them. The greater the number of PACs making contributions to a specific member of Congress, the greater the likelihood that the claims of one on his or her loyalties will be opposed by the claims of another. In the words of Representative Barney Frank, a Democrat from Massachusetts, "Business PACs invest in incumbents. It's the banks against the thrifts, the insurance companies against the banks, the Wall Street investment banks against the money center commercial banks. There's money any way you vote."[13]

A caveat to that conclusion is, however, in order. The mechanism of offsetting, countervailing group activity probably best fits policy disputes over the larger issues that are part of broader ideological positions—over issues such as Medicaid funding or hazardous waste disposal. The model works less well when the dispute is single-sided, where the activity of one set of interests does not jolt another set of interests, perhaps those of consumers, into action. The nonresponding interests may be too general, too invisible, or of too low a priority to warrant political action. So the hypothesis of countervailing interests meshes well with the conclusion that PACs have their greatest impact on the less visible politics of narrow and particularistic interests in which the conflicts, and thus the controls, of pluralism are not joined.

Critics of Tony Coelho and the DCCC raise an issue with a new twist on the money-votes relationship. If it is in fact true that the money, especially the PAC money, follows the voting records of incumbents, why can't incumbents change the record to lure the money? That, they charge, is exactly what the House Democrats did under Coehlo's lead-

---

13. Quoted in Robert Kuttner, "Ass Backward," *New Republic*, April 22, 1985, p. 22.

ership in the early 1980s. It is true that Democrats began to attract more business money then and that Coelho unabashedly urged the party to do so. It is also true that PACs closely scrutinize the voting records, or "scores," of incumbents. The argument suffers, however, from the monism that haunts the subject: the belief that money explains all. Why the assumption that the Democrats are politically so free to move to the center—that the influence of money rather than the mood of voters governs their political calculus? What, too, about the countervailing influence of other contributors, especially those of organized labor, that fight for a move *away* from the center? Logic and assumptions aside, however, the central factual premise of the argument does not hold up. The ratings of the roll call positions of House members by the AFL-CIO, the U.S. Chamber of Commerce, the Americans for Democratic Action, and the American Conservative Union all give House Democrats collectively a more liberal score in 1990 than they had in 1980.[14]

That an increasingly national "contributor constituency" has entered American electoral politics seems beyond contest. Electoral politics remain local because the constituencies are geographically defined with only one representative and two senators per constituency and because the American political parties have been decentralized and local. Now PACs and other representatives of national interests find a small but measurable additional edge in electoral politics. They increasingly ally themselves with the lobbying of the interests they share, and it becomes increasingly difficult to say whether their victories come through contributing or lobbying. It is far easier to say simply that contributions have become one more limited means among many in the pursuit of policy goals—one more piece of evidence that the localism of American electoral politics is increasingly anomalous. Campaign

---

14. The specific scores of the liberal groups rose: the AFL-CIO score rose from 67 in 1980 to 82 in 1990, the ADA score from 57 to 71. The acceptability scores of the conservative groups dropped in the same span of years; the chamber's score went from 59 to 34, the ACT score from 30 to 20.

finance serves as a shaper of national politics as well as one of its consequences.

## THE PURCHASE OF ELECTIONS

"As a general rule," Benjamin Disraeli once said, "nobody has money who ought to have it."[15] It is precisely on the maldistribution of campaign money, especially the paucity of it in the hands of challengers, that the second great argument of the post-1974 regime centers. After the alleged buying of the Congress, it is the alleged buying of the elections to the Congress that most worries Americans. Many of them are convinced that incumbents are winning reelection at such stunning rates precisely because the incumbents have too much money and their challengers have too little.

The facts are undeniable. Challenger financing has deteriorated in the 1980s by all measures. In 1980 the average House major-party challenger running against an incumbent in the general election spent $100,458 in the entire campaign; by 1990 that figure was only $109,377, and only $54,563 in 1980 dollars. The average incumbent spent $165,509 in 1980 and $399,310 in 1990 ($199,197 in 1980 dollars). Obviously the incumbent-challenger gap was opening; the ratio was 1.6:1 in 1980 but 3.7:1 in 1990. General-election challengers found it increasingly difficult to raise money from PACs; PACs gave them 25.8 percent of their contributions to House candidates in 1980 but only 6.7 percent in 1990. House challengers, in fact, became increasingly dependent on their own resources in the 1980s. Data for 1980 are unavailable, but in 1984 general-election challengers, in a combination of contributions and loans to themselves, accounted for 11 percent of their receipts. By 1990 they provided 19 percent of their receipts; PACs accounted for only 17 percent.

For mass opinion and its shapers, such data lead to an easy conclu-

---

15. The aphorism is cited in Laurence J. Peter, *Peter's Quotations* (New York: Morrow, 1977), but its source is not given.

sion. Incumbents win so often because they outspend their opponents so greatly, and challengers fall to win because they lack the resources with which to mount a winning campaign. For the scholarly community the conclusion does not come as easily, for once again it sees a problem in simultaneous cause. Do candidates win because they spend more money, or do they get more money, and spend it, because they win? The structure of causal problems is much like the problem of simultaneous cause in PAC contributions and policy outcomes in the Congress: is the financial contribution made because of the expectations about the recipient's victory some months hence, or does the contribution buy the campaigning that shapes the election outcome? That is, do underfunded candidates fail because contributors think their fate is sealed months before election day?

The other side of the argument is equally straightforward: challengers lose because they cannot spend enough. It is a fact not only that challengers in the aggregate fail to raise and spend the sums incumbents do but also that the challengers who spend the most collectively win the greater share of the two-party vote. The percentage of challengers' general-election vote rises as they narrow the incumbent-challenger spending ratio or as they increase their dollar spending in the campaign (see table 1).

Before one leaps to the conclusion that incumbents win and challengers lose because of the state of their campaign resources, there are contrary bits of data to reckon with. House incumbents won reelection at rates well above 90 percent long before they established their present funding superiority; the cumulative reelection percentage of House incumbents from 1950 through 1970 was 91.8 percent.[16] Furthermore, the general political strength of incumbents can easily be traced, not to their campaign treasuries but to all the advantages of office they enjoy. The postal frank, their easy access to the media, their district offices,

---

16. That is, 4,064 of 4,428 incumbents seeking reelection were successful. Data from Norman J. Ornstein, Thomas E. Mann, and Michael J. Malbin, *Vital Statistics on Congress, 1989–1990* (Washington, D.C.: Congressional Quarterly Press, 1990), p. 56.

TABLE 1.    Relationship between Challenger Spending and Challenger Vote Share:
            1984–1988

| | MEDIAN GENERAL ELECTION VOTE (%) | | |
| --- | --- | --- | --- |
| | *1984* | *1986* | *1988* |
| *Challenger:Incumbent\* Spending Ratios* | | | |
| Up to 1:3 | 28 | 27 | 27 |
| 1:3 to 1:2 | 36 | 35 | 37 |
| 1:2 to 1:1 | 43 | 41 | 40 |
| 1:1 to 2:1 | 45 | 38 | 43 |
| More than 2:1 | 46 | 41 | 39 |
| *Challenger Total Spending Ranges* | | | |
| Up to $5,000 | 24 | 23 | 24 |
| $5,000 to $25,000 | 27 | 26 | 26 |
| $25,000 to $75,000 | 32 | 30 | 29 |
| $75,000 to $250,000 | 38 | 35 | 36 |
| More than $250,000 | 45 | 43 | 42 |

\*Includes only major-party, general-election House challengers running against an incumbent in the
general election.
SOURCE:  Federal Election Commission.

and their staffs for "servicing" constituents all have grown in recent
decades, at least partly to buttress their reelection chances.[17] Less obviously, perhaps, the growing difference between the receipts and the
expenditures of incumbents—their larger sums of cash on hand—suggests that contributors give to them not to help them win but because
they are going to win, a conviction that accounts for the PACs having
reduced their support of challengers. But all these clues aside, the major
attack on this problem in simultaneity has come in the scholarly work
of Gary Jacobson.

The problem is easily defined. The percentage of the vote the challengers get is related to the sums they spend: the greater the dollars, the
greater the votes. Money and votes are reciprocally related, however,

17. On the use of congressional perquisites for developing constituent support generally,
see Morris A. Fiorina, *Congress: Keystone of the Washington Establishment* (New Haven: Yale
University Press, 1977).

because challengers raise money on expectations about their ability to get votes. So how to show that the spending of challengers actually does affect the size of the vote they get? One way is through the same two-stage least squares procedures Janet Grenzke used to stipulate the direction of cause in the similar problem of the correlation between PAC contributions and the roll call votes of their recipients in Congress. A second is to use poll data to relate incremental changes in spending to incremental changes in probable vote stage by stage during the campaign. Both avenues brought Jacobson to the conclusion that challenger spending did indeed lead to increases in challenger votes.[18]

The dynamic that relates challenger money to challenger votes can then be outlined. Spending money in the campaign buys visibility and greater "likely support" for challengers, which also means that spending results in the rising expectations that enable them to raise even more money. As Jacobson put it, "Candidates are given money according to how well they are expected to do, but campaign expenditures have an independent effect on how well they actually do, because without them, the expectation would not be realized. The process is largely recursive because elite perceptions and strategies determine how much is spent in campaigns, and the level of campaign spending in turn determines how much is known about candidates and therefore how much support they actually receive from voters. Elite expectations about how the vote will go are only fulfilled if they do, in fact, supply enough money to the candidate."[19] The problem, therefore, is that although money would help them greatly, challengers have increasing trouble in raising it in the first place.

The importance of campaign funds for challengers, moreover, was

18. Gary C. Jacobson, *Money in Congressional Elections* (New Haven: Yale University Press, 1980). See also Jacobson's restatement and reconsideration in "Money and Votes Reconsidered: Congressional Elections, 1972–1982," *Public Choice* 34 (1985): 7–62. For another view of the theoretical problem and additional poll data, see Jacobson, "The Effects of Campaign Spending in House Elections: New Evidence for Old Arguments," *American Journal of Political Science* 34 (May 1990): 334–62.

19. Jacobson, *Money in Congressional Elections*, p. 162.

highlighted by Jacobson's conclusion that incumbent spending produced no increase in the incumbent's share of the vote. In fact, the more
incumbents spent, the worse they did—not because their spending lost
them votes, but because they had to spend more when challengers began
to encroach on their electoral margins. Other scholars have challenged
that finding about incumbent spending, and the debate is yet to be
resolved.[20] Nonetheless, few would argue that the effect of incumbent
spending matches that of challenger spending; it seems likely, at least,
that one increment of challenger spending (an extra $25,000 perhaps)
has more effect on voter awareness than does the same increment in
incumbent spending. If the challenger is spending at lower levels than
is the incumbent, challenger spending will also be more efficacious per
increment because of the decreasing marginal utility—the smaller suc-
cessive impact on the vote of each increment—of campaign spending.

Incumbents continue to outspend and then to outpoll their challengers, but to conclude that incumbents "buy" reelection or that spending leads to the margin of victory misstates the problem somewhat.
Incumbents build support in their constituencies largely by virtue of
the perquisites of office and by reason of the visibility and name recognition they routinely achieve. Ultimately the greatest advantage the
incumbents have is not their campaign money; it is the expectation early
in the election cycle that they can and will win reelection. It is that
expectation that makes it so difficult for challengers to raise the money
by which they might effectively overcome the incumbents' advantage
in the campaign and election.

For Americans who value competitiveness in elections, the issue is
of the greatest magnitude. It is simply that the campaign finance system
offers challengers no weapons with which to overcome the advantages
of incumbency. The challengers lack money because the incumbents'
reelection prospects are so strong as to discourage both the emergence

---

20. Contra the Jacobson conclusion, see Donald P. Green and Jonathan S. Krasno,
"Salvation for the Spendthrift Incumbent: Re-estimating the Effects of Campaign Spending
in House Elections," *American Journal of Political Science* 32 (November 1988): 884–907.

of appealing challengers and the willingness of potential contributors to invest in electoral politics. The solution to the problem, therefore, rests either in reducing the advantages of incumbency or in getting money to challengers in time to entice both strong candidates and more contributors. The post-1974 regime faces no greater challenge.

## ARTFUL DODGING AND SKILLFUL AVOIDING

The conventional wisdom is right at last: the regulatory vessel is in fact leaking. Important activity and individuals escape its requirements for reporting, and money flows outside of its controls in swelling torrents. One need only tick off the specifics: bundling, soft money, brokers, independent spending, fund-raisers netting six-figure totals in America's urban centers. However one may wish to describe the structural flaws—as "leaks" or "loopholes"—the integrity of the post-1974 regulatory structure is at grave risk.

The assault on the structure of regulation—the statutorily defined campaign finance system—comes in various ways. There are, first, the actors and the activity in violation of explicit statutory limits. The individuals exceeding the $25,000 annual limit on contributions are the most widely publicized case; ambitious investigators now vie to find new miscreants in the computer records of the FEC. Second are the invisible brokers and transactions that remain only partially within the governance of the system; the money they raise and its origins are reported, but neither their role nor the aggregate sums they organize are. Similar are the formal bundlers, many of whom press the limits of permissible control over contributions. Third are the sums raised and spent outside the limits of the system. Soft money (previously discussed) and independent spending provide the major examples. The 1974 amendments to the FECA set strict limits on the sums of money that groups or citizens could spend independently in a campaign—that is, without the control or even the knowledge of any candidate. Like everything else in the FECA, those provisions have a history. Spending by groups other than the candidates had been the stock device for dodging earlier attempts to control spending and ensure full reporting of all contributions. The Supreme Court, however, struck down those limits in *Buckley v. Valeo*, leaving only the requirement that independent expenditures be reported to the FEC.

Enter John Terrence ("Terry") Dolan, founder and executive director of the National Conservative Political Action Committee (NCPAC). NCPAC surfaced for the first time in the election of 1978, but it became a household acronym in 1980 after spending $3.3 million independently in the presidential and congressional campaigns of that year. It spent $1.1 million of that total to challenge six liberal Democratic senators running for reelection: Birch Bayh of Indiana, Frank Church of Idaho, Alan Cranston of California, John Culver of Iowa, Thomas Eagleton of Missouri, and George McGovern of South Dakota. Bayh, Church, Culver, and McGovern were defeated, and NCPAC boldly took the credit. There were other less arresting explanations for the losses—the Reagan and conservative triumphs of 1980, the growing gulfs between the losers and their conservative constituencies, for example; but they were pallid stuff next to the swashbuckling of NCPAC. A potent new political tactic, independent spending, had arrived.

The post-1974 beginnings of independent spending are obscure. Record keeping at the FEC was in its infancy in 1976, and its data on independent spending in that cycle are incomplete; the best guess is that about $2 million was spent independently, with all but $400,000 spent in the presidential campaign. Another $300,000 or so was spent in the 1978 congressional elections, and then came the eye-grabbing jump to a total of $16.1 million in 1980 (see table 2). NCPAC alone accounted for almost half of the $2.3 million spent independently on congressional races in 1980, and, flushed with the successes of 1980, it exceeded that mark in 1982 with $3.1 million of the $7.1 million spent on races for Congress. NCPAC's dominance ended slowly after that, but independent spending hit its highest level in congressional campaigns in 1986: $9.4 million. By 1990 it had fallen back to a total of $1.8 million in the

TABLE 2.   Independent Spending in Presidential and Congressional Elections:
           1980–1988

| | PRESIDENTIAL | | | CONGRESSIONAL | | |
| Year | Total (in millions of $) | Against Incumbent (in percent) | Republican (in percent) | Total (in millions of $) | Against Incumbent (in percent) | Republican (in percent) |
|---|---|---|---|---|---|---|
| 1980 | $13.75 | 5.9% | 96.6% | $2.34 | 58.9% | 83.9% |
| 1982 | .19 | .8 | 50.2 | 7.10 | 72.5 | 75.9 |
| 1984 | 17.47 | 4.8 | 93.4 | 5.95 | 44.3 | 49.7 |
| 1986 | .84 | 5.4 | 88.9 | 9.36 | 14.2 | 58.9 |
| 1988 | 14.13 | 24.8 | 94.9 | 7.21 | 16.5 | 64.1 |
| 1990 | .50 | 35.1 | 98.0 | 1.77 | 15.7 | 48.6 |

SOURCE: Federal Election Commission.

House and Senate campaigns. Amid all the ups and downs, independent spending has been constant in one way: except for the congressional elections of 1984, it has been consistently pro-Republican, often overwhelmingly so (see table 2). No other kind of spending in all of American campaign finance has so consistently favored one party by such margins.

Even at their zenith, independent expenditures on congressional elections never accounted for major sums. The record $9.4 million in 1986 was only 2 percent of the cash expenditures ($450.3 million) by all candidates in that year's campaigns. Moreover, the effective sums were greatly exaggerated. The splashiest spenders in the 1980s—NCPAC and an assortment of PACs supporting Republican presidential candidates—were PACs without parent organizations, "nonconnected PACs" in the parlance of the FEC. They raised their money in costly direct-mail solicitations; and with no parent to pay overhead, not to mention fund-raising expenses (postage, printing, computerized mailing lists), they had to absorb all of these costs out of the money they raised. Estimates vary, but shrewd and careful reports found that only 5 to 20 percent of their receipts went into campaign activity as it is usually understood—into television or newspaper ads or campaign brochures or mailings. Nevertheless, NCPAC and its siblings systematically overstated their campaigning by reporting solicitation costs as a part of their independent spending because the solicitation letter contained a plea for action in support of or opposition to specific, named candidates.[21]

Such scrupulous reporting to the FEC helped create a myth. The NCPAC millions took headlines in 1980 and 1982, although totals in the hundreds of thousands of dollars might not have. Moreover, NCPAC and Terry Dolan cultivated an image that combined the arts of guerrilla warfare (targeting, hit lists) and a new amoral Machiavellianism. That Dolan should so baldly say that "a group like ours could lie through its teeth and the candidate it helps stays clean" was titillating enough;[22] that it should come from a thirtyish executive director with the youthful looks and seeming innocence of a choir boy made it the stuff of sensation. NCPAC and independent spending merged to create the archetype of a ruthless ideological, single-issue politics.

Although the great ideological PACs dominated independent spending in its palmiest years, they did not monopolize it. A Californian by the name of Michael Goland spent $1.1 million in 1984 to urge the defeat of Illinois senator Charles Percy, a liberal Republican. It was by far the largest sum spent by an individual in the post-1974 regime. Percy got only 48 percent of the vote, losing to Democrat Paul Simon, but even experienced analysts find it hard to assess the impact of the billboards and other ads Goland bought. Closed-mouthed about his political agenda, Goland owns up only to a concern for animal rights and people with disabilities. Goland-watchers add a deep concern for Israel and conservative Republicanism to that list. Goland reappeared in the 1988 campaign, indicted after it was over for making illegal contribu-

---

21. For example, the researches of Michael J. Malbin on the subject are reported in Ronald Brownstein, "On Paper, Conservative PACS Were Tigers in 1984—but Look Again," *National Journal*, June 29, 1985, p. 1504. The rules of the FEC require that letters raising money for a specific candidate or candidates be treated as independent expenditures themselves; it is not clear to me that all of the indirect costs in getting that letter to the reader must also be reported.

22. Quoted in Myra MacPherson, "The New Right Brigade," *Washington Post*, August 10, 1980.

tions of more than $100,000 to an American Independent Party candidate for the U.S. Senate.

It would be wrong to suggest that independent spending has been entirely in the hands of the political buccaneers. By the late 1980s a few large-membership PACs, such as the Realtors PAC and the American Medical PAC, began to spend independently in congressional elections; generally their interventions were in favor of candidates, with only a few smaller PACs making the kind of "negative" expenditures NCPAC had made famous. AMPAC spent $1.6 million on behalf of fourteen congressional candidates in 1986, and the Realtors PAC spent $1.7 on behalf of six; in 1988 the level of spending dropped to $.8 million by AMPAC and $1.3 million by the Realtors PAC. In neither year did either PAC spend a cent to oppose a candidate.

In the mid-1980s, in fact, it seemed that some larger PACs would incorporate such spending into their contribution strategy, putting a second arrow in the quiver. There was even talk of retreating to it if the Congress further restricted PAC contributions. But that prospect faded along with the heyday of NCPAC and its clones. Independent spending created intraorganizational problems for the PACs that tried it; some of their donors either did not approve of it generally or were outraged at the PACs' choice of targets. It also raised the wrath of incumbents, especially when it was spending in favor of challengers, and they quickly learned to ignite voter backlash to it. Indeed, candidates complained even when the spending favored them; none of them wanted any part of what the public sees as their campaigns to be beyond their control.

Those explorations by mainline PACs opened up another issue that had festered for some years: the meaning of independence. How, for instance, could a large PAC making contributions to congressional candidates and discussing their campaigns with them also make independent expenditures in which there was no cooperation or contact with the candidate? Or what of an independently financed media campaign supporting candidate J when the commercials are designed and placed by the same media consultants working for candidate J's campaign? And how are voters to know who is responsible for independent expenditures on television when the credit line is invisible to most viewers? Independence comes down in the end to small but important details.

Independent expenditures happen to exploit a gap in the regulatory system created by the Supreme Court's application of the First Amendment to it. Soft money, however, flows in presidential campaigns as a result of an intended exclusion from the system and the constitutional status of American federalism. Most of the bundling and high-stakes brokering result from the failure of the authors of the FECA, whether out of faintheartedness or lack of foresight, to place intermediaries securely within the regulatory structure. So, the natures of the leaks differ; they are far too varied in both origin and purpose to bear the single pejorative label of loophole. Calling them loopholes blurs moral and ethical distinctions in a subject in which moral and ethical judgments abound.

Such judgments are the first reason for concern about the integrity of the regulatory structure. Its impairments invite and receive public denunciation of campaigns, campaigners, and campaign finance. Americans do not take kindly to avoidance, no matter how legal or even ethical, of systems of regulation; avoidance carries the stigma of self-servingness compounded by excessive cleverness. Independent spenders may be exercising a First Amendment right in the most open and direct way, but they are not treated much more charitably than the trimmers and shavers who bundle ever more creatively to escape the statutory limits on the size of contributions. In short, breaches in the integrity of the structure give rise to blanket judgments untempered or ungraded by any fine distinctions among the kinds of breaches.

The problems, however, extend beyond those of public judgment. The breaches create massive administrative problems, especially in reporting. Again, independent spending is a splendid case in point. The only other spending in the campaign permitted by the FECA is that by the candidates and the party committees, both of which must register with the FEC and make periodic reports to it. Their officials become institutionalized reporters and trained compliers, most of them also aided by accountants, lawyers, and computer software. A Michael Goland must report his independent spending, but he is not in the same sense institutionalized, nor is he a trained complier with the FECA. He is not registered with the FEC, and he does not have to report his contributions to actors who are. Similarly, many of the ad hoc groups making independent expenditures in presidential campaigns are transient, striking tent as soon as the election is over. It is neither a secret nor a surprise that the FEC has had to work hard to piece together full reports on independent spending in an election cycle.

On this and other matters of administration and enforcement, the FEC suffers from an uncertain authority. The placement of exchanges and flows of money on the peripheries of the regulatory system means, in effect, that they also sit on the peripheries of the FEC's authority. One need only cite the great controversies, including the intervention of the federal district court for the District of Columbia, over the FEC's handling of the soft money controversy. It has been almost equally vexed by the bundling inventions of the National Republican Senatorial Committee. Underfunded by the Congress and kept on a short leash for fifteen years, the FEC has never been able to establish its independence as a regulator; its even division between three Democrats and three Republicans has made it additionally difficult for the commission to deal with problems that are inevitably partisan. These leaks in the regulation system have only further embarrassed it and given its sterner critics more reason for criticism.[23]

Administrative problems are closely related to mechanisms of responsibility. The major institutionalized actors—PACS, parties, and candidates—respond to various systems of control or responsibility: voters, members, parent organizations, representative bodies, public officials, or mass opinion, as the case may be. On the other hand, brokers

---

23. See, for example, Brooks Jacobson, *Broken Promise: Why the Federal Election Commission Failed* (New York: Priority Press, 1990).

such as Charles Keating or a well-heeled individual contributor make
no reports to the FEC, and no other institutions or responsible bodies
stand behind them. With no visibility and no long-term interest in the
political system, the brokers may have no political reputation at stake;
often, too, they offer no target at which the wrath of voters can be
directed. The political controls of reputation and the ballot box are
imperfect at best, but they do work more effectively on visible, committed political actors with continuing stakes in politics.

When the integrity of the regulatory system suffers, so too do the
morale and the law-abidingness of those clearly within the regulatory
perimeters. Compliance with both the letter and the spirit of a regulatory
structure cannot easily survive the impression that the structure catches
only some of the players while others go free. The belief that "I've been
playing by the rules while those guys have been getting away with
murder" has a corrosive effect on compliance, and compliance is that
act of self-enforcement on which all legitimate and effective systems of
regulation depend.

It almost goes without saying that breaches in the regulatory system
sabotage the achievement of the initial purpose of the regulation. If the
purpose was to limit PAC contributions to $5,000 per candidate per
election, any modus operandi that permits groups of potential PAC
contributors to give their cash instead as individuals defeats both the
limit and the congressional intent that their money be identified with
the interest that recruited it.

## ARE CAMPAIGNS TOO EXPENSIVE?

Each round of debates over congressional campaign finance is, in the
words of Yogi Berra, déjà vu all over again. Putting a cap on campaign
expenditures was high on the agenda of a reform in 1974, and it still is.
The Supreme Court struck down the FECA's limits on all spending in
*Buckley,* and reformers have been trying to find a way of restoring them
ever since. So strongly convinced are the American people that campaigns cost too much, so firmly placed on the agenda of reform is the

issue, that it flourishes in the 1990s despite the stability of expenditures in congressional campaigns. Not only does the issue persist, but its rhetoric about skyrocketing and escalating expenditures remains impervious to any new realities.

It is virtually a truism that the case for spending limits rests on the premise that the costs of campaigning are too great. For many American adults the standards for making such a judgment are implicit; the spending is just "too much"—too much perhaps by standards of middle-class personal finance, too much because of the imagined rate of runaway increase in them. Or too much perhaps in terms of value, in terms of the worth of the product or service the money produces. The campaigns, or the parts of them they happen to notice, are simply not worth those sums, just as $40 is not too much for a good steak dinner but is an outrageous price for a bad one.

The many cries of "too much" reflect negative judgments about politics and the entire public sector. Those judgments similarly govern public opinion about the salaries of public officials. Inherent in them is a double standard, one code of behavior for the private sector and another for the public sector. Political scientists are fond of making the public-private comparison in campaign finance with data on advertising expenditures, for advertising campaigns are, like campaigns for public office, an exercise in information and persuasion. Americans are shocked by total expenditures of $445.2 million in the congressional campaigns of 1990, but in that same year Sears Roebuck, the giant merchandiser, had an advertising budget in excess of $1.4 billion.

The case against present spending levels is much stronger on pragmatic or consequential grounds. These arguments are, however, not about spending per se but about the need to raise the money in order to spend it. They go this way:

- Present levels of spending are too high because, in order to raise the funds to spend, elected public officials must take too much time and energy from their public responsibilities. It is now almost a commonplace that a U.S. senator must raise $12,000 a week for six years in order to amass the $3.5 to $4 million for a typical Senate campaign.

■ The pressures to raise those sums for a Senate race, or close to half a million for a House campaign, drive candidates to seek money in large sums at a time when contribution limits are shrinking because of inflation. Initially, candidates replaced small individual contributors with large PAC contributions, and now even the usual PAC contribution is small compared to the take at a brokered fund-raiser in Los Angeles. A senator can make a flying trip to a distant spot for a quick reception and return to Washington with $50,000 or $100,000 in campaign resources. Spending levels, that is, affect how money is raised, where it is raised, and with whose help it is raised.

■ The ability to raise funds becomes a substantial qualification for candidates. Candidates of knowledge, experience, and even wisdom may lack the skills or the stomach for begging funds from people they scarcely know; the need to do it may discourage them from seeking office. Worse than such a shrinking of the pool of talent is the possibility that the consequence will be to recruit and elect candidates whose skills in raising money and conducting a campaign are their chief or even their only major attributes.

The problem with elevated spending levels seems to be that one needs to raise the money in the first place.

Probably the most direct and reasonable judgments about spending levels are the ones based on a stipulated minimum campaign. If the candidate needs at least to be able to do A, B, and C in order to run a competitive campaign that also honors the need for an informed electorate, then the minimum cost of A, B, and C, with appropriate staff and overhead, frames a reasonable cost for the campaign. One recent and authoritative manual for campaigners posits a budget of $600,000 for a House challenger. Its direct-mail figures total about $150,000 for only two mailings to the approximately 200,000 households of a congressional district; it also provides $100,000 for radio and television commercials, a sum that will yield three high-visibility campaigns for three television spots in many metropolitan markets.[24] The budget is perhaps overweighted with personnel and overhead costs, but it is hard to avoid the conclusion that a campaign of $500,000–$600,000 is something less than profligate.[25] In view of the fact that the average major-party general election candidate spent less than half of $500,000 in 1990 and that even the average open-seat candidate spent $484,000, one can make a plausible argument that candidates spend too little, not too much, in congressional campaigns.

Leaving aside the strength of popular and reformist feelings on the point, there is a basic conceptual problem here. Not one but two issues are entwined: the need for the money and the costs to the system of raising it. It is easier to justify the spending levels than the effort that has to go into raising the cash in the first place. So we are raising too much money and yet not really spending enough in the campaigns for Congress. It is a paradox that recalls Mark Twain's observation about good bourbon: "Too much is hardly enough."[26]

REALITY AND REFORM

Even the experts and activists find it difficult to reach a judgment about American campaign finance. The mass public necessarily comes to its understandings about it without any profound knowledge, often with-

---

24. For the Minneapolis–St. Paul television market, by no means one of the country's most expensive, one pays about $100 a "rating point" for television advertising (i.e., $100 for reaching 1 percent of households once); so for a single campaign ad campaign $30,000 will yield approximately 300 points, or 80 percent of households three or four times.

25. S. J. Guzzetta, *The Campaign Manual: A Definitive Study of the Modern Political Campaign Process*, 2d rev. ed. (Alexandria, Va.: Political Publishing, 1987). The proposed budget is on p. 83.

26. I am indebted to Charls Walker for the Twain quotation. Neither he nor I know the occasion on which, or the essay in which, Twain made the observation.

out even basic information. Citizens are compelled to watch the shadows projected on the vast wall in front of them. They take their conclusions and judgments as they see them in the dance of distorted images. Of necessity, their judgments are the judgments of those who project the images.

In the opinions on all of the major concerns about the post-1974 system, the consonances and dissonances are consistent. Whether it is the PAC-Congress connection, the impact of money on the winning of elections, or the judgments about spending levels, mass opinion and image-making opinion are in agreement. Their consensus, moreover, diverges in all three instances from much of scholarly and other expert opinion.[27] It is hardly a novel outcome, for expert opinion is often at odds with mass opinion over the analysis of public problems and policy solutions. It is, in fact, one of the oldest and most troubling dilemmas in the governance of mass, popular democracies.

The successes and failures of the post-1974 regime present the dilemma in a heightened form. Mass opinion about campaign finance increasingly feeds a cynicism about, even a rejection of, basic democratic processes. Any threat to mass involvement in or acceptance of electoral politics threatens the essence of representative government. The resulting conflict of equities could not be more disturbing. Is one to adopt policies that address the real problems of the system, as the informed best understand them, or ought one to devise change that will lay to rest the fears and anger of a disaffected public? Can we indeed win back disaffected citizens and solve real public problems at the same time? It is the hardest of the policy questions, this intersection of image and reality, of mass politics and expert prescription—especially when the

27. I want to be clear that in referring to scholarly opinion I am talking about more than my judgments. I have cited examples of scholarly opinion about the first two issues; as for the question of spending levels, see, inter alia, Larry J. Sabato, *Paying for Elections: The Campaign Finance Thicket* (New York: Priority Press, 1989), especially chapters 2 and 3.

divergence is not only over ultimate policy goals but over the reality of the problem itself.

Whether by accident or prescience, the justices of the U.S. Supreme Court recognized the dilemma in the majority opinion in *Buckley v. Valeo*. Congress could act to limit the constitutionally protected flow of campaign money only in the case of "corruption or the appearance of corruption," either in the instance of certifiable corruption by some unspecified standards or in the instance of some widespread belief that institutions were being corrupted. So Congress might apparently act on the basis of one reality or the other, on the basis of the image behind the viewer or the image projected on the wall. Is it to make no difference if one reality could meet standards of truth or validity and the other could not? The answer, in the world of democratic politics, depends on crafting reforms that serve both reality and its appearances.

# Campaign Finance Regulation: Faulty Assumptions and Undemocratic Consequences

## Bradley A. Smith

This selection was originally published as Cato Policy Analysis no. 238, September 13, 1995. Bradley A. Smith, an associate professor at Capital University Law School in Columbus, Ohio, provides an enlightening overview of the history of the financing of political campaigns in the United States. He also presents a useful summary of the current limitations on federal contributions and expenditures.

Smith finds that campaign finance regulation has had a detrimental effect on the electoral process contradictory to its stated purposes. This is because it has been based, as are proposals for further "reform," on false assumptions.

Smith's conclusion is that deregulation is a more appropriate way to achieve the objectives of reform than is further regulation. Cato Institute's web site is www.cato.org.

Efforts to control political campaign spending have met with little ideological resistance since the turn of the century, and efforts over the past twenty-five years to reform campaign finance, primarily by limiting contributions to and spending by campaigns, have been exceptionally popular.

However, despite its popularity, there is no serious evidence that campaign finance regulation has actually accomplished any of the goals set out for it by its supporters. Rather, continued support for campaign finance reform by groups such as Common Cause seems to stem more from habit than from any serious argument that those reforms already enacted are working or that proposed reforms might meet their stated goals. In fact, efforts to regulate campaign finance have been little short of disastrous. They have distorted the political process, hindered grassroots political involvement, infringed on First Amendment rights, and helped to entrench incumbents in office while doing nothing to address the allegedly corrupting influence of money in politics.

This paper examines the fundamental assumptions behind campaign finance reform efforts and finds them largely flawed.[1] Because these assumptions are flawed, campaign finance reform will not achieve the objectives set out for it and, in fact, has already had a detrimental effect on the electoral process. Rather than continue down the path of greater government regulation, the country would be best served by deregulating the electoral process, as intended by the drafters of the Constitution.

## THE STRUCTURE OF CAMPAIGN FINANCE REGULATION

The first state laws regulating campaign finance were passed in the latter part of the nineteenth century. These laws were typically limited to minimal disclosure requirements of campaign donations and expenditures, although four states also banned all corporate contributions beginning in 1897.The first federal law, a narrow provision banning some corporate contributions, was passed in 1907. Over the next six decades, the federal government passed several laws requiring disclosure of contributions and the filing of reports, but these laws remained generally toothless and were largely ignored. Only with passage of the Federal Election Campaign Act in 1971 and, more important, the 1974 amendments to FECA, did campaign finance regulation become a significant factor on the American political landscape.[2]

## THE FEDERAL ELECTION CAMPAIGN ACT

The 1974 amendments to FECA constituted the first effort to establish a comprehensive, national system of campaign finance regulation. Spe-

1. For purposes of this paper we focus primarily on regulation of federal campaigns, recognizing that many states have adopted similar regulatory schemes with similar bad effects. These state laws share the assumptions and basic structure of the federal regime.

2. Robert E. Mutch, *Campaigns, Congress, and Courts: The Makings of Federal Campaign Finance Law* (New York: Praeger, 1988), pp. xvii, 7–42.

cifically, the amendments established the following framework of contribution and spending limits for federal campaign finance:

- Individual contributions were limited to $1,000 per candidate per election, with primary and general elections counting as separate elections.

- Individuals were limited to $25,000 per calendar year in total contributions to candidates, party committees, and political action committees (PACs).

- PACs and party committees were limited to contributing $5,000 per candidate per election.

- Candidates were limited to personal spending of $25,000 in House races and $35,000 in Senate races, a provision later struck down as unconstitutional by the Supreme Court.

- Absolute ceilings were placed on the amount that could be spent in any campaign: $70,000 for a House seat and $100,000, or eight cents per eligible voter, in the Senate. That provision was also struck down by the Supreme Court.

- Independent expenditures by nonparty committees—that is, expenditures on behalf of a candidate without the cooperation or knowledge of the candidate—were limited to $1,000 per candidate per election. That, too, was struck down by the Supreme Court.

- Political party committees, in addition to being limited in the amounts they could directly contribute to candidate campaigns, were limited in spending on behalf of their candidates to $10,000 in House campaigns and $20,000 in Senate campaigns. Both figures were indexed for inflation, and the Senate figure also allowed for adding spending based on population.[3]

3. Federal Election Campaign Act, U.S. Code, vol. 18, sec. 608. Party senatorial com-

In addition, the 1974 amendments established the presidential financing system of matching funds to candidates for amounts raised in contributions of $250 or less, established overall spending limits for eligibility to receive matching funds, and provided for public funding of major party candidates in the general election for president.

In the years surrounding the passage of the 1974 amendments to FECA, many states passed similar laws regulating the financing of state campaigns. The amendments and their state counterparts were hailed at the time as marking an end to the corrupt system of elections that the United States had used since its founding.

### BUCKLEY V. VALEO

One of the more remarkable features of the decades-long effort to regulate campaign finance, which culminated in the 1974 amendments to FECA, was the almost total absence of ideological opposition to regulation.[4] Yet scarcely had FECA been enacted when a formidable ideological and constitutional challenge against it was launched in the federal courts.

In *Buckley v. Valeo*,[5] a coalition of liberals and conservatives attacked FECA as a violation of First Amendment guarantees of free speech. Restrictions on campaign contributions and spending, they pointed out, constitute restrictions on speech as surely as would a statute directly prohibiting an individual from speaking.

> Presumably dollars are not stuffed in ballot boxes. . . . The mediating factor that turns money into votes is speech. More money leads to more communications supporting the candidate. More communications sup-

---

mittees were allowed to contribute up to $17,500 per candidate per election. By 1991 indexing had raised the amounts that political party committees could give to candidates to $26,500 in House races and as much as $1,166,493 for California's Senate seat. See Frank Sorauf, *Inside Campaign Finance* (New Haven, Conn.: Yale University Press, 1992), p. 10.

4. Mutch, *Campaigns, Congress, and Courts*, p. 54.

5. *Buckley v. Valeo*, 424 U.S. 1 (1976).

porting the candidate leads to additional votes. . . . Advocacy cannot be proscribed simply because it may be effective.[6]

In a lengthy opinion, the Supreme Court agreed that campaign finance restrictions burdened First Amendment rights but declined to strike down the entire statute. Citing the government interest in preventing the "appearance of corruption," the Court upheld restrictions on the size of campaign contributions but struck down limits on candidate spending and independent expenditures in support of a candidate. The Court held that the provision of taxpayer funds to support campaign activity could be conditioned on a candidate's agreement to limit total campaign expenditures. It also held that Congress could require the disclosure of campaign donors' names, addresses, and amounts contributed.[7]

The net result of the *Buckley* decision is that Congress and state legislatures can limit the amount an individual or entity can give to a campaign and can require disclosure of campaign donors and expenditures. However, Congress cannot limit the amount a campaign spends, nor can it limit the amount individuals or organizations spend on their own to support a candidate's campaign so long as these expenditures are made independent of the campaign. It is within these limits that proposals to regulate campaign finance must operate.

In a partial dissent from the judgment in *Buckley*, Chief Justice Warren Burger warned that contribution limits would restrict the amount of political speech and have a "chilling" effect on grassroots political activity. The loss of "seed money" in the form of early, large contributions would, he argued, discriminate against many candidates. He further argued that the legislation, and in particular its provisions for public funding of presidential campaigns, would be used by incum-

---

6. Brief of United States p. 53, *Buckley v. Valeo*, p. 1, cited in Mutch, *Campaigns, Congress, and Courts*, p. 56.
7. *Buckley v. Valeo*, p. 1.

bents to disadvantage challengers, third parties, and independent candidates.[8]

In the twenty years since the *Buckley* decision, all of Burger's fears have been realized. However, supporters of campaign finance limitations continue to argue for still more regulation. This regulatory approach is doomed to fail, not only because the reformers have incorrectly assessed the probable results of legislation but also because they have based their legislation on faulty assumptions.

FAULTY ASSUMPTIONS OF CAMPAIGN FINANCE REFORM

John Gardner, founder of the interest group Common Cause, once stated, "There is nothing in our political system today that creates more mischief, more corruption, and more alienation and distrust on the part of the public than does our system of financing elections."[9] In a nutshell, Gardner's statement sums up the general assumptions underlying the arguments made in favor of campaign finance regulation: first, there is too much money being spent in political campaigns; second, this money has a corrupting influence, buying both votes and elections and thereby excluding ordinary citizens from the political process; and, finally, the growth in campaign spending has made the electoral process in some way less "democratic."[10] However, as Professor Frank Sorauf of the University of Minnesota, the nation's foremost commentator on campaign finance, points out, "Very few aspects of American politics better fit the metaphor of Plato's cave than the realities of American campaign finance." What most political scientists and other experts know as reality is vastly different from the "grotesque images projected onto the wall of the cave." The common public perception of the role of money is, in

8. Ibid., pp. 236–55 (Burger, J., dissenting).
9. Quoted in Fred Wertheimer and Randy Huwa, "Campaign Finance Reforms: Past Accomplishments, Future Challenges," *New York University Review of Law and Social Change* 10 (1981): 43–44.
10. Elizabeth Drew, *Politics and Money* (New York: Macmillan, 1983); Cass R. Sunstein, "Political Equality and Unintended Consequences," *Columbia Law Review* 94 (1994): 1390, 1391–92.

Sorauf's words, "difficult to square with the evidence."[11] But any rational policy discussion of campaign finance must be based on the world as it is, not on the distorted images projected onto the wall of the cave and heralded as reality by the campaign finance reformers. Close scrutiny of the assumptions underlying most campaign finance reform efforts is long overdue.

## Do We Spend Too Much on Campaigns?

One often hears that too much money is spent on political campaigns.[12] Indeed, the language in which campaigns are described in the general press constantly reinforces that perception. Candidates "amass war chests" with the help of "special interests" that "pour" their "millions" into campaigns. "Obscene" expenditures "careen" out of control or "skyrocket" upward.[13] Rarely is there a dispassionate discussion of actual expenditures on politics. For the campaign finance regulators, this lack of calm discussion is a good thing. If truth be told, there is substantial reason to believe that Americans spend too little on political campaigns.

To say that too much money is spent on campaigning is to beg the question, compared to what? For example, Americans spend more than twice as much money each year on yogurt as on political campaigns.[14] As the *Washington Post* reported recently, "Close to $100 million will be spent promoting the 'Seinfeld' launch into syndicated reruns this fall—more than it costs to run a presidential campaign."[15] In the two-year election cycle culminating in November 1994, approximately $590

---

11. Sorauf, *Inside Campaign Finance*, p. 26.

12. One poll found that 90 percent of respondents agreed with the proposition that "there is way too much money in politics." See Terry Ganey, "To Campaign Finance Reform Advocates, the Webster Scandal Was Proof Positive," *St. Louis Post Dispatch*, October 23, 1994, p. 1B.

13. Sorauf, *Inside Campaign Finance*, p. 26, and sources cited therein.

14. George F. Will, "So We Talk Too Much," *Newsweek*, June 28, 1993, p. 68.

15. Roxanne Roberts, "The Remote Controllers," *Washington Post*, June 10, 1995, p. B1.

million was spent by all congressional general election candidates.[16] Although this set a new record for spending in congressional races, the amount is hardly exorbitant, amounting to roughly $3 per eligible voter over the two-year period. Total direct campaign spending for all local, state, and federal elections, including Congress, over the same period can be reasonably estimated at between $1.5 billion and $2.0 billion, or somewhere between $7.50 and $10 per eligible voter.[17] When one considers that money was spread over several candidates, it is hard to suggest that office seekers are spending obscene sums attempting to get their messages through to voters. By comparison, Americans spent two to three times as much money in 1994 alone on the purchase of potato chips.[18] Procter & Gamble and Philip Morris Company, the nation's two largest advertisers, spend roughly the same amount each year on advertising as is spent by all political candidates and parties.[19]

If it is hard to suggest that too much money is spent on political campaigns in some absolute sense, it may be fairly suggested that the perception that too much is spent stems from a belief that what is spent is largely ineffective. In other words, the problem, on closer examination, may not be that too much is spent but that too little benefit seems

16. As noted in "Post-Election Reports Point to New Records," *Political Finance & Lobby Reporter,* December 28, 1994, p. 1, this includes amounts spent by victorious primary candidates. An additional $76 million was spent by primary election candidates who lost.

17. The author is aware of no hard data yet compiled on state and local election spending in this cycle. Drawing from Herbert Alexander and Monica Bauer's 1991 study of 1988 spending, Sorauf estimates that total 1988 direct spending was $1.7 billion (*Inside Campaign Finance,* p.29). This figure includes approximately $370 million, or about $2 per eligible voter, spent on the presidential campaign and approximately $1.33 billion in direct spending on all other local, state, and national campaigns. If local and state spending since that time increased at the same rate as congressional spending (roughly 25 percent, according to Sorauf, *Inside Campaign Finance,* p. 30), this would yield a 1993–94 direct spending total of approximately $1.66 billion. Although this is a rough estimate, there is little reason to think that total 1993–94 spending at all levels exceeded $2 billion, and it was probably closer to $1.5 billion.

18. Clare Ansberry, "The Best Beef Jerky Has Characteristics Few Can Appreciate," *Wall Street Journal,* April 4, 1995, pp. 1, 4, cites annual spending on chips in excess of $4.5 billion.

19. Roy A. Schotland, "Proposals for Campaign Finance Reform: An Article Dedicated to Being Less Dull Than Its Title," *Capital University Law Review* 21 (1992): 429, 444.

to come out of it. Voters are tired of what they perceive as the relentless negativity of televised campaign advertisements, and they do not believe that political advertisements add significantly to their store of real political knowledge.

This perception may itself be influenced by press reporting and editorials critical of campaign advertising.[20] But whether modern, televised campaign advertising is overly negative may simply be a matter of individual voter preference. Negative advertising is popular for a simple reason: it works. Indeed, as Bruce Felknor, former executive director of the Fair Campaign Practices Committee,[21] states, "Without attention-grabbing, cogent, memorable, negative campaigning, almost no challenger can hope to win unless the incumbent has just been found guilty of a heinous crime."[22] It is a mistake to assume, as many campaign finance reformers do, that the elimination of negative campaigning would necessarily serve the public. Negative advertising that is relevant to the issues can serve the public well. Felknor notes that without negative campaigning aimed at showing up an opponent's bad side, "any knave or mountebank in the land may lie and steal his or her way into the White House or any other elective office." To suggest that candidates should not point to each other's perceived shortcomings, writes Felknor, is "preposterous."[23] Negative campaigning—that is, ef-

---

20. See, for example, Robin Toner, "Bitter Tone of '94 Campaign Elicits Worry on Public Debate," *New York Times*, November 13, 1994, p. 1; Stuart Elliott, "Ketchum Protests Political Ads," *New York Times*, November 10, 1994, p. D23 (quoting an advertising executive that "negative ads [are] political filth that is not advertising and shouldn't be dignified by being called advertising"); John Balzar and Doug Connor, "With Foley, Noble Era Will End," *Los Angeles Times*, November 10, 1994, p. 1 (asserting that negative ads constitute "special interest intrusion" and "the dark streak of American politics"); Charles Krauthammer, "Political Suicide," *Washington Post*, October 28, 1994, p. A27.

21. The Fair Campaign Practices Committee was a private, nonpartisan organization that sought to make public, and thereby discourage, unfair campaign tactics and advertisements. It operated from 1954 through the 1980 election, with some level of success. See Bruce L. Felknor, *Political Mischief: Smear, Sabotage and Reform in U.S. Elections* (New York: Praeger, 1992), pp. 226–34.

22. Ibid., p. 29.

23. Ibid.

forts to expose corruption, unpopular positions, or weak character in an opponent—has been prevalent in American elections since 1796.[24]

Even if one concedes that the elimination of negative advertising would be a good thing, efforts to limit spending on campaigns—either directly, through spending limits, or indirectly, through contribution limits—bear no relationship to the negativity of the campaign. Less spending only reduces the amount of communication, not any negative tone of that communication.

Increased campaign spending does translate into a better informed electorate. Gary Jacobson's extensive studies have shown that "the extent and content of information [voters] do have has a decisive effect on how they vote."[25] Voter understanding of issues clearly increases with the quantity of campaign information received.[26] In short, spending less on campaigns will not elevate the level of debate, but it will result in less public awareness and understanding of issues. This reduction in the flow of information may even make well-produced negative advertising more valuable, as candidates will need to get the maximum political mileage from each expenditure and a poorly informed electorate may be more susceptible to misleading political advertisements.

There are no objective criteria by which to measure whether "too much" is spent on political campaigns. What is spent, we might fairly say, is the amount that individuals feel is worthwhile to contribute and candidates find is effective to spend. Considering the importance of elections to any democratic society, it is hard to believe that the expenditure of less than $10 per voter for all local, state, and national campaigns every two years constitutes a crisis requiring government regulation and limitations on spending.

24. Ibid., pp. 29–44.
25. Gary Jacobson, *Money in Congressional Elections* (New Haven, Conn.: Yale University Press, 1980), pp. 31–32.
26. Stephen E. Gottlieb, "The Dilemma of Election Campaign Finance Reform," *Hofstra Law Review* 18 (1989): 213, 266.

## Does Money Buy Elections?

The second assumption of campaign finance reform is that money buys elections in some manner incompatible with a functioning democracy. Of course, it is true that a candidate with little or no money to spend is unlikely to win most races. Furthermore, the candidate spending more money wins more often than not.[27] But correlation is not the same as cause and effect, and one must be careful not to make too much of such simple numbers. The correlation may stem simply from the desire of donors to contribute to candidates who are likely to win, in which case the ability to win attracts money rather than the other way around.[28] Similarly, higher levels of campaign contributions to and spending by a candidate may merely reflect a level of public support that is later manifested at the polls.[29]

Moreover, higher spending does not necessarily translate into victory. Michael Huffington, Lewis Lehrman, Mark Dayton, John Connally, and Clayton Williams are just a few of the lavish spenders who wound up on the losing end of campaigns. As Michael Malbin, director of the Center for Legislative Studies at the Rockefeller Institute of Government, explains, "Having money means having the ability to be heard; it does not mean that voters will like what they hear."[30] In the end, so long as voters have the final say among various candidates of differing views, the democratic process is well served.

Although money does not ensure election, those few studies that have attempted to quantify the effect of campaign spending on votes have found that additional spending does affect a limited number of votes.[31] The positive effect of added spending, however, is significantly

27. Herbert Alexander, *Financing Politics: Money, Elections, and Political Reform* (Washington, D.C.: Congressional Quarterly Press, 1984), p. 20.

28. Stephanie D. Moussalli, *Campaign Finance Reform: The Case for Deregulation* (Tallahassee, Fla.: James Madison Institute, 1990), p. 4.

29. Ibid.

30. Quoted in ibid., p. 9.

31. Ibid. and sources cited therein.

greater for challengers than for incumbents. In fact, studies show an inverse relationship between incumbent spending and incumbent success. Heavy spending by an incumbent usually indicates that the incumbent is in electoral trouble and facing a well-financed challenger.[32] But the incumbent's added spending is likely to have less effect on vote totals than the challenger's added spending. Thus, limits on campaign spending would hurt challengers more than incumbents. Accordingly, efforts to limit spending, whether mandatory or through incentive-based "voluntary" caps, should not be viewed as benign. Incumbent lawmakers will always have an incentive to draw campaign regulations to their advantage; commentators have noted that campaign finance legislation routinely favors the party or candidate putting forth the proposal and always favors incumbent legislators.[33]

Incumbency is already the single best predictor of electoral success. Limits on campaign financing can tend to add to political ossification. Although incumbent reelection rates have been consistently above 75 percent since the turn of the century, they have risen to record heights in this era of extensive campaign finance regulation.[34] Even in the November 1994 elections, which resulted in significant political realignment, 91.4 percent of congressional incumbents seeking reelection were victorious.[35] The Republican gains came primarily from the GOP's near sweep of "open" seats—that is, seats to which the incumbent did not seek reelection. Although money can help buy votes, it buys far more

---

32. Ibid., p. 5.

33. David Mason and Steven Schwalm, *Advantage Incumbents: Clinton's Campaign Finance Proposal* (Washington, D.C.: Heritage Foundation, 1993); Daniel H. Lowenstein, "On Campaign Finance Reform: The Root of All Evil Is Deeply Rooted," *Hofstra Law Review* 18 (1989): 301, 335. See also Bradley A. Smith, "Judicial Protection of Ballot Access Rights," *Harvard Journal of Legislation* 28 (1991): 167, 212–16, for a description of how incumbent lawmakers draft electoral legislation—in this case, ballot access laws—to disadvantage challengers.

34. John H. Fund, "Term Limitation: An Idea Whose Time Has Come," *Cato Institute Policy Analysis*, no. 141 (October 30, 1990): 5.

35. Edward Zuckerman, "Money Didn't Matter for Most Challengers Who Won," *Political Finance & Lobby Reporter*, November 23, 1994, p. 1.

votes for challengers than for incumbents. This being the case, money is an equalizer in the system, helping challengers to overcome the otherwise tremendous advantages of incumbency.[36] Despite all the alarmist rhetoric, it is once again difficult to see what all the fuss is about.

## Does Money Buy Votes in the Legislature?

Many Americans have come to view legislative politics as a money game. Indeed, states with few restrictions on campaign spending are frequently referred to as "pay to play" states. For many casual observers, legislative politics in the U.S. Congress can be summed up in the words of former representative Ozzie Myers (D-Pa.), who was caught on videotape taking a bribe while declaring, "Money talks, bull . . . walks!" The fact that Representative Myers was expelled from the House is often overlooked.

In fact, those who have studied voting patterns on a systematic basis are almost unanimous in finding that campaign contributions affect very few votes in the legislature. The primary factors in determining a legislator's votes are party affiliation, ideology, and constituent views and needs.[37] That has been reflected in study after study over the past 20 years.[38] Where contributions and voting patterns intersect, it is

36. Ruy A. Teixeira, "Campaign Reform, Political Competition, and Citizen Participation," in *Rethinking Political Reform: Beyond Spending and Term Limits*, ed. Ruy A. Teixeira, L. Sandy Maisell, and John J. Pitney Jr. (Washington, D.C.: Progressive Foundation, 1994), pp. 10–11.

37. Larry Sabato, "Real and Imagined Corruption in Campaign Financing," in *Elections American Style*, ed. A. James Reichley (Washington, D.C.: Brookings Institution, 1987), p. 160.

38. Moussalli, p. 6; Frank J. Sorauf, *Money in American Elections* (New Haven, Conn.: Yale University Press, 1988), p. 316; Michael Malbin, "Looking Back at the Future of Campaign Finance Reform," in *Money and Politics in the United States*, ed. Michael Malbin (Chatham, N.J.: Chatham House Publishers, 1984), p. 232; Janet Grenzke, "PACs and the Congressional Supermarket: The Currency Is Complex," *American Journal of Political Science* 33 (1989): 1. Compare W. P. Welch, "Campaign Contributions and Legislative Voting: Milk Money and Dairy Price Supports," *Western Political Quarterly* 35 (1982): 478–79, who writes, "The influence of contributions is small, at least relative to the influences of constituency, party, and ideology"; but see Lowenstein, "On Campaign Finance Reform," pp. 301, 313–22, who argues that such studies are seriously flawed.

primarily because donors contribute to candidates believed to favor their positions, not the other way around.[39]

In response to these repeated studies showing little or no "vote buying," campaign reformers generally offer a simple response: experience and human nature generally tell us that legislators, like other people, are influenced by money, even when it goes not directly to their pockets but to their campaigns. Yet the issue is not so simple, and to accept the findings of the repeated studies does not require us to check our common sense at the door.

First, people who are attracted to public office generally do have strong personal views on issues. Second, there are institutional and political incentives to support party positions. Third, money is not the only political commodity of value. For example, in 1993–94, the National Rifle Association contributed nearly $2 million to congressional campaigns through its PAC.[40] However, the NRA also has 2.8 million members "who focus intently, even solely, on NRA issues in their voting."[41] Groups advocating gun control often complain that the NRA outspends them but rarely mention that the NRA also outvotes them. Is the NRA's influence based on dollars or votes? When the NRA faced a liberal Congress and president in 1993–94, money did not gain the NRA victory over the Brady Bill or the assault weapons ban. Yet a fourth reason why campaign contributions have minimal effect on legislation is that large campaign contributors are usually offset in legislative debate by equally well-financed interests who contribute to a different group of candidates. In fact, large PACs and their parent organizations frequently suffer enormous losses in the legislative process.[42]

If campaign contributions have any meaningful effect on legislative voting behavior, it appears to be on a limited number of votes that are

39. Moussalli, *Campaign Finance Reform*, pp. 5–6.
40. "The Top 100 PACs of the 1993-94 Election Cycle," *Political Finance & Lobby Reporter*, April 26, 1995, p. 3.
41. Sorauf, *Inside Campaign Finance*, p. 166.
42. Ibid., p. 165.

generally related to technical issues arousing little public interest.[43] On such issues, prior contributions may provide the contributor with access to the legislator or legislative staff. The contributor may then be able to shape legislation to the extent that such efforts are not incompatible with the dominant legislative motives of ideology, party affiliation and agenda, or constituent views.[44] Whether the influence of campaign contributions on these limited issues is good or bad depends on one's views of the legislation. The exclusion of knowledgeable contributors from the legislative process can just as easily lead to poor legislation with unintended consequences as their inclusion.[45] But in any case, it must be stressed that such votes are few.[46]

Campaign finance reformers seem to envision a world in which career officeholders, freed from the corrupting influence of money, lobbyists, and—dare it be said?—public opinion, would produce good, wise, and fair legislation. This notion of the philosopher-bureaucrat, popular during the Progressive Era at the turn of the century, has been discredited as an unattainable and, indeed, undesirable ideal.[47] And although campaign finance reformers have long posed as disinterested citizens seeking only good government, Lillian BeVier of the University of Virginia Law School has surveyed reform efforts and found that campaign finance regulators have targeted certain types of campaign activities, "at least in part because [those activities] are closely tied to political agendas the reformers oppose."[48] In other words, the motivation for efforts to limit campaign contributions and spending may not

43. Ibid.; Sabato, "Real and Imagined Corruption," p. 160.
44. Ibid., pp. 160–61.
45. David A. Strauss, "Corruption, Equality, and Campaign Finance Reform," *Columbia Law Review* 94 (1994): 1369, 1378–79.
46. Sabato, "Real and Imagined Corruption," p. 160.
47. See, for example, Dwight Lee and Richard McKenzie, *Failure and Progress* (Washington, D.C.: Cato Institute, 1993); Geoffrey Brennan and James Buchanan, "The Normative Purpose of Economic Science: Rediscovery of an Eighteenth Century Method," *International Review of Law and Economics* 1 (1981): 155.
48. Lillian R. BeVier, "Money and Politics: A Perspective on the First Amendment and Campaign Finance Reform," *California Law Review* 73 (1985): 1045, 1060.

be that money sways votes in the legislature but that those being elected to office reflect ideologies and voting tendencies with which many campaign finance reformers do not agree. The reformers therefore favor regulation that would tilt the electoral process in favor of preferred and, as it turns out, largely liberal candidates.

Given the popular perception otherwise, it simply cannot be stated strongly enough: no significant causal relationship has been found between campaign contributions and legislative voting patterns. In the end, just as money can buy speech but cannot ensure that voters will like what they hear, money can buy access to officials but cannot ensure that those officials will like what they hear. The safeguard is an informed voting public.

## Has the Growth in Campaign Spending Altered the Democratic Nature of the Process?

The final basic assumption motivating efforts to limit campaign contributions and spending is the notion that the growth in campaign expenditures over the past thirty years has created an unequal distribution of electoral power, in which monied interests dominate the system. Like the notion that money buys elections and legislative votes, this assumption contains a kernel of truth surrounded by a heavy coating of myth.

Contrary to the image created by campaign finance reformers, there has never been a "golden age" of American politics in which money was unimportant and the poor participated on the same level as the rich. Wealth has always been important in democratic politics, and never have more than a small minority of Americans contributed to politics with their dollars.

Indeed, in early U.S. elections, most campaign expenses were paid directly by the candidates. Such expenses were relatively minimal, such as publishing an occasional campaign pamphlet and, especially in the South, treating voters to food and drink at public gatherings and rallies. Candidates did not "run" for election but "stood" for office, relying on their reputations and personal recommendations to carry them to victory. Far from being more "democratic" than current campaigns, however, elections in this early period were generally contested by candidates representing aristocratic factions before a relatively small, homogeneous electorate of propertied white men.[49]

This genteel system of upper-class politics began to change in the 1830s, when Martin Van Buren organized the first popular mass campaigns around Andrew Jackson and the Democratic Party. It was the very democratization of the process that created the need for significant campaign spending. Money became necessary not only for the traditional expenditures on food and liquor but also for advertisements, widespread pamphleteering, organization of rallies, and logistic support. Even the new, mass parties, however, obtained financing from a small number of sources. Funding for the new style of mass campaigning initially fell on those who benefited most directly from gaining and/or retaining power: government employees. Absent a professional civil service, all government employees relied on their party retaining power if they were to retain their jobs. It became common practice to assess those employees a percentage of their salaries to support the party's campaigns.

Similarly, would-be officeholders allied with the opposition served as a major source of challenger funds.[50] As late as 1878, roughly 90 percent of the money raised by the Republican congressional committee came from assessments on federal officeholders.[51] However, after the passage of the Pendleton Act in 1883, which created a federal civil service, and similar laws in the states, campaign money from assessments on officeholders began to dry up. Only then did politicians look for new sources of funds. Two dominant sources emerged: wealthy individuals and corporations.

The acceleration of northern industrialization that accompanied

49. Mutch, *Campaigns, Congress, and Courts*, pp. xvii, 7–42.
50. Ibid., p. xvi.
51. Ibid.

and followed the Civil War created the new phenomenon of large, national corporations. These corporations and government regulation grew in a symbiotic relationship. Wartime government contracts created the foundations of many a corporation, and government land and cash grants to railroad companies became common. Corporations also benefited as Republican Congresses sheltered many industries behind high tariff walls.[52] To tame the corporate power it had helped to create, in 1883 Congress created the Interstate Commerce Commission. More business regulation followed, including the Sherman Antitrust Act in 1890. State regulation of railroad rates, business competition, and working conditions became common.

With both state and federal governments claiming previously unprecedented powers to both regulate and subsidize industry, corporate America recognized the need for political participation. The goal was not to buy votes but to elect candidates supportive of corporate interests. By 1888, roughly 40 percent of Republican national campaign funds came from manufacturing and business interests. State parties were probably even more reliant on corporate funding. In the last years of the nineteenth century, Republican national chairman Mark Hanna systematized these contributions through a system of assessments on banks and corporations.[53] In 1904, corporations contributed more than 73 percent of Theodore Roosevelt's presidential campaign funds. The Democratic Party relied less on corporate contributions but was also heavily wedded to funding from the personal wealth of a handful of wealthy industrialists. Industrialist Thomas Fortune Ryan and banker August Belmont contributed roughly three-quarters of the Democrats' 1904 presidential campaign fund ($450,000 and $250,000, respectively); Henry Davis, a mine owner and the party's vice presidential candidate, contributed much of the rest.[54]

---

52. Daniel K. Tarullo, "Law and Politics in Twentieth Century Tariff History," *UCLA Law Review* 34 (1986): 285, 286.

53. Mutch, *Campaigns, Congress, and Courts*, p. xvii.

54. Ibid., p. 3.

In other words, contrary to the myths of campaign finance reformers, the role of the average citizen and the small contributor in financing campaigns has not been reduced over the years. For most voters, familiarizing themselves with the candidates and voting in elections have always been the extent of political involvement. Today, approximately 10 percent of Americans make a financial contribution to a political party, candidate, or PAC in an election cycle.[55] That represents a far broader base of financial support than has historically existed. Yet few would argue that it has made the political system more democratic or responsive. Just as it is a mistake to assume that reliance on a small number of contributors is necessarily undemocratic, it is a mistake to believe that large expenditures are inherently undemocratic. If, for example, we assume that reliance on numerous small contributions makes a campaign in some way more democratic, then the U.S. Senate campaign of Oliver North was the most democratic of all 1994 campaigns. Yet it was also one of the most expensive, costing nearly $20 million.[56] Despite his reliance on small donations from many people, North was roundly castigated by many campaign finance reformers for the high cost of his campaign. Yet North lost.

Unfortunately, campaign finance regulation actually limits voter choice by discouraging challengers and favoring political insiders. Neither increased campaign spending nor reliance on a small fund-raising base is inherently undemocratic. Those who seek to broaden the fundraising base by limiting large contributions are searching for a Holy Grail that never was, and their efforts tend to make the system less democratic rather than more so.

55. Sorauf, *Inside Campaign Finance*, p. 29, citing data from the University of Michigan National Election Study.

56. According to Michael J. Malbin, "Most GOP Winners Spent Enough Money to Reach Voters," *Political Finance & Lobby Reporter*, January 11, 1995, pp. 8, 9, North spent almost $20 million on his campaign, more per eligible voter than did Huffington in California. Most of North's money was raised in small, individual contributions.

SUMMARY

The pressure for campaign finance regulation has been based on assumptions that are, at best, seriously flawed. Campaigns are not particularly costly; the total spent every two years on congressional campaigning amounts to roughly the cost of one home video rental per eligible voter. Expenditures do not buy elections; large campaign expenditures are subject to diminishing returns, especially for incumbents, which strongly suggests that heavy spending cannot buy a seat if the voters do not like the message the campaign puts out. Finally, there is no serious evidence documenting a causal link between campaign contributions and the voting patterns of elected representatives. Nevertheless, although these assumptions lack empirical support, it is on them that the American system of campaign regulation has largely been based.

This is not to suggest that money is not without its problematic aspects.[57] But the greater threat to the democratic nature of our system comes less from the growth of campaign expenditures than from ill-conceived regulation that threatens to close off electoral politics to outsiders, hinder grassroots political involvement, and trample First Amendment rights to free speech.

THE UNDEMOCRATIC CONSEQUENCES OF
CAMPAIGN FINANCE REGULATION

If campaign finance regulation is founded on faulty assumptions, the continued call for additional regulation seems to be driven by a single-minded determination to ignore the consequences of such regulation on the electoral process. The goal of campaign finance reform has been to lower the cost of campaigning, reduce the influence of special interests, and open up the system. In all three aspects, the FECA amendments

---

57. See, for example, Frank J. Sorauf, "Politics, Experience, and the First Amendment: The Case of American Campaign Finance," *Columbia Law Review* 94 (1994): 1348; Sunstein, "Political Equality," p. 1390; Strauss, "Corruption, Equality, and Campaign Finance Reform," p. 1369; Lowenstein, "On Campaign Finance Reform," p. 301.

of 1974 appear to have been a fantastic failure. Congressional campaign spending, in constant dollars, nearly tripled between 1974 and 1992. Congressional election contributions by PACs, in constant 1992 dollars, increased from $101 million to $179 million over the same period, while the number of PACs rose from 608 to 4,268.[58] House incumbents, who in 1976 outspent challengers by a ratio of 1.5 to 1, by 1992 outspent challengers by almost 4 to 1.[59] Meanwhile, incumbent reelection rates in the House reached record highs in 1986 and 1988 before declining slightly in the 1990s.[60]

In an examination of the effects of campaign finance laws on American elections and American political life, it becomes apparent that campaign finance regulation helps close off political challenge and ossify the political system, stifles grassroots political activity, artificially constricts the political debate and the voices heard in that debate, distorts the political process in favor of the wealthy and powerful, and is ultimately incompatible with the First Amendment to the Constitution. In short, campaign finance regulation is undemocratic.

### Campaign Finance Regulation Favors Incumbents

Although limits on campaign contributions increase candidate reliance on small contributors, such limits are undemocratic if by *democratic* we mean a political system that is open to challenge by outsiders and that allows challengers and those already in power to compete on relatively equal footing. The undemocratic nature of campaign finance limitations is most readily seen in the way such limitations favor incumbents over challengers.

As previously discussed, higher levels of spending tend to benefit challengers more than incumbents. Incumbents begin each election with significant advantages in name recognition. They are able to attract

58. Mason and Schwalm, *Advantage Incumbents*, p. 3.
59. Fred Wertheimer and Susan Manes, "Campaign Finance Reform: A Key to Restoring the Health of Our Democracy," *Columbia Law Review* 94 (1994): 1126, 1133.
60. Sunstein, "Political Equality," p. 1402, table 2.

press coverage because of their office, and they often receive assistance from their office staffs and government-paid constituent mailings. Through patronage and constituent favors, they can add to their support.[61] To offset these advantages, challengers must spend money. By limiting the ability of challengers to raise and spend money, campaign finance laws lock into place the advantages of incumbency and disproportionately harm challengers.[62]

Campaign finance laws also tend to favor incumbents by making it harder for challengers to raise money vis-à-vis incumbents. With campaign contribution limits, candidates cannot raise money quickly from a small number of dedicated supporters. Yet the ability to raise campaign cash from a large number of small contributors lies with those candidates who already have in place a database of past contributors and an intact campaign organization and who are able to raise funds on an ongoing basis from PACs. In other words, campaign finance limitations benefit incumbents, as shown by the escalating spending advantage incumbents have obtained since 1974.

Campaign finance laws pose a particularly high hurdle to unknown candidates because of the difficulties faced by those with low name recognition in raising substantial sums from small contributors. Contributors are less likely to give to unknowns.

However, even well-known public figures challenging the status quo have historically relied on a small number of wealthy patrons to fund their campaigns. For example, Theodore Roosevelt's 1912 Bull Moose campaign was funded almost entirely by a handful of wealthy supporters. Senator Eugene McCarthy's 1968 antiwar campaign relied on seed money from a few six-figure donors, including Stewart Mott, who gave approximately $210,000, and Wall Street banker Jack Dreyfus Jr., who may have contributed as much as $500,000. It is interesting to consider that, had the 1974 FECA amendments been in effect, it is likely that

61. Gottlieb, "Dilemma of Election Campaign Finance Reform," pp. 213, 224.
62. Jacobson, *Money in Congressional Elections*, pp. 195-96.

neither campaign would have gotten off the ground. In that case, Roosevelt would not have paved the way for Woodrow Wilson's election as president by splitting the Republican vote in 1912, and Lyndon Johnson would almost certainly have sought reelection in 1968. More recently, John Anderson would probably have had more success in his independent campaign for the presidency in 1980 had his wealthy patron, the ubiquitous Stewart Mott, been able to contribute unlimited amounts to his campaign.[63] And whereas Ross Perot's 1992 campaign was made possible by the Supreme Court's holding in *Buckley* that an individual may spend unlimited sums to advance his own candidacy, the contribution limits upheld in *Buckley* would make it illegal for Perot to bankroll the campaign of a more plausible challenger, such as Colin Powell or Paul Tsongas, in the same manner. Despite recent polls showing strong voter interest in a third-party or independent candidate for president in 1996, FECA makes a serious independent challenge by anyone other than Perot virtually impossible by limiting such a candidate's fund-raising ability.

Of course, the fund-raising disadvantage applies to challengers for all federal offices, not just the presidency. To offset the advantages incumbents have in raising funds and to secure adequate time to raise cash from small contributions, challengers must declare their candidacies at ever earlier points in the election cycle. Incumbents, in turn, resort to regular fund-raising to stay ahead of challengers. The result, in addition to record-high reelection rates for incumbents, has been an endless cycle of campaign fund-raising. In the end, the 1974 FECA amendments were something of a Faustian bargain for incumbents. In return for higher reelection rates, they are now subjected to a seemingly endless parade of fund-raisers. The weary public loses on both counts.

---

63. See Stewart Mott, "Independent Fundraising for an Independent Candidate," *New York University Review of Law and Social Change* 10 (1981): 135. See also Statement of Stewart R. Mott, exhibit to deposition of Stewart R. Mott, *Buckley v. Valeo*, p. 1, describing Mott's political expenditures from 1963 to 1974.

## Campaign Finance Regulation Favors Special Interests over Grassroots Activity

Limitations on contributions and spending, by definition, require significant regulation of the campaign process, including significant reporting requirements as to amounts spent and sources of funds. Such regulation creates opportunities to gain an advantage over an opponent through use of the regulatory process, and litigation has now become a major campaign tactic.[64] Typically, regulation favors insiders already familiar with the regulatory machinery and those with the money and sophistication to hire the lawyers, accountants, and lobbyists needed to comply with complex filing requirements.[65] Indeed, there is some evidence that campaign enforcement actions are disproportionately directed at challengers, who are less likely to have staff familiar with the intricacies of campaign finance regulation.[66]

Perhaps those most likely to run afoul of campaign finance laws are unaffiliated individuals engaged in true grassroots activities. For example, in 1991 the *Los Angeles Times* reviewed Federal Election Commission (FEC) files and found that sixty-two individuals had violated FECA contribution limits by making total contributions of more than $25,000 to candidates in the 1990 elections. As the *Times* noted, though many of these sixty-two were "successful business people" who "usually have the benefit of expert legal advice on the intricacies of federal election laws," the next largest group of violators consisted of "elderly persons . . . with little grasp of the federal campaign laws."[67] Political involvement should not be limited to those with "the benefit of expert legal advice on the intricacies of federal election laws."

---

64. Moussalli, *Campaign Finance Reform*, p. 9.
65. Mott, "Independent Fundraising," p. 135.
66. See *Pestrak v. Ohio Elections Commission*, 926 F.2d 573 (1991), brief of amicus curiae American Civil Liberties Union of Ohio Foundation, at 13–16, noting that the Ohio Election Code has been enforced almost exclusively against challengers.
67. Sara Fritz and Dwight Morris, "Federal Campaign Donors' Limits Not Being Enforced," *Los Angeles Times*, September 15, 1991, p. A1.

Even more chilling is the story of Margaret McIntyre. In 1988 McIntyre, an Ohio housewife, was fined by the Ohio Elections Commission for the peaceful distribution of truthful, homemade campaign literature outside a public meeting.[68] The fine was based on a complaint brought by the assistant school superintendent in McIntyre's hometown of Westerville after a local school levy, which McIntyre campaigned against, failed on two occasions. The charges, filed months after the election, accused McIntyre of distributing anonymous campaign literature in violation of Ohio law;[69] McIntyre had signed her brochures simply "Concerned Parents and Taxpayers." After seven years of litigation, the Supreme Court finally overturned McIntyre's conviction in April 1995.[70]

The McIntyre case illustrates the manner in which campaign finance laws can trip up ordinary citizens and threaten them with years of litigation and legal fees, even if those citizens are ultimately exonerated. Significantly, immediately after the Supreme Court's decision, both the Ohio secretary of state and the state's attorney general indicated their belief that the Court's ruling does not prohibit enforcement of the law against "groups," just individuals.[71] This suggests that grassroots coalitions are still in danger whenever they engage in speech without first consulting a lawyer. Federal law and the law of every state save California contain provisions similar to that under which McIntyre was fined.

Even sophisticated interest groups have found campaign finance laws a substantial hindrance to grassroots campaign activity and voter education efforts. In 1994, for example, under threats of litigation from the FEC, both the U.S. Chamber of Commerce and the American Medical Association decided not to publish and distribute candidate endorsements to thousands of their dues-paying members. Under FEC

---

68. *McIntyre v. Ohio Elections Commission*, 67 Ohio St.3d 391 (1993).

69. Ibid. Federal law contains similar disclosure provisions for campaign literature.

70. *McIntyre v. Ohio Elections Commission*, 115 S.Ct. 1511 (1995).

71. Roger K. Lowe, "Justices Strike Down Ohio Law," *Columbus Dispatch*, April 20, 1995, p. 1.

regulations, only 63 of the chamber's 220,000 dues-paying members qualified as members for the purposes of receiving the organization's political communications. Similarly, the FEC had held it to be unlawful for the AMA to distribute endorsements to some 44,500 of its members. One AMA lawyer noted that, under the circumstances, communicating endorsements to its dues-paying members was not "worth the legal risk."[72]

But if campaign finance laws, and FECA in particular, have contributed to the decline of grassroots political activity,[73] they have also favored select elites—in particular, media elites. For example, although most corporations are limited in what they may contribute to a particular campaign, newspapers, magazines, and television and radio stations can spend unlimited sums to promote the election of favored candidates. Thus, Rupert Murdoch has at his disposal the resources of a media empire to promote his views, free from the campaign finance restriction to which other persons are subjected. Donald Graham, publisher of the *Washington Post,* can run editorials and shape news coverage in favor of a preferred candidate seven days a week, as can the publishers of *Time* and *Newsweek.*[74] Rush Limbaugh and Jim Hightower can take to the airwaves daily to support their choices for public office. Yet the Supreme Court has allowed states to limit even independent expenditures by nonmedia corporations to candidate races.[75]

The increased power that campaign finance restrictions give to media elites emphasizes the fact that efforts to limit campaign spending and contributions do not eliminate inequalities in political participation. Rather, such restrictions neutralize one type of political resource,

72. Edward Zuckerman, "Speechless in DC," *Political Finance & Lobby Reporter,* November 9, 1994, p. 1.

73. Gottlieb, "Dilemma of Election Campaign Finance Reform," p. 225 n. 61, and sources cited therein.

74. For a journalist's view of this power, see Jonathan Rowe, "The View from the Hill: Government's Opinion of the Capital Press Corps," *Columbia Journalism Review* 33 (July 1994): 47.

75. *Austin v. Michigan Chamber of Commerce* 494 U.S. 652 (1990).

thereby strengthening the position of those with other, nonmonetary resources. For example, restricting the flow of money into campaigns increases the relative importance of in-kind contributions and so favors those who are able to control large blocks of manpower rather than dollars. Thus, limiting contributions and expenditures does not particularly democratize the process; it merely shifts power from those whose primary contribution is money to those whose primary contribution is time—for example, from small business to People for the American Way.

Other beneficiaries of campaign finance limitations include political middlemen: public relations firms conducting "voter education" programs on behalf of special interest groups; lobbyists; PACs such as Emily's List, which "bundle" large numbers of $1,000 contributions; and political activists. These individuals and groups may or may not be more representative of public opinion than the wealthy philanthropists and industrialists who financed so many campaigns in the past. One thing is clear, however: that campaign finance restrictions do not make the system more responsive. Efforts to ensure "equality" of inputs into the campaign process are less likely to guarantee popular control than is the presence of multiple sources of political power.[76] FECA and state campaign finance laws attempt to limit certain power bases—for example, those based on monetary contributions—but leave others intact, thereby decreasing the number of voices and increasing the power of those groups whose form of contribution remains unregulated.

By helping to entrench incumbents in office and by adding to the power of media elites and careerist political operatives, campaign finance limitations have added to the public demand for term limits and to the general public negativity toward politics and politicians.

*Campaign Finance Limitations Favor Wealthy Candidates and Parties*

Campaign finance restrictions have also helped create the modern phenomenon of the "millionaire candidate," of whom Michael Huffington

---

76. Gottlieb, "Dilemma of Election Campaign Finance Reform," pp. 271–73.

and Ross Perot are only the most celebrated examples. In the *Buckley* decision, the Supreme Court held that Congress could not limit the amount that candidates could spend on their own campaigns. Under FECA and similar state laws limiting the size of campaign contributions, however, candidates are forced to raise funds from the public in small amounts. The ability to spend unlimited amounts, coupled with FECA's restrictions on raising money, favors those candidates who can contribute large sums to their own campaigns from personal assets. A Michael Huffington, Herb Kohl, or Jay Rockefeller becomes a particularly attractive candidate precisely because personal wealth provides a direct campaign advantage that cannot be offset by a large contributor to the opposing candidate.[77]

At the same time that campaign finance restrictions help wealthy candidates, they tend to harm working-class political interests. Historically, candidates with large constituencies among poor and working-class people have obtained their campaign funds from a small base of wealthy donors.[78] If the law limits the ability of a Stewart Mott or August Belmont to finance these efforts, working-class constituencies may suffer. Their supporters simply do not have the funds to compete with other constituencies and candidates. As Stephen Gottlieb points out,

---

77. In 1994 Huffington spent approximately $25 million of his own fortune to run for the U.S. Senate, and by September 30, 1994, Kohl had contributed almost $4 million to his 1994 reelection effort. Edward Kennedy and Mitt Romney each loaned $2 million to their campaigns for the U.S. Senate from Massachusetts ("Senate Candidates Add $31.5 Million to Their Own Campaigns," *Political Finance & Lobby Reporter*, October 26, 1994, p. 1). According to Edward Roeder, Bill Frist of Tennessee was another big ($3.75 million) spender ("Big Money Won the Day Last November," *Cleveland Plain Dealer*, December 25, 1994, p. 1-C). (This article, incidentally, is typical of newspaper bias when reporting on campaign finance, arguing that in 1994, "the fat cats bought more elections for Republicans than for Democrats." Although Roeder does note that FECA has favored incumbents, created a cottage industry of professional middlemen, and harmed grassroots activity, his curious conclusion is that Congress should enact still more campaign finance laws.) On the House side, Republican Gene Fontenot ($2.0 million) and Democrat Robert Schuster ($1.1 million) provided the bulk of their own campaign funds (Zuckerman, "Money Didn't Matter," p. 1).

78. Gottlieb, "Dilemma of Election Campaign Finance Reform," p. 221.

"Candidates with many supporters who can afford to give the legal limit may be relatively unscathed by 'reform' legislation. As a consequence, it appears that national campaign 'reform' legislation has benefitted the wealthy at the expense of the working class."[79]

## How Campaign Finance Reform Threatens the Right to Free Speech

In the eighteen years since *Buckley* was decided, the Supreme Court has struggled to develop principled limits on what Congress and the states can do to regulate campaign donations and spending. Operating within the *Buckley* framework, the Court has found all the following distinctions to be of constitutional dimension in deciding what a state may or may not regulate in the way of campaign contributions and spending:

- The right of individuals to spend unlimited amounts on their own campaign versus the right of those same individuals to contribute unlimited amounts to other people's campaigns[80]

- The right of a candidate to spend money versus the right of a contributor to give money[81]

- Contributions to a candidate versus independent expenditures in support of a candidate[82]

- Spending by ideological corporations versus spending by non-ideological corporations[83]

- Spending on ballot issues versus spending on candidate races[84]

- Contributions made from a corporation's general fund versus contributions made from a segregated corporate fund[85]

79. Ibid.
80. *Buckley v. Valeo*, p. 1.
81. Ibid.
82. *FEC v. National Conservative Political Action Committee*, 470 U.S. 480 (1985).
83. *FEC v. Massachusetts Citizens for Life, Inc.*, 479 U.S. 238 (1986).
84. *First National Bank of Boston v. Bellotti*, 435 U.S. 765 (1978).
85. *Austin v. Michigan Chamber of Commerce*, p. 652.

- Campaign expenditures by media corporations versus campaign expenditures by nonmedia corporations[86]

- Campaign expenditures by corporations versus campaign expenditures by unincorporated entities such as labor unions[87]

In other words, the *Buckley* standard has created a doctrinal nightmare for the Court. Having conceded that Congress and the states can regulate campaign contributions and spending despite the First Amendment, the Court has been unable to define clear limits to this regulation short of the complete gutting of the First Amendment. As a result, the Court's attempted distinctions between fact situations seem less and less a matter of constitutional principle and more and more a matter of policy preference.

The problematic nature of these distinctions can be seen most vividly in the Court's 1990 decision in *Austin v. Michigan Chamber of Commerce.* In this case, the Michigan Chamber of Commerce challenged a state law prohibiting it from spending corporate funds to run a newspaper advertisement in support of a candidate for the Michigan State Senate. In an earlier decision, *FEC v. Massachusetts Citizens for Life (MCFL)*,[88] the Court had held that FECA, in requiring all corporate expenditures on campaigns to be made from a segregated fund (i.e., a PAC), impermissibly burdened the First Amendment rights of ideological corporations. The Chamber of Commerce sought to invoke MCFL to protect its right to spend funds from its general treasury in support of a candidate for office. However, the Court held that whereas MCFL was an ideological corporation, the Chamber of Commerce was not. Such a discovery would have been shocking to many Michigan lawmakers, but the Court cited as examples of the chamber's nonideological nature a seminar it held on product liability losses and lawsuits and the

---

86. Ibid.
87. Ibid.
88. *FEC v. Massachusetts Citizens for Life,* p. 238.

fact that the chamber, though a nonprofit organization, accepted contributions from for-profit businesses.[89]

The Court also attempted to justify the different treatment of labor unions and corporations under the Michigan law by finding that unions do not gain significant "state-conferred" advantages. Here the Court's position borders on the ludicrous, given the protection given to union members and organizers under the National Labor Relations Act and Michigan state law.[90] The Court further struggled to explain why media corporations could be exempted from the law and be allowed to expend unlimited sums from their corporate treasuries to engage in political activities. In this effort, the Court pointed to the important role of the "institutional press" in "informing and educating the public, offering criticism, and providing a public forum for discussion and debate."[91] Yet this is exactly what the chamber sought to do through independent newspaper ads in support of its favored candidate. Apparently, the Court would allow the chamber to spend unlimited sums from its corporate treasury if it purchased a newspaper or radio station but not if it simply chose to advertise with one. The notion that the state can choose certain types of individuals or organizations to serve as the approved "public forum for discussion and debate," entitled to special privileges and exemptions from the law, should be alarming to all First Amendment activists.

Historically, the most controversial First Amendment issues have centered on whether certain types of speech, such as pornography or commercial speech, or symbolic acts, such as flag burning, are protected by the amendment. What has been undisputed is that the First Amendment must protect political speech.[92] Having decided in *Buckley*, how-

---

89. *Austin v. Michigan Chamber of Commerce*, pp. 663–64.
90. See Michigan Statutes Annotated 17 (Callaghan 1991).
91. *Austin v. Michigan Chamber of Commerce*, p. 667.
92. Even scholars who have criticized judicial protection of pornography and other types of speech have recognized the obvious applicability of the First Amendment to political speech. See, for example, Robert Bork, "Neutral Principles and Some First Amendment Problems," *Indiana Law Journal* 47 (1971): 1.

ever, that admittedly political speech can be regulated if the state has a strong "compelling interest," the Court has left itself with no logical stopping point. There can be few state interests more compelling than the electoral process. Thus, the Court's announced test favors significant state regulation of the content of campaign speech. Yet this is precisely the type of speech that the First Amendment was most clearly enacted to protect. By emphasizing the state's interest in regulating speech, the Court has turned the First Amendment on its head. Whereas the Founders saw government regulation of political speech as a great danger to self-government, the Court sees unregulated political discourse as the threat to self-government.

FECA and its various state counterparts are profoundly undemocratic and profoundly at odds with the First Amendment.

## PUBLIC FUNDING IS NOT THE ANSWER

Many have argued that the solution to the perceived evils of money in politics lies in public financing of campaigns.[93] Public financing would, it is suggested, remove the alleged corrupting influence of money, place candidates for office on equal footing, and relieve candidates of the need for constant fund-raising. In fact, public financing is unlikely to achieve these goals and raises significant problems in its own right.

Most public financing proposals are tied to limitations on the expenditure of private funds. Although the Supreme Court has held that Congress may not directly limit spending by candidates, it may link the receipt of public funds to voluntary spending limits.[94] If, however,

93. For example, see Wertheimer and Manes, "Campaign Finance Reform," pp. 1142–44; and Jamie Raskin and John Bonifaz, "The Constitutional Imperative and Practical Superiority of Democratically Financed Elections," *Columbia Law Review* 94 (1994): 1160, who argue that the Constitution requires public financing of campaigns.

94. *Buckley v. Valeo*, p. 1. However, the penalties for failing to accept "voluntary" limits may not be so steep as to amount to de facto compulsion, under the Court's doctrine of "unconstitutional conditions." For example, see Kathleen M. Sullivan, "Unconstitutional Conditions," *Harvard Law Review* 102 (1989): 1413. President Clinton's 1993 campaign finance proposal probably crossed the line on unconstitutional conditions through signif-

public financing of campaigns becomes a surrogate for spending caps, it will have the effect of favoring incumbents against challengers. This is because, as discussed above, added spending tends to benefit challengers more than incumbents. Thus, far from equalizing the field, public financing tied to spending limits will further add to incumbent advantages.[95]

In response, some political scientists have suggested that public financing should not serve to cap expenditures but rather to create a floor for them.[96] Under this theory, public financing would be used to ensure that each major party candidate has sufficient funds to run a minimally competitive race for office. Candidates could then supplement their public funds with unlimited private spending. Such an approach would avoid the disadvantages of spending and contribution limits and would perhaps help to make more campaigns competitive. However, several problems remain.

To begin with, public financing is undemocratic in a most fundamental way: it is generally opposed by the public. A December 1990 NBC News/*Wall Street Journal* poll found public funding opposed by 55 percent to 38 percent. A January 1990 ABC News/*Washington Post* poll found 31 percent opposed, 20 percent in favor, and 49 percent undecided.[97] Although some polls have shown more favorable responses to public financing,[98] the general public has also refused to support

---

icant penalties against candidates who did not accept the voluntary limits coupled with substantial added subsidies to their competitors. S 3, 103d Cong., 1st sess.

95. Further, incumbents will have incentives to set spending limits at a level that works in their favor. For example, as Mason and Schwalm (*Advantage Incumbents*) write, recent elections have shown that a challenger for a seat in the House must spend roughly $600,000 to have a realistic shot at defeating an incumbent (p. 10). Not surprisingly, the administration's 1993 proposal would have capped spending just at this level. See also Lowenstein, "On Campaign Finance Reform," pp. 301, 335, who notes that President Bush's 1989 campaign finance proposals would have favored Republicans.

96. See, for example, Sabato, "Real and Imagined Corruption," p. 160.

97. Sorauf, *Inside Campaign Finance*, p. 145.

98. Sorauf notes, for example, that a 1990 Greenberg/Lake poll found 58 percent in favor and 33 percent opposed. However, the same survey also showed that voters were 60

public financing at the ballot box or through tax returns; voters have defeated public financing referenda in California, Ohio, and Arizona, and fewer than 20 percent of Americans contribute to the presidential campaign fund through checkoffs on their tax returns.[99]

Public funding is undemocratic in other ways as well. As does campaign finance regulation generally, public funding favors those already in power. The presidential system, for example, automatically grants public funding for the general election and nominating convention to any party that received more than 25 percent of the vote in the previous election. New parties or independent challengers are in most cases ineligible for such funds and, in a best-case scenario, receive less money than the two major parties.[100]

Worse still, most public financing proposals call for the distribution of public funds to be tied to the candidates' popularity in opinion polls or proven fund-raising ability, as does the matching fund system used in presidential primaries. That type of public financing actually compounds funding inequalities and the benefits of prior name recognition, generally to the detriment of candidates with disproportionate support among less affluent voters.[101] For example, a $500 contribution to Bill Clinton would yield $500 in matching funds; a $20 contribution to Jesse Jackson would yield just $20 in matching funds. Yet the alternative—making funds available regardless of proven support—is unappealing to most Americans.

Indeed, even when disbursement of funds is tied to some measure of popular support, it is likely that public funds will also flow to those

---

percent to 29 percent against public financing when told that it would result in taxpayers paying for negative advertising (*Inside Campaign Finance*, p. 145). See also Russ Hemphill, "Public Rejects Paying for Campaigns," *Phoenix Gazette*, September 22, 1993, p. B3, who reports that 75 percent of voters polled opposed public financing.

99. Sorauf, *Inside Campaign Finance*, p. 141. Minnesota's state checkoff system also has participation rates below 20 percent (ibid., p. 143).

100. Elizabeth Rada, David Cardwell, and Alan Friedman, "Access to the Ballot," *Urban Law* 13 (1981): 793, 808.

101. Gottlieb, "Dilemma of Election Campaign Finance Reform," p. 223.

on the fringes of American politics. For example, Lenora Fulani of the ultraleft New Alliance Party received nearly $3 million in public funding over the course of the 1988 and 1992 presidential elections,[102] although her level of public support never reached even 1 percent. Perennial presidential candidate and convicted felon Lyndon LaRouche took in a cool $825,000 in taxpayer-provided matching funds in 1988 alone.[103] As far back as 1777, Thomas Jefferson wrote, "To compel a man to furnish contributions of money for the propagation of opinions which he disbelieves, is sinful and tyrannical."[104] This is true when the money goes to Bob Dole and Bill Clinton; that taxpayers are forced to fund Lyndon LaRouche and Lenora Fulani as well only drives the point home.

Finally, public financing is expensive at a time of ongoing deficit spending by government. For example, the provision of $300,000 in public funds, the minimum needed for an effective campaign, to each of 870 candidates for the U.S. House of Representatives would cost more than $260 million per congressional election. Add in senatorial candidates, funding for primary candidates, or funding for third-party and independent candidates, and the amounts go higher still. Given that the shortage of challenger funds could be largely resolved by re-pealing contribution limits already in effect, public financing appears to be a serious boondoggle.

CONCLUSION

Efforts to regulate campaign finance, in particular, the Federal Election Campaign Act, have been based on mistaken assumptions about the role of money in politics and on the mistaken belief that eliminating or reducing money will in some way make the process more fair, the playing field more level. In fact, spending on political campaigns is hardly extravagant, amounting to only a few dollars per eligible voter every

---

102. Mason and Schwalm, *Advantage Incumbents*, p. 13.
103. Sorauf, *Inside Campaign Finance*, p. 138, table 5.1.
104. Thomas Jefferson, "A Bill for Establishing Religious Freedom," in *The Portable Thomas Jefferson*, ed. Merrill D. Peterson (New York: Viking Press, 1975), p. 252.

two years. Because there is no a priori correct allocation of political advantages, including money, efforts to control this one feature of the political landscape have tended to have serious detrimental side effects, including the entrenchment of incumbents and the stifling of new, alternative political choices. FECA and its state counterparts have served to limit grassroots political activity and to enhance the power of campaign professionals and insiders. Overall, campaign finance regulation has served to make the political process less open and less democratic.

Moreover, efforts to limit campaign contributions and expenditures run directly counter to the assumptions of the First Amendment. The First Amendment was based on the belief that political speech is too important to be regulated by the government. Campaign finance laws operate on the directly contrary assumption—that campaigns are so important that speech must be regulated. The result has been a series of Supreme Court decisions making largely arcane, questionable distinctions between different types of entities, campaigns, and campaign activities. These decisions are hard to justify under the First Amendment and have clearly limited the opportunities for Americans to engage in what at least one sitting justice has recognized as "core political speech."[105]

After nearly twenty-five years, FECA has done nothing to change the alleged evils that led to its adoption. This suggests either that the evils are inevitable, if not beneficial, or that the solution to the alleged problems must lie elsewhere—in measures such as term limitations, abolition or modification of legislative seniority and pension systems, or other structural reforms from which Congress has shied away.

In short, the solution to the alleged problems of campaign finance is far simpler than the arcane web of regulations that leads to citizens being fined for distributing homemade leaflets, to trade groups being prohibited from communicating with their members, and to personal

---

105. Roger K. Lowe, "High Court Takes Up Westerville Woman's Case," *Columbus Dispatch*, October 13, 1994, p. 1, quoting Justice O'Connor.

wealth serving as an indicator of a viable political candidate. The solution is to recognize the flawed assumptions of the campaign finance reformers, dismantle FECA and the FEC bureaucracy, and take seriously the system of campaign finance regulation that the Founders wrote into the Bill of Rights: "Congress shall make no law . . . abridging the freedom of speech."

# PACs and Parties

## Larry J. Sabato

This chapter first appeared in *Money, Elections, and Democracy: Reforming Congressional Campaign Finance*, edited by Margaret Lotus Nugent and John R. Johannes (Boulder, Colo.: Westview Press, 1990), pp. 187–204. In "PACs and Parties," Sabato, a professor of political science at the University of Virginia and the author of several books on the American political process, considers the relationship between political action committees and political parties, especially since the passage of the campaign finance legislation of the 1970s.

Sabato finds that PACs are not nearly as pernicious as journalists would make them out to be. Special interest money has always found its way into the political arena, Sabato notes; the growth of PACs since the legislation of the 1970s is its current manifestation and makes special interest money more visible than it was before reporting requirements were instituted. Sabato also finds that PACs as well as parties have a legitimate and important role in the political process.

He would, however, prefer to strengthen parties rather than PACs and to this end suggests less restrictive limits on contributions of individuals and PACs to political parties (these limits were not indexed for inflation, and their real value has thus eroded over the years) and even tax incentives for contributions.

VALUES AT STAKE

The relationships between political action committees and political parties are at once symbiotic and parasitic. Both parties work hard to cultivate PACs and secure their money, and most PACs energetically endeavor to be of use bipartisanly (at least to incumbents of both parties). At the same time, PACs and parties are rivals for the attentions of candidates, the favors of officeholders, and the devotions of voters. More important, the success of narrow-based PACs necessarily comes partly at the expense of broad-based parties. As parties decline, PACs gain, and in some ways PACS have greased the skids of party decline.

This decline of parties and the preeminence of PACs comes at the expense of important democratic values, for PACs and parties perform very different functions in our electoral and governmental system. PACS provide avenues for participation and political liberty but have questionable effects on competition, accountability, governmental legitimacy, and effectiveness. Parties allow for the expression of more broad-based interests, provide channels for representation and accountability, legitimacy and effectiveness. Given the symbiotic relationship of parties and PACs, both have a valuable role in our campaign finance system, but democratic values could be better served by increasing the significance of the parties and diminishing that of PACs. In other words, I am partial to parties, but not anti-PAC, so this paper will simultaneously *defend* both types of political organization while arguing the case for tilting the electoral system's balance in favor of the parties.[1]

## ASSESSING CRITICISMS AGAINST PACS

It in easy to conclude that political action committees are the root of all campaign financing evils—if one's sources are restricted to news media coverage of politics. Journalists' obsession with PACs, reinforced by the predilections of various public interest groups, has focused attention on PAC excesses to the near exclusion of other concerns in the area of political money. Why is there such an obsession with PACs, and what charges against them generate such emotion?

Although a good number of PACs of all political persuasions existed before the 1970s, it was during this decade—the decade of campaign reform—that the modern PAC era began. Spawned by the Watergate-inspired revisions of the campaign finance laws, PACs grew in number from 113 in 1972 to 4,268 by the end of 1988, and their contributions to congressional candidates multiplied almost eighteenfold, from $8.5 million in 1971–1972 to $151.3 million in 1987–1988 (see table 1). This

---

1. This paper will draw information and arguments from three of my other works in the subject area: *PAC Power: Inside the World of Political Action Committees* (New York: W. W. Norton, 1984); *The Party's Just Begun: Shaping Political Parties for America's Future* (Boston: Little, Brown/Scott, Foresman, 1988); and *Paying for Elections: The Campaign Finance Thicket* (New York: The Twentieth Century Fund, 1989).

TABLE 1.   Growth in PAC Numbers and Congressional Contributions, 1972–
1988 (in $ millions)

| Year | Number of PACs | Contributions to Candidates [a] |
|------|----------------|----------------------------------|
| 1972 | 113 | 8.5 |
| 1974 | 608 | 11.6 |
| 1976 | 1,146 | 20.5 |
| 1978 | 1,653 | 34.1 |
| 1980 | 2,551 | 65.2 |
| 1982 | 3,371 | 83.6 |
| 1984 | 4,009 | 106.3 |
| 1986 | 4,157 | 132.7 |
| 1988 | 4,268 | 151.3 |

[a] As of December 31 of each year, for the two-year election cycles ending in years shown.
SOURCE: Federal Election Commission.

rapid rise of PACs has inevitably proven controversial, yet many of the charges made against political action committees are exaggerated and dubious.

It is said that PACs are dangerously novel and have flooded the political system with money, mainly from business. Although the widespread use of the PAC structure is new, the fact remains that special interest money of all types has always found its way into politics and that before the 1970s, it did so in less traceable and far more disturbing and unsavory ways. And yes, in absolute terms PACs contribute a massive sum to candidates, but it is not clear that there is proportionately more interest group money in the system than before. The proportion of House and Senate campaign funds provided by PACs has certainly increased since the early 1970s, but individuals, most of whom are unaffiliated with PACs together with the political parties, still supply about three-fifths of all the money spent by or on behalf of House candidates and three-quarters of the campaign expenditures for Senate contenders. So although the importance of PAC spending has grown, PACs clearly remain secondary as a source of election funding and therefore pose no overwhelming threat to our system's legitimacy.

Apart from the argument over the relative weight of PAC funds, PAC critics claim that political action committees are making it more expensive to run for office. There is some validity to this assertion. Money provided to one side funds the purchase of campaign tools, which the other side must then match in order to stay competitive. In the aggregate, American campaign expenditures seem huge. All 1988 U.S. House of Representatives candidates taken together spent about $256 million, and the campaign of the average winning House nominee cost more than $392,000. Will Rogers's 1931 remark has never been more true: "Politics has got so expensive that it take lots of money to even get beat with." Yet $256 million is far less than the annual advertising budgets of many individual commercial enterprises. These days it is expensive to communicate, whether the message is political or commercial. Television time, polling costs, consultants' fees, direct mail investment, and other standard campaign expenditures have been soaring in price, over and above inflation.[2] PACs have been fueling the use of new campaign techniques, but a reasonable case can be made that such expenses are necessary and that more, and better, communication is required between candidates and an electorate that often appears woefully uninformed about politics. PACs therefore may be making a positive contribution by providing the means to increase the flow of information during elections and thus enhancing political liberty.

PACs are also charged with reducing competition, and, except for the ideological ones, PACs do display a clear, overwhelming preference for incumbents. But the same bias is apparent in contributions from individuals. On the other hand, the best challengers are usually generously funded by PACs. Well-targeted PAC challenger money clearly helped the GOP win a majority in the U.S. Senate in 1980, for instance, and in turn aided the Democrats in their 1986 Senate takeover. I share Maisel's belief that PACs limit the number of strong challengers by

---

2. See Larry Sabato, *The Rise of Political Consultants: New Ways of Winning Elections* (New York: Basic Books, 1981); see also *National Journal* 15 (April 16, 1983): 780–81.

giving so much early money to incumbents, money that helps to deter potential opponents from declaring their candidacies. But the money that PACs channel to competitive challengers late in the election season may then increase the turnover of officeholders on election day. PAC money also normally invigorates competitiveness in open seat congressional races—races without an incumbent candidate.

The fourth major criticism of PACs concerns their influence on legislature behavior—or "vote buying." As Grenzke notes, there is the potential for influence under certain circumstances, but the magnitude of the problem is greatly exaggerated. Furthermore, PACs are influenced in those cases where traditional lobbies—many of whom have merely supplemented their arsenals with PACs—also succeed.

One last line of attack on PACs is more justified. As David Adamany has noted, many PACs are inadequately accountable to donors or voters—a condition most apparent in many of the ideological nonconnected PACs, which lack a parent body and whose freestyle organization makes them accountable to no one and responsive mainly to their own whims.[3] Many corporate PACs can hardly be considered showcases of democracy either. In a few PACs the chief executive officers completely rule the roost, and in many the CEOs have inordinate influence on PAC decisions.

As this brief examination of the charges made about political action committees has suggested, PACs are misrepresented and unfairly maligned as the embodiment of corrupt special interests. Contemporary political action committees are another manifestation of what James Madison called *factions*. Through the flourishing of competing interest groups or factions, said Madison in his *Federalist No. 10*, liberty would be preserved.

In any democracy, and particularly in one as pluralistic as the United States, it is essential that groups be relatively unrestricted in advocating

---

3. David Adamany, "The New Faces of American Politics," *The Annals of the American Academy of Political and Social Sciences* 486 (July 1986): 31–32.

their interests and positions. Not only is unrestricted political activity by interest groups a mark of a free society, but it provides a safety valve for the competitive pressures that build on all fronts in a capitalistic democracy. It also provides a means to keep representatives responsive to legitimate needs.

## THE BENEFITS OF PARTIES

The PACs have stolen the media spotlight, but the parties, an important check on the abuses of PAC power, are holding their own in the long-term battle for political supremacy. This is a surprise since the party system in the United States has declined and deteriorated in major ways in the last several decades. Prematurely counted out by many political observers, the parties have surprised many critics by regenerating themselves at the national level through the use of direct mail and other tools of the new campaign technology.[4] The Republican Party has led the way, spurred by the hope of breaking out of its minority status, and the Democrats have lately followed, prompted by the party's 1980 election disasters and the need to catch up with the GOP. Despite the press's focus on political action committees, the parties are about as healthy as the PACs. When all national party spending is taken together, the two parties raised $391 million in 1987–88, compared to about $370 million for all PACs.

The Democrats are clearly the junior partner in the arena of campaign finance. Of the $391 million total in 1988, the Republicans raised two-thirds. The GOP has traditionally been more successful at fundraising, but the gap began to grow after 1968 and to accelerate rapidly in the mid-1970s. During this time the Republicans made an enormous success of their direct-mail program while the Democrats continued to rely solely on large donors to whittle away at accumulated campaign debts.[5]

4. See Sabato, *The Party's Just Begun*, chapter 3.
5. Rhodes Cook, "Democrats Develop Tactics: Laying Groundwork for 1984," *Congressional Quarterly Weekly* 40 (July 3, 1982): 1595.

TABLE 2.   Political Party Finances, 1976–1988ᵃ (in $ millions)

| | TOTAL RECEIPTS | | TOTAL CONTRIBUTIONS | |
|---|---|---|---|---|
| Year | Democrats | Republicans | Democrats | Republicans |
| 1976 | 18.2 | 45.7 | 3.9 | 6.3 |
| 1978 | 26.4 | 84.5 | 2.3 | 8.9 |
| 1980 | 37.2 | 169.6 | 6.6 | 17.0 |
| 1982 | 39.3 | 215.0 | 5.1 | 19.9 |
| 1984 | 98.6 | 297.9 | 11.6 | 25.0 |
| 1986 | 64.8 | 255.2 | 10.7 | 17.7 |
| 1988 | 127.9 | 263.3 | 19.6 | 26.1 |

ᵃ Includes total for the national senatorial and congressional committees as well as all other reported national and state/local spending. All presidential, Senate, and House candidates are included.

SOURCE: Federal Election Commission.

The contemporary Republican Party has organizational strength unparalleled in American history and unrivaled by the Democrats. The Republicans have outraised the Democrats by enormous margins in all recent election cycles, never by less than 2 to 1 and usually by a considerably higher ratio (see table 2). This GOP fund-raising edge inevitably enhances the aid provided party nominees (see table 2). The Republicans have been able to give nearly the legal maximum gift (both in direct contributions and in coordinated expenditures) to every reasonably competitive Senate and House candidate; frequently the money is given "up front," immediately after a primary when a nominee's war chest is depleted and the need is greatest.

In the House of Representatives' contests, parties are limited to direct gifts of $5,000 per candidate per election (with the primary and general election counted separately).[6] But in House races these party contributions are being multiplied since the national party committee,

6. This assumes that the party committee or PAC is a multicandidate committee. See Sabato, *PAC Power*, pp. 7–8. If the committee or PAC has not qualified as a multicandidate committee, then a gift of only $1,000 maximum is permitted.

the state party committee, and the national party's congressional campaign committee are usually each eligible to give the $5,000 maximum. Thus, as much as $30,000 ($5,000 × 2 elections [primary and general] × 3 separate party committees) can be directly contributed to every party nominee for the United States House. In Senate elections, the national party committee and the senatorial campaign committee may give a combined maximum of $17,500 to each candidate; another $10,000 can be added from the state party committee for a total of $27,500 in direct gifts.

The parties' direct contributions can be significantly augmented with coordinated expenditures-party-paid general election campaign expenditures (for television advertising, polling, etc.) made in consultation and coordination with the candidate.[7] The coordinated expenditure limits are set surprisingly high. For House candidates the national and state parties may each spend $10,000 plus an inflation adjustment; the party committees together could thereby spend $46,100 in 1988 on behalf of each House nominee. Senate candidates are the beneficiaries of even higher limits on coordinated expenditures. The national and suggested state parties can each spend $20,000 (plus inflation), or two cents per voter, whichever is greater. In 1988 the party expenditure limits amounted to $92,200 in the eight smallest states to more than $1.9 million in California—or a national total maximum of about $12.8 million for each party in the thirty-three Senate contests. Importantly, the national party committee is permitted to act as the state party committee's spending agent; that is, with the state party's agreement, the national committee can assume the state party's permitted portion of the coordinated expenditures. This privilege centralizes power in the national committees and unburdens weaker state party committees that otherwise might not be able to contribute the maximum.

The candidate contribution totals in table 2 actually understate by a considerable margin the Republican Party's lead. Because the GOP so

7. Under 2 U.S.C. 441a(d).

frequently bumps up against the allowable ceiling on contributions and expenditures, it sends additional aid through back channels: soft money, individuals' donations solicited and collected for specific candidates by the party (and thus counted as individual gifts despite the party's role), and cut-rate party in-kind services for media, polling, and consultants. One journalist estimated that the GOP had at least a $30 million advantage just in the closest 1986 Senate races when money from all sources was taken into account.[8]

The Democratic Party lagged far behind Republicans until massive Democratic defeats in 1980 forced the party to modernize its approach to raising and contributing funds. Even after the better part of a decade, Democrats still trail their competitors by virtually every significant measure of party activity. Although the GOP has consistently maintained a large edge, however, the Democrats have considerably increased their total receipts. That is no small achievement.

## WHY PARTIES OVER PACS?

Whereas individuals and PACs represent particular interests and further the atomization of public policy, the parties encompass more general concerns and push the system toward consensus. There are no more unappreciated institutions in American life than the two major political parties. Often maligned by average citizens and many politicians alike as the repositories of corrupt bosses and smoke-filled rooms, the parties nonetheless perform essential electoral functions for our society. The enormous good that parties do for American society can be suggested by a brief discussion of several purposes served by the parties.

### Voting and Issue Cues

The political parties provide a useful cue for voters, particularly the least informed and least interested, who can use their party affiliation as a shortcut or substitute for interpreting issues and events they may little

---

8. Thomas B. Edsall, writing in the *Washington Post*, October 17, 1986, p. A1.

comprehend. But even better educated and more involved voters find party identification an assist. After all, no one has the time to study every issue carefully or to become fully knowledgeable about every candidate seeking public office. The result may be increased participation in elections.

## Mobilizing Support and Aggregating Power

The effect of the party cue is exceptionally helpful to elected leaders. They can count on disproportionate support among their partisans in time of trouble, and in close judgment calls they have a home court advantage. And because there are only two major parties, pragmatic citizens who are interested in politics or public policy are mainly attracted to one or the other standard, creating natural majorities or near majorities for party officeholders to command. The party creates a community of interest that bonds disparate groups together over time— eliminating the necessity of creating a coalition anew for every campaign or every issue. More effective government that is broadly accepted as legitimate is the consequence.

## Forces for Stability

As mechanisms for organizing and containing political change, the parties are a potent force for stability. They represent continuity in the wake of changing issues and personalities, anchoring the electorate as the storms that are churned by new political people and policies swirl around. Because of its unyielding, pragmatic desire to win elections (not just contest them), each party in a sense acts not only to promote competition but also to moderate public opinion. The party tames its own extreme elements by pulling them toward an ideological center in order to attract a majority of votes on election day.

## Unity, Linkage, Accountability

Parties provide the glue to hold together the diverse parts of the fragmented American governmental apparatus. The Founding Fathers designed a system that divides and subdivides power, making it possible to preserve individual liberty but difficult to coordinate and produce timely action. Parties help compensate for this drawback by linking all the institutions and loci of power one to another, enhancing governmental effectiveness. Although rivalry between the executive and legislative branches of American government is inevitable, the partisan affiliations of leaders of each branch constitute a common basis for cooperation, as any president and his fellow party members in Congress frequently demonstrate. Similarly, the federalist division of national, state, and local governments, while always an invitation to conflict, is made more workable and easily coordinated by the intersecting party relationships that exist among officeholders at all levels. Party affiliation, in other words, is a sanctioned and universally recognized basis for mediation and negotiation laterally among the branches and vertically among the layers. The party's linkage function does not end there, of course. The party connection is one means to ensure or increase accountability in election campaigns and in government. Candidates on the campaign trail and elected party leaders in office are required from time to time to account for their performance at party-sponsored forums and in party nominating primaries and conventions.

The increased money and services from both Democratic and Republican organizations may be drawing candidates much closer to their parties since the parties are contributing in tangible ways to their nominees' election. Whether or not any gratitude or obligation to the party is created in this fashion, such services as training schools, party issue papers, and institutional advertising put officeholders through a "homogenizing" process that may predispose them more favorably to the "party line" in government. Party leaders and political observers differ about whether such a development is really taking place, but all are agreed on one point: the parties remain less influential than they would be otherwise because alternative sources of funding are available to candidates. And the most available "alternative source" for incumbents is PACs.

## Promotion of Civic Virtue and Patriotism

Because identification with a party is at the core of most Americans' political lives, the prism through which they see the world, many voters accept and adopt the parties' values and view of responsible citizenship. These values include involvement and participation; work for the "public good" in the "national interest" (as conceived in partisan terms, naturally), and patriotism and respect for American society's fundamental institutions and processes.

### THE SYMBIOTIC RELATIONSHIP OF PACS AND PARTIES

On paper one can make a strong case that PACs and the political parties are bound to be competitors. They both raise money from the same limited universe of political givers, large and small. They both try to elect candidates, but in doing so they adopt very different perspectives: most PACs act on the basis of relatively narrow or even single-interest viewpoints, while the parties operate from a fish-eye, broad-based, over-arching vantage point. And they both vie for the attention, affection, and loyalty of candidates and officeholders.

Although there is in fact evidence of considerable competition between PACs and parties, what is more surprising is that, despite their natural tensions, the two have learned to coexist symbiotically: they use one another quite well. PACs need the information about candidates, intelligence about congressional contests, and access to political leaders that parties can provide. The parties seek PAC money for their candidates and their own organizations, which of late have modernized and expanded at a rate that matches the growth of PACs.

The still-developing relationship between PACs and the political parties can be characterized in many ways, for the diversity of the PAC world makes sweeping generalizations difficult. For example, most PACs are determinedly bipartisan, as befits their primary goal of access to officeholders. Business and trade PACs are commonly believed to be Republican-oriented, yet since 1978 more than a third of corporate PAC gifts and well over 40 percent of all trade PAC donations in congressional races have gone to Democratic candidates. In recent election cycles, business and trade PACs have been even more closely divided between the two parties, causing great consternation among Republican Party officials.[9] In some years business committees alone have supplied as much or more money to Democrats than have the traditionally heavily Democratic labor PACs. Unlike the business and trade PACs, labor union committees make no pretense of bipartisanship; an average of 94 percent of all labor PAC money has flowed to the Democrats since 1978. In return, fifteen seats on the DNC Executive Committee are reserved for labor officials.

Democrats have also worked hand in hand with many liberal non-connected PACs such as Pamela Harriman's Democrats for the '80s. Although no set of PACs is as closely tied to the GOP as labor is to the Democrats, the Republicans have had very smooth working relationships with many of the corporate, trade, and coordinating business PACs over the years. The independent oil PACs, for example, have been very supportive of many GOP candidates and party needs since the mid-1970s.

But the parties' relationships with some other PACs are more difficult. The ideological PACs lead the list of party antagonists and there is concern about them in both parties. The rhetoric and actions of many New Right PACs have been anti–Republican Party. The GOP has been termed a "fraud" and "a social club where rich people go to pick their noses" by one New Right leader, while others have called for the party's disbanding and the establishment of a new "conservative party."[10] In some cases the conservative PACs have attempted to usurp the functions of the party and establish themselves as substitutes by recruiting and training candidates and creating pseudo-party organizations of their own.[11] Senator Jesse Helms' Congressional Club has tried to supplant

9. See, for example, David S. Cloud, "Feud between GOP PACs Stings Candidates," *Congressional Quarterly Weekly* 46 (September 3, 1988): 2447–2450.

10. Sabato, *PAC Power*, pp. 150–51.

11. See Margaret Ann Latust, "Assessing Ideological PACs: From Outrage to Under-

the regular Republican Party organization in North Carolina, to the consternation of some GOP officials in the state.[12] NCPAC, which has been accused of stealing contributors' names from Republican Party finance report lists,[13] seriously considered declaring itself to be a political party in 1982.[14]

Even though the New Right groups usually end up supporting Republican candidates (or opposing Democratic ones), their antagonism has caused some GOP leaders to take a critical view of their activities.[15] So, too, have Democrats looked askew at the efforts of NCPAC's liberal counterparts. As one Democratic National Committee officer put it:

> I believe the independent PACs are a problem for two reasons. There's a finite pool of political money, and we simply can't afford thin drain to them, gambling that they'll spend it wisely. . . . Second, unlike the parties, many of the independent PACs are essentially computer-driven mail-order operations that have no membership and are accountable to no-body.[16]

Fortunately for both parties, the independent, nonconnected ideological PACs have fallen on hard financial times, and many (including NCPAC) are mere shadows of their former selves. The parties have easily withstood the assaults of the antiparty PACs, and the latter's heyday may well be over.

---

standing," in *Money and Politics in the United States: Financing Elections in the 1980's*, edited by Michael J. Malbin (Washington, D.C.: American Enterprise Institute/Chatham House, 1984), pp. 157–59.

12. See *Congressional Quarterly Weekly* 40 (March 6, 1982): 499–505.

13. See *Political Finance/Lobby Reporter* 3 (July 21, 1982): 188. In response to the GOP charges, the FEC forbade NCPAC from soliciting Republican donors NCPAC had copied from financial disclosure reports. NCPAC had not yet solicited them, though the FEC agreed with the GOP that NCPAC's intent to solicit eventually was clear.

14. See Political *Finance/Lobby Reporter* 3 (September 22,1983): 252.

15. Sabato, *PAC Power*, p. 151.

16. Ann Lewis, as quoted in Sabato, *PAC Power*, 151.

Most PACs fall between the proparty and antiparty poles; in fact most could perhaps best be described as indifferent to parties. That does not mean the effects PACs have on party organization and development are neutral, of course. Overall, there is little evidence for the widespread claim that PACs have contributed greatly to the long-term decline of the political party system in the United States. Rather, PACs may be one more manifestation of the atomizing forces that have made the parties less appealing to Americans.[17]

Nonetheless, PACs provide an alternative source of funding and support services for a candidate, weakening his ties with the party and lessening his fear of severe electoral consequences if he is disloyal to his party. But at the same time the competition from PACs is one of many factors stimulating a dramatic surge in party organization, technology, programs, and fund-raising that has drawn candidates much closer to the national parties. Parties can now do—or refuse to do—much more to elect their nominees than they could in the past. These party advances were occurring during the same years the PAC movement was maturing, and just as PACs have in some ways limited the parties' influence, so too have the invigorated parties acted as a check on PACs.

Finally, since candidates want campaign cash and PACs have it, there is inevitably a mating dance between the two groups, and the political parties act as matchmakers and, occasionally, chaperons. A multicandidate PAC is permitted to give $15,000 each year to all national party political committees combined, and although few contribute that large an amount, about a third of all multicandidate PACs donated some amount to the parties in recent years. PACs swelled the parties' treasuries by a total of nearly 87 million in 1985–86 for instance. Although this sum comprised a modest 5 percent of all PAC contributions, the money was not insubstantial and was welcomed especially by the financially hard-pressed Democrats. The Democrats received $5.74 mil-

17. See, for example, Frank J. Sorauf, "Political Parties and Political Action Committees: Two Life Cycles," *Arizona Law Review* 22, no. 2 (1980): 449–50.

lion to the Republicans' $1.11 million, an edge attributable in part to the GOP's desire to steer all available PAC money to its candidates.

Most PACs secure some of their information about candidates and elections at regular party briefings and through party newsletters, but PACs are naturally somewhat wary of the slant they receive at briefings. The party's built-in bias is apparent to seasoned PAC managers, and most PACs have learned the committees' backing losers. The GOP, for example, received a great deal of criticism from the PAC community after the 1986 elections, when many of the Senate and House candidates they claimed were on the verge of victory in fact were defeated.

As PACs have become more sophisticated, they have begun to demand more precise and accurate information from the parties, and both parties are attempting to provide it. The RNC and associated committees have established numerous programs and channels of communication with the PACs. For example, any PAC contributing $5,000 or more to the RNC each year gains a PAC 40 membership, entitling it to meet with Republican congressional leaders for off-the-record breakfasts once a month at the Capitol Hill Club in Washington.

Also, briefings for the PACs are provided by both the congressional and senatorial committees on a quarterly basis in Washington and in major cities around the country. And the GOP usually pays attention to the needs of its candidates, particularly unknown challengers. When a challenger comes to Washington, the appropriate Republican committee will help to set up appointments with PAC mangers in the capital and to design a PAC solicitation program tailor-made to the candidate's strengths.

The Democrats have also recently devoted greater efforts to securing corporate and trade PAC money. From 1981 to 1986 then Representative Tony Coelho (D-Calif.), chairman of the Democratic Congressional Campaign Committee (DCCC), made a concerted appeal to business to "not let your ideology get in the way of your business judgment."[18]

---

18. As quoted in Paul Taylor, "For Business PACs This Year, Suitable Targets Are in

Coelho's approach, using access to a Democratically controlled House (and now Senate) has clearly worked, as demonstrated by figures on business/trade PAC gifts to Democratic candidates (cited earlier).

Democrats have also followed the Republican lead in using exclusive clubs and offering special access to attract the PACs. For instance, the DNC has a Business Council, which PACs can join with a $15,000 annual contribution, and a $2,500-per-year PAC Council, which is the rough equivalent of the RNC's PAC 40 Club. Like its GOP counterpart, the PAC Council gathers together legislators and PAC officials for monthly breakfasts. Reflecting labor's prominent role in the Democratic Party, there is a separate DNC Labor Council whose price is $15,000 a year for a PAC and a whopping $50,000 for a labor union proper. Democratic services to PACs and party candidates have improved, too.

The party committees have expanded the size of their PAC liaison staffs, conduct regular briefing sessions for PACs, and distribute informational newsletters about key races.

In essence, the role of icebreaker is the fundamental one played by both parties with the PACs. The parties' uneasy alliance with PACs is formed and maintained of necessity—to elect party candidates. Republican and Democratic leaders alike may understand the competing nature of PACs and parties, but they also realize that, under the current system of campaign finance, PAC money gives congressional contenders an often crucial competitive edge. So PACs and parties learn to support each other.

REFORMS TO STRENGTHEN PARTIES AND DIMINISH PACS

Despite how well the symbiotic relationship between PACs and parties works for them, concerns about the welfare of our representative democracy suggest that some changes might enhance the promotion of important values, including governmental effectiveness, legitimacy, and

---

Short Supply," *Washington Post*, July 27, 1982, p. A6. See also *National Journal* 14 (August 7, 1982): 1368–73.

accountability. Because PACs and parties are so interrelated, giving preferential treatment to the parties will indirectly lessen the influence of PACs and the adverse consequences they have. The current limits of contributions to party committees ($20,000 a year for an individual and $15,000 for a multicandidate PAC) should be substantially increased. Additionally, individuals as well as corporations, labor unions, and trade associations should be permitted to underwrite without limit the administrative, legal, and accounting costs parties incur, with full disclosure of all donations.

Another way to lessen the importance of PACs is to increase the pool of alternative money. To begin with, the $1,000 limit on an individual's contribution to each candidate per election should be raised to recover its loss to inflation since 1974. (A $1,000 gift in 1974 is worth less than half that today.) Both the $1,000 cap and the companion limit of $25,000 that an individual is permitted to donate to all candidates taken together in a calendar year should also be permanently indexed to the inflation rate. Restoring the value of individual contributions will offset somewhat the financial clout of the PACs.

Even more important would be the enactment of a tax credit to benefit the parties. Before landmark tax reform legislation was passed in 1986, federal taxpayers were granted a 50 percent tax credit for all contributions to candidates, PACs, parties, and political committees of up to $50 for an individual and $100 on a joint return. Unfortunately this credit was one of those eliminated in the tax revision, and currently there is no credit for political gifts. The credit ought to be re-established not only to the 50 percent level but all the way to 100 percent, at least for candidate and party gifts. Such a move would clearly encourage small donations that have few if any real strings attached; the parties not only would remain unencumbered by the perceived debts that come with large contributions, but both parties would have an exceptionally valuable tool to use in expanding their donor and membership base.[19]

---

19. A 100 percent tax credit would almost certainly increase party giving. The California

This would be all the more so if income-taxing states agreed to offer a similar 50 percent credit if the federal government refused to give more than 50 percent; taxpayers in these forty-three states[20] would, in effect, get a 100 percent credit.[21]

Realistically, in an era when gigantic budget deficits threaten even essential existing programs, the prospects of securing either a 50 percent or 100 percent credit at the federal level do not appear promising. In one survey, when respondents were asked whether they would favor or oppose "giving people a full tax credit for contributing money to a political party," a solid majority of 55 percent to 39 percent disapproved (5 percent had no opinion.)[22] This is somewhat surprising since the public is usually inclined to approve tax credits that might provide some benefit to it. Respondents' negative reactions might signify concern about the budget deficit or, more likely, estrangement from political parties.

Luckily, there is another option that could win both public and legislative favor: a tax "add-on" that permits a citizen to channel a few dollars of his income tax refund to the party of his or her choice. Both parties would clearly gain funds, but the budget deficit would be none the worse for it. The voluntary nature of this self-imposed tax will appeal to conservatives and Republicans, while the ready cash will draw the assent of money-starved Democrats and liberals. In its ideal form, the federal 1040 (short and long form) and every annual income tax form on the state level should include an add-on provision that gives a tax-

---

Commission on Campaign Financing found that 35 percent of state residents would either increase their political gifts or give for the first time if there were a 100 percent credit. See California Commission on Campaign Financing, *The New Gold Rush: Financing California's Legislative Campaigns* (Sacramento: State of California, 1985), p. 15.

20. Only the states of Alaska, Florida, Nevada, South Dakota, Texas, Washington, and Wyoming have no income tax.

21. Minnesota and the District of Columbia already provide a 50 percent tax credit for political contributions.

22. Cited in Sabato, *The Party's Just Begun*, pp. 213–14.

payer the opportunity to check off a gift of $2, $5, $10, $25, $50, or $100 to the party he or she designates.

Will any significant number of taxpayers give money using this device? Several states (including Maine, Massachusetts, Montana, and Virginia) currently have some form of add-on. The Virginia experience is typical, with only about 2.2 percent of all eligible taxpayers contributing in recent years, though even this tiny portion has provided several hundred thousand dollars cumulatively to the parties (actually, Virginia is a little on the low side compared to other states; participation rates in an add-on plans combined have averaged about 4 percent.)[23] Although giving even small amounts to the political parties will doubtless never become the rage among beleaguered taxpayers anticipating a refund, it is likely that the present minuscule percentage of participation could be substantially augmented by a joint two-party educational advertising campaign undertaken at tax time. The campaign might profitably be keyed to patriotic themes, urging citizens to demonstrate their civic commitment in this small but crucial way. If afforded the add-on's superb opportunity for financial advancement by the federal and state governments, the parties certainly must take full advantage and capitalize on this golden entry on the tax forms. Such a cost-free reform should be among the highest priorities of both national parties and all state parties where an add-on does not now exist.

Fortunately for those who see the compelling need for stronger parties, the political parties are progressing on many fronts already. There are winds at the parties' backs today, forces that are helping to reverse decades of decline. None may be more important than the growing realization of the worth of political parties by many journalists and officeholders, as well as the continued advocacy of party-building reforms by many academics and political practitioners. The resolve of recent national party leaders, such as Republican National Committee

23. See Holly Wagner, "Costly Campaigns Attract Special Interest Dollars," *State Government News* 29 (October 1986): 20.

chairmen William Brock and Frank Fahrenkopf and Democratic Party leaders Paul Kirk (Democratic National Committee chairman) and Tony Coelho (chairman until 1987 of the Democratic Congressional Campaign Committee), has been of paramount significance to the ongoing revival of political party organizational and financial might.

These suggested reforms in campaign finance are certainly not enough to cure all the ills of the American party system. A separate agenda—which I have elaborated elsewhere—is necessary to revive partisan affiliation in the electorate and to increase volunteer strength in the party organizations.[24] But at least these proparty changes in campaign finance can enhance the role of the parties while tilting the structure's balance somewhat more to parties and somewhat less to PACs. In society's interests, for sustained health of our representative democracy, these are modest changes worth making.

---

24. See Sabato, *The Party's Just Begun*, chapter 6.

# Liberty of the Press under Socialism

## Williamson M. Evers

This selection was excerpted from *Social Philosophy & Policy* 2, no. 6 (spring 1989): 211–34. This article is especially relevant to proposals to give Congress the power to legislate limitations on campaign contributions and spending.

The basic point is that control of resources is a fundamental means of censorship; indeed, it is all that is necessary. Socialist regimes, which control the resources—the newsprint, the ink, the broadcast towers, the studios—essential to communications, often do not explicitly censor. Blue-pencil censorship is by their own admission unnecessary.

Instead they control the press and speech by controlling the resources used to publish and communicate. Evers cites evidence primarily for the Soviet Union and Eastern Europe. In some Latin American countries as well, sometimes the press, formally privately owned, has been controlled by reducing government advertising (and thus important revenues) and by calling loans made to newspapers, even loans made by supposedly private banks.

In describing the controls over the press in existing socialist societies, it is wrong, for example, to speak simply of censorship. In a centrally planned economy in which the means of production have been nationalized, the resources used by the communications media are completely under the economic control of the government. As Paul Lendvai points out, in existing socialist societies "literally everything" needed by the publishing industry, from "the printing plant, working capital and newsprint" to "the typewriters, stationery and waste paper baskets," must be provided by government departments.[1]

Manes Sperber emphasizes the effect of economic dependency when he writes that "everything belongs to these omnipotent regimes—the streets, the cities, the workshops, the factories, everything that is produced. Plus all printing presses, periodicals, and publishing houses. They

---

1. Paul Lendvai, *The Bureaucracy of Truth* (London: Burnett Books, 1981), p. 19.

do not even require censorship, for nothing can be printed that does not suit them."[2]

Sperber perhaps overstates the case, since some socialist governments have found direct coercion and censorship useful as ways of double-checking. On the other hand, the fact that the socialist government in Hungary has never set up a formal censorship apparatus supports Sperber's point. Socialist Romania abolished its censorship in 1977 but still controls the press.[3]

An officially approved Hungarian account of the institutions of the press says, in effect, that, because the state owns the equipment, because the state distributes the paper supplies and so forth, censorship by the police is not needed:

> The effective provisions of Hungarian press law do not insist on the submission of manuscript for the purpose of licensing (i.e., prepublication censorship). This is in charge of the competent specialized agencies or institutions of an economic character, and not of the police authorities. Consequently these provisions governing licensing are not of a policing character, and rely on the fact that the printing offices, publishing companies, and so forth are in public ownership, and that governmental organs are in charge of paper or newsprint.[4]

The Bolsheviks' own analysis of the press under existing socialism focuses on control of resources. I maintain that the history of the press

2. Manes Sperber, *Man and His Deeds*, trans. Joachim Neugroschel (New York: McGraw-Hill. 1970), p. 45. See also Milovan Djilas, *The New Class* (New York: Praeger, 1957), p. 143; Dragoljub Jovanovic, quoted in Vojislav Kostunica and Kosta Cavoski, *Party Pluralism or Monism*, East European Monographs, no. 189 (New York: Columbia University Press, 1985), p. 161.

3. Lendvai, *Bureaucracy of Truth*, pp. 30, 119–24.

4. Peter Schmidt, "The Citizens' Freedoms," in Imre Szabo et al., *Socialist Concept of Human Rights*, Series in Foreign Languages of the Institute for Legal and Administrative Sciences of the Hungarian Academy of Sciences, nos. 1 and 2 (Budapest: Akademiai Kiado, 1966), pp. 256–57.

in the Soviet Union shows that, under socialism, economic structure and economic policy decide the fate of freedom of the press.[5]

During the Bolshevik-led Soviet seizure of power in late October 1917,[6] Soviet forces seized or shut down approximately twenty nonsocialist newspapers.[7] On October 27, only two days after the successful Soviet revolution, in its Decree on the Press—the first law issued by the new Council of People's Commissars—the government gave itself the authority to close down all newspapers that printed false information or promoted resistance to Soviet power. The text of the decree described these measures as temporary.[8] Some non-Bolshevik newspapers continued to publish under censorship.

Ten days later, the Central Executive Committee of the All-Russian Congress of Soviets passed a resolution confirming the government's Decree on the Press. This resolution, drafted by Trotsky and backed by the Leninist Bolsheviks, took a further step. It stated that restoring seized printing facilities to nonsocialist owners would constitute "capitulation to the will of capital" and was "indubitably counterrevolutionary." This resolution also stated that the "next measure" should be Soviet expropriation of all private printing facilities and supplies of newsprint.

On November 15, the Council of People's Commissars decreed that all paid advertising was henceforth to be a monopoly of government publications. That meant that no private advertising could appear in

---

5. For an excellent brief discussion of why the Soviet Union is the appropriate existing socialist society on which to concentrate in considering the socialist project, see Peter Berger, *The Capitalist Revolution* (New York: Basic Books, 1986), pp. 174–76.

6. For Russian history before February 1/14, 1918 I use the Julian calendar, rather than the Gregorian one.

7. Peter Kenez, *The Birth of the Propaganda State* (Cambridge: Cambridge University Press, 1985), p. 38; N. N. Sukhanov, *The Russian Revolution 1917*, ed. and trans. Joel Carmichael (1955; repr. Princeton: Princeton University Press, 1984), pp. 649–51; Albert Resis, "Lenin on Freedom of the Press," *Russian Review* 36, no. 3 (July 1977): 285–86.

8. James Bunyan and H. H. Fisher, eds., *The Bolshevik Revolution, 1917–1918* (Stanford: Stanford University Press, 1934), p. 220; Yuri Akhapin, ed., *First Decrees of Power* (London: Lawrence & Wishort, 1970), pp. 29–30.

nongovernmental newspapers.[9] But much more devastating than this advertising ban were expropriations of facilities and paper supplies and the business conditions after the October revolution.[10]

The economic institutions of the press have remained fundamentally the same: state ownership or ownership by cooperatives that are creatures of the state.[11] Roy Medvedev notes that, by 1929, "there was not a single non-Party publication left, nor any privately owned publishing houses that might serve as vehicles for oppositionist views."[12]

*Samizdat* is a form of private publishing that takes place despite the fact that the state forbids private ownership of capital equipment (means of production) for the mass production of intellectual products.

Rare and brief periods of genuine liberty of the press do occur under existing socialism—for example, during the 1968 Prague Spring period

9. Bunyan and Fisher, *Bolshevik Revolution*, pp. 222–23; Reed, *Ten Days That Shook the World*, ed. Bertram D. Wolfe (New York: Modern Library, 1960), pp. 365, 391–92; Resis, "Lenin on Freedom of the Press," p. 292.

10. See Kenez, *Birth of the Propaganda State*, p. 42.

11. There were two exceptions: (1) During the civil war, the Bolsheviks permitted pro-Soviet non-Bolshevik political parties and groups to operate and to publish their own newspapers under censorship. (2) Under the liberalized conditions of the NEP, beginning in 1921, private capitalists and independent cooperatives published books. Such private ventures together with the mildness of the government's literary censorship at this time permitted a literary renaissance in the 1920s. On literary policy during the NEP, see Kenez, *Birth of the Propaganda State*, pp. 239–45.

This was the time of greatest liberalism in Soviet literary policy. See Ernest J. Simmons, "Introduction: Soviet Literature and Control," in Simmons, ed., *Through the Class of Soviet Literature* (New York: Columbia University Press, 1953), p. 6. On the limits of freedom of expression during the NEP, see Jean Elleinstein, *The Stalin Phenomenon*, trans. Peter Latham (London: Lawrence & Wishart, 1976), p. 65; Raphael R. Abramovitch, *The Soviet Revolution*, ed. Anatole Shub, trans. Vera Broido-Cohn and Jacob Shapiro (New York: International Universities Press, 1962), pp. 225–26; Leszek Kolakowski, *Main Currents of Marxism*, trans. P. S. Falla (Oxford: Clarendon Press, 1978), vol. 3, pp. 7, 45.

12. R. Medvedev, "New Pages from the Political Biography of Stalin," in Robert C. Tucker, ed., *Stalinism* (New York: Norton, 1977), p. 205. See also Elleinstein, *Stalin Phenomenon*, p. 87; Nicola A. de Basily, *Russia under Soviet Rule* (London: George Allen & Unwin, 1938), pp. 431–32.

in Czechoslovakia and during the 1980–81 period in which the Solidarity labor union operated publicly in Poland.[13]

Why, according to the critics of existing socialism, do such societies not enjoy long-term liberty of the press? Skeptics about the liberty of the press under socialism point to two major difficulties. The first is the absence of opportunities for independent, nongovernmental employment. The second is the absence of opportunities to organize independent institutions for the gathering and dissemination of information, the creation and exhibition of cultural works, and so forth.

Let us turn to socialist policies on income and their effect on liberty of expression. Socialists at all times have complained that proletarians, with their low incomes, cannot effectively exercise liberty of expression. Some, such as Upton Sinclair, simply point to the higher income that they maintain workers will enjoy under socialism as a further assurance of freedom of expression.[14]

In addition, twentieth-century socialist theorists are aware that the authorities in existing socialist societies have not hesitated to demote or fire dissidents in order to stifle their voices.[15] C. B. Macpherson proposes a guaranteed income as one way of protecting a dissident from his or her employer—the state.[16]

13. See John Downing, *Radical Media* (Boston: South End Press, 1984), section three.

14. Upton Sinclair, *The Brass Check* (Pasadena, Calif.: Author, 1920), p. 409.

15. See, for example, the discussion of job discrimination in existing socialist societies in R. Medvedev, *On Socialist Dissent: Interviews with Piero Ostellino* (New York: Columbia University Press, 1980), pp. 19, 22; R. Medvedev, *Political Essays* (Nottingham: Spokesman Books, 1976), pp. 15, 89; Zdenck Mlynar, *Relative Stabilization of the Soviet System in the 1970s*, Research Project: Crises in Soviet-Type Systems, Study No. 2 (Cologne: Index, 1983), pp. 6, 15; Ota Sik, *The Communist Power System*, trans. Marianne Grund Freidberg (New York: Praeger, 1981), p. 103; Berger, *The Capitalist Revolution*, p. 63. Richter anticipated the problem of political job discrimination under socialism. See Eugen Richter, *Henry Wright* (London: Swan Sonnenschein, 1893), p. 16.

16. C. B. Macpherson, *Democratic Theory: Essays in Retrieval* (Oxford: Clarendon Press, 1973), pp. 153–54. See also Bertrand Russell, *Proposed Roads to Freedom* (New York: Henry Holt, 1919), pp. 177–78; Paul G. Chevigny, "Reflections on Civil Liberties under Socialism," *Civil Liberties Review* 2, no. 1 (winter 1975): 55–57. I am indebted to Robert Hessen for bringing Chevigny's article to my attention.

Spargo, Liehm, and Hook, with somewhat different emphases, also rely on the right to work or the right to one's job as a guarantee of freedom of expression. Liehm envisions a right to see one's ideas realized. Hook proposes to extend the prerogatives of academic freedom to the publishing industry.[17]

Let us now turn to socialist production policies and their consequences for freedom of expression. On the production side, some socialists advocate setting aside sites in socialist societies for the public expression of views—Hyde Parks, if you will, in public meeting places, in the press, and on broadcast programs. For example, Norman Thomas in *America's Way Out* proposes that the state set aside places for Hyde Park–like forums. He proposes that the state aid the efforts of political parties to publicize their positions via the mails or broadcasting. Alternatively, he suggests, the socialist state should itself undertake this task: the state should provide the members of society with "intelligible accounts" of the views of the various political parties.[18] Some socialists favor huge subsidies to culture. Liehm, for example, wants the state to guarantee each film artist that his or her ideas will be turned into films and shown to the public.[19]

These proposals raise numerous questions. Thomas is aware of the fact that allocation decisions will have to be made about every means of expression because he specifically says that political groups should be entitled to prime time for broadcasting their views.[20] But he does not

17. John Spargo, *Applied Socialism* (New York: B. W. Hebsch, 1912), p. 227; Liehm, "On Culture, Politics, Recent History," p. 80; Sidney Hook, "Is Freedom of the Press Possible in a Planned Society? Discussion Notes," May 4, 1942, unpublished ms., Sidney Hook Papers, Hoover Institution Archives, Stanford University, p. 2; Hook, *Political Power and Personal Freedom*, 2d ed. (New York: Collier Books, 1962), p. 405.

18. Norman M. Thomas, *America's Way Out* (New York: Macmillan, 1931), pp. 210–11.

19. Liehm, "On Culture, Politics, Recent History," p. 80. On the supply and demand for public assistance to culture, see Milton Friedman, *Capitalism and Freedom* (Chicago: University of Chicago Press, 1962), p. 18.

20. For an example of a socialist theorist's dismissal of economic constraints as applying

begin to address the problems that will arise. For example, an auditorium can perhaps be used for five meetings a day. Many groups will want to use the facility at times convenient to them. The government will have to decide who uses it and when. Even if the government adheres formally to the requirements that Thomas proposes, it has a monopoly of the means of communication; it should therefore have no difficulty in effectively relegating to obscurity whomever and whatever it finds disagreeable.[21]

Similarly, the authorities can easily distort a publish-at-cost rule in the name of needed economy measures. The authorities can distort such a rule by placing low ceilings on the numbers of copies of unofficial publications the state prints. Officials might authorize the state printing house to print only a handful of copies of unofficial publications because of, say, a supposed paper shortage or some other supposed emergency situation. At the same time, these officials might deem it vital to print millions of copies of works of governmental propaganda.

Finally, under socialism the state will distribute all products. It can stifle dissent through its control of the distribution network.[22]

Indeed, the authorities in existing socialist societies have been able to use this economic dependency to reestablish their control following periods (the Prague Spring, for example) in which many persons—including those working in the communications industry—enjoyed liberty of an anarcho-syndicalist sort. The authorities reestablished con-

---

to cultural products in a socialist society, see Karl Kautsky, *The Social Revolution* (Chicago: Charles H. Kerr, 1905), pp. 181–83.

21. See Eugen Richter, *Picture of the Socialist Future*, trans. Henry Wright (London: Swan Sonnnschein, 1893), p. 85.

22. H. G. Wells and Upton Sinclair, for example, are most emphatic that distribution must remain in the hands of the government. Wells, *New Worlds for Old* (New York: Macmillan, 1919), p. 281; Upton Sinclair, *The Brass Check* (Pasadena: Author, 1920), p. 409. See also Edward Bellamy, *Looking Backward, 2000–1887*, ed. John L. Thomas (Cambridge: Belknap Press of Harvard University Press, 1967), p. 199; G.D.H. Cole, *Fabian Socialism* (London: Allen & Unwin, 1943), p. 41; P.J.D. Wiles, *Economic Institutions Compared* (New York: John Wiley, 1977), pp. 462, 466.

trol in part by having the police coerce dissidents. But much more important in making such "normalization" and stabilization possible is an ideology and a reality of economic dependency.

So long as a command economy remains in place, power will flow back to the authorities—even after a time of revolt and anarcho-syndical freedom—because they are the only employers and because they are the bosses of the societal coordinating mechanism that seems to make the economy run.

Nonetheless, one cannot rely on a social system that gives an important role to unknowable and changeable visions and motives. Far more trustworthy is a social system where the structures and incentives hedge power, do not permit the morally corrupt to exercise unchecked coercion, and encourage the exposure and accountability of those corrupted by power. In the absence of suitable institutional supports, even the favorable intentions of most political officeholders in a socialist society will not suffice to sustain liberty of the press over the long run.

Another proponent of liberty of the press under socialism might contend that the authorities in socialist societies will observe the laws upholding liberty of the press if the public is vigilant.[23] But is it not likely that the public will defer to the government and that public opinion will be shaped by the government when the government is in charge of all schools (as would be the case in most models of socialism[24])? What can one expect when there is no independent press

23. R. H. Tawney, "We Mean Freedom," *Review of Politics* 8, no. 2 (April 1946): 237.

24. For example, Wilhelm Liebknecht, *Socialism: How It Is and What It Seeks to Accomplish*, trans. May Wood Simmons (Chicago: Charles H. Kerr, 1897), pp. 57–58. It might seem from Engels's criticism of a draft of the Erfurt Program of the German Social Democrats that he favored permitting private educational institutions under socialism. A passage in this piece in which Engels says that one cannot forbid religious persons from founding their own schools with "their own funds" is cited by Hunt as revealing Engels's "liberal and Victorian sense of decency." Richard N. Hunt, *The Political Ideas of Marx and Engels* (Pittsburgh: University of Pittsburgh Press, 1974–1984), vol. 2, pp. 181–82. But Engels's reference to the religious persons' "own funds" shows that he is talking about educational reform and church disestablishment in what he considered capitalist societies, not about

to speak out for liberty of the press and other liberties and to propagandize for them?

Yet the issue goes deeper than this. What is at issue is clearly suggested in the following remarks of Irving Howe:

> While there is no reason to suppose that . . . an intense political consciousness is a "normal" or even desirable feature of human life at all times, there can be no guarantee of minority rights except insofar as they are cherished in consciousness—and this is true for all societies.[25]

As one looks back across the various proposals for the press under socialism, it appears that they are, most often, a partial rejection of pure, orthodox socialist principles—somehow partially exempting intellectual work and intellectual products from the purview of state ownership and planning. The proposals are attempts to produce some of the features of property rights while retaining most of the subsidies and many of the controls of pure socialism.

In these proposed exemptions and modifications of socialism, one can see an effort by members of the intelligentsia to carve out a special sphere of privilege for themselves under socialism. Such exemptions and modifications are for brain workers, not hand workers.[26]

---

private schooling under Marxian socialism, which from the outset of proletarian rule would have a moneyless economy.

25. Irving Howe, "An Answer to Critics of American Socialism," review of *Socialism and American Life*, ed. Stow Persons and Donald Drew Egbert, *New International* 18, no. 3, whole no. 154 (May–June 1952): 131.

26. For at least tacit acknowledgment that such measures are deviations from a thoroughgoing application of socialist planning principles, see Kautsky, *Social Revolution*, pp. 182–83; Bellamy, pp. 200, 204; Russell, pp. 180–81 ; G.D.H. Cole, *Fabian Socialism*, pp. 40–41 ; Spargo, p. 298; Annie Besant, "Industry under Socialism," in George Bernard Shaw, ed., *Fabian Essays in Socialism* (London: George Allen and Unwin, 1931), pp. 148–49; Wells, pp. 275–83; Sidney and Beatrice Webb, *Consumer's Co-operative Movement* (London: Longmans, Green, 1921), p. 412; Hook, *Political Power*, pp. 403–4; Robert G. Picard, *The Press and the Decline of Democracy* (Westport: Greenwood Press, 1985), p. 67; James A. Yunker, *Socialism in the Free Market* (New York: Nellen Publishing Company, 1979), pp. 200–1; William E. Connolly, *Appearance and Reality in Politics* (Cambridge: Cambridge University

But the dynamics of actually existing socialist societies—in particular, the effects of the sociology of control over resources and the resulting sociology of power—seem to overwhelm such efforts to carve out a special sphere for the press. Three interconnected phenomena block the emergence of a free and independent press: the absence of liberal institutions of private property, the privileged status of the *nomenklatura* (the Soviet political elite), and the concentration of power inherent in central planning.[27]

In sum, it could be argued that the possibilities for freedom of the press under socialism are open to grave doubts. Perhaps these doubts could be resolved by more work on such topics by socialist theorists. They could certainly be resolved by the existence of a pluralistic socialist society. Until that time, the obstacles in the way of freedom of the press under socialism will continue to look formidable.

---

Press, 1981), p. 190. Compare Bukharin, quoted in Stephen Cohen, *Bukharin and the Bolshevik Revolution* (New York: Knopf, 1973), p. 205.

27. On the sociological implications of the *nomenklatura* and central planning for liberty of the press under socialism, see Williamson M. Evers, "Limits of Liberty of the Press in Political Theory from Milton to Hocking," Ph.D. dissertation, Stanford University, 1987, pp. 301–6, 324–25, 331–62.

# Why Congress Can't Ban Soft Money

## David M. Mason

This article first appeared in *Heritage Backgrounder*, no. 1130 (July 21, 1997). In this article David Mason explains soft money and the constitutional protection for political speech that prevents Congress from limiting it by legislating what can and cannot be done or said and how much money may be spent doing so. In fact Supreme Court decisions over the years have declared unconstitutional any but voluntary restrictions on campaign spending, while leaving in place a variety of limitations on contributions.

From the view point of the authors of the bills Mason discusses, "soft" money, money that is not under the contribution and expenditures controls and reporting requirements of the federal government, is evil. Soft money has always existed, Mason points out, but with limits on hard money—money specifically going to candidates' campaigns—soft money, free from limitations on amounts that can be contributed, expands. Thus contributions to parties and PACs increase. It becomes difficult to tell whether party-building activities really support a particular candidate and should count in spending limitations.

If such spending is also constrained, money will flow to independent special interest groups—the many organizations from the Sierra Club to the Christian Coalition that work on behalf of ideas that they wish to see supported by candidates and eventually embodied in legislation. Is their issue advocacy too to be brought under the control of the Federal Election Commission because it comes too close to supporting candidates in an election?

Mason's lesson is that this is a slippery slope and that what divides the players on the issue is whether they choose to stand atop the slope or slide right down to the mud at the bottom.

Eliminating political party "soft money" and regulating similar spending by groups other than political parties are central features of many proposals that would reform campaign financing. Soft money (defined as money raised and spent outside the regulatory structure for federal election campaigns) has played a growing and increasingly controversial role in politics for a decade; in fact, most of the fund-raising abuses alleged to have occurred during the 1996 elections involved soft money.

One of the leading reform proposals is the Bipartisan Campaign

Reform Act of 1997 (S. 25), introduced by Senators John McCain (R-Ariz.) and Russell Feingold (D-Wisc.). Both McCain-Feingold and H.R. 493, a companion bill introduced in the House by Representatives Christopher Shays (R-Conn.) and Martin Meehan (D-Mass.) would impose extensive restrictions and regulations on soft money activities. Another proposal from a group of House freshmen would ban soft money donations to political parties and impose government regulation on "issue advertising" that refers to specific candidates or officeholders. Shays, Meehan, and President Clinton have petitioned the Federal Election Commission (FEC) to ban or limit soft money donations to political parties.

Efforts to ban, limit, or regulate soft money and related spending such as issue advertising are complicated by constitutional limits on government power, difficulties in defining targeted activities, and the relative ease with which political activists avoid targeted regulations that are constitutionally valid. Specifically,

- Most soft money activities already have been approved by the Supreme Court as exercises of First Amendment rights.

- Although Congress has some authority to regulate national political parties, even those regulations must be focused narrowly on preventing fraud or corruption.

- Regulation of the soft money activities of nonparty groups and individuals is both subject to the strictest constitutional scrutiny and nearly always constitutionally invalid.

Regulating advertising because it includes the name or likeness of a public official, for example, is clearly unconstitutional.

Congressional motives and interests also should be examined. Campaign laws and regulations clearly tend to favor incumbents,[1] and con-

---

1. David M. Mason and Steven Schwalm, "Advantage Incumbents: Clinton's Campaign Finance Proposal," *Heritage Foundation Backgrounder*, no. 945 (June 11, 1993), and Bradley

gressional statements indicate that efforts to limit soft money issue advertising are motivated by incumbents' desire to suppress criticism of their actions. In other words, it appears that some politicians are trying to use public dissatisfaction with their own actions and campaigns as an excuse to expand government regulation of, and reduce citizen participation in, the political process.

In considering any limited steps it might take on soft money, Congress should recall that existing practices are direct responses to previous attempts to regulate political activity. As "hard money" (direct expenditures on campaigns) was limited and regulated, activists simply changed tactics. It is arguable that total political spending has increased as a result; it is certain that there is a less complete and less open accounting of such spending and wholly foreseeable that political activists will discover legitimate ways to avoid any new regulations by pursuing behavior that is more objectionable and less accountable than the activities targeted by regulation.

Rather than embark on another pointless and constitutionally suspect cycle of regulatory expansion, Congress should reexamine existing regulations on hard money, lifting and easing regulations in order to encourage donors and activists to move toward entities like parties, campaigns, and political action committees (PACs) that already are subject to regulation and disclosure. The real solution to the problem of soft money lies in minimizing, not expanding, government controls.

## ROOTS OF A CONTROVERSY

This controversy has arisen because of the size of certain soft money donations (more than $1 million in some cases); the growing use of soft money by political parties, labor unions, and other groups; and certain practices involved in the raising of soft money. White House coffees and sleepovers during the 1996 campaign, for example, allegedly were

---

A. Smith, "Campaign Finance Regulation," Cato Institute Policy Analysis, no. 238, September 3, 1995.

associated with soft money fund-raising efforts by the Democratic National Committee (DNC).

A series of laws passed in the 1970s[2] limited the source and size of donations to federal election campaigns and required the extensive reporting and disclosure of campaign expenditures. These limited and reportable funds became known as hard money: contributions made directly to candidates by individuals and political action committees. Certain spending, such as internal communications by corporations and labor unions and spending on headquarters space by political parties, was exempt from most regulatory requirements. Other activities, like spending on state campaigns, were not addressed by federal statutes.

In 1976, in *Buckley v. Valeo*,[3] the U.S. Supreme Court struck down significant parts of the Federal Election Campaign Act (FECA) and established strict limits on the government's ability to regulate political activity. Subsequent decisions expanding on *Buckley* declared various activities by parties and other groups to be exempt from FECA and other government regulation. Activities exempt from the FECA escape its donation limits of $1,000 (for individuals) and $5,000 (for political committees), bans on union and corporate donations, and requirements for disclosure of donors and spending. As parties and other groups have adjusted their tactics to take advantage of these features, soft money has grown.

Originally, the term *soft money* was applied solely to labor union spending for political advocacy among union members. Internal activities could be financed by dues from the union's general treasury; political communications with the general public had to be paid for through voluntary contributions and reported to the FEC. The distinction between hard and soft union activity goes back to 1943 and 1947 legislative prohibitions on union donations to, or spending on, elections.

---

2. The Federal Election Campaign Act of 1971, which was amended in 1974, 1976, and 1979, and the presidential campaign funding provisions of the Tax Act of 1971.

3. 424 U.S. 1 (1976).

After passage of FECA, as political parties explored the distinctions between regulated federal campaign activities and other party functions, the term was applied to unregulated party activities, including voter registration, headquarters construction, and state and local political activity. Later, politically active groups began to provide voter scorecards and other printed materials under the "express advocacy" exemption specified in the *Buckley* ruling. Issue-related television and radio advertising became a significant factor in campaigns beginning in 1994, when independent term limits, tax reform, and conservative religious groups ran ads to alert voters to candidates' positions on various issues. In 1996, unions and environmental organizations made extensive use of such issue advertising, and business and independent conservative organizations responded in kind.

In many 1996 races, this advertising by organizations independent of candidates and political parties was seen as a major factor. This had been the case in a few races in 1994 and only rarely before that time.

As with nonparty efforts, political party issue advertising had been present, but generally as a minor factor, before 1996, when it exploded in both scope and significance. Clinton adviser Dick Morris cites the DNC's issue advertising effort as one of the key elements in Clinton's reelection.[4] From 1992 to 1996, overall soft money receipts by the national political parties grew more than threefold, from $86 million to $262 million. At the state level, soft money receipts appear to have grown even more rapidly as a result of a vigorous Democratic effort to channel soft money donations directly to state parties.

The rapid growth in soft money means that these largely unregulated funds represent a far larger proportion of total political spending. Soft money represented just 16 percent of national party receipts during the 1992 election cycle but 30 percent during the 1996 elections. The DNC, the most dependent on soft money of all major party organizations,

4. Dick Morris, *Behind the Oval Office: Winning the Presidency in the '90s* (New York: Random House, 1996).

received almost 50 percent of its 1995–1996 income in soft dollar donations: $102 million as opposed to $108 million in hard dollars. Comparable figures for the Republican National Committee were $113 million and $193 million. Today, the term *soft money* is applied to activities as diverse as an internal union newsletter touting a candidate endorsement, the "Harry and Louise" ads on the Clinton health plan, and donations to state political campaigns. The only common element is that these activities are not regulated under FECA.

## SOFT MONEY, ISSUE ADVOCACY, AND FREE SPEECH

The problems involved in regulating soft money begin with its definition, as evidenced by the wide variety of activities to which the term is applied. In terms of contributions to political parties, soft money is a donation that is outside limits established by FECA, either because it is above specified dollar limits ($20,000 per year for an individual) or because it comes from a "prohibited source" (a corporation or labor union). In terms of spending, soft money is literally anything other than donations to, or spending in behalf of, federal election campaigns.

Some soft money proposals address only political party fund-raising. President Clinton and House sponsors of the Shays-Meehan Bill have petitioned the FEC to take regulatory action to ban or limit contributions to parties, other than those already subject to FECA. This appeal is based on the commonly repeated (but incorrect) claim that the FEC "created" soft money. In fact, it merely defined the parameters of regulation of campaigns and political parties, establishing accounting rules to keep regulated and unregulated activities separate and to allocate shared expenses. Such regulations are essential, considering the limits of the FEC's authority under FECA and the Constitution. To argue that because the FEC has defined certain attributes of soft money, either the FEC or Congress can abolish or arbitrarily limit the practice is the same as saying that Americans' political liberties are granted by the government and may be altered or abolished at any time.

Other soft money proposals, such as one drafted by a bipartisan group of House freshmen, would combine a ban on soft money fund-raising by political parties with restrictions on issue advertising by non-party groups. Still other legislation, including the McCain-Feingold proposal (similar to the Shays-Meehan Bill in the House), would attempt to subject issue advertising and many other soft money activities to the same FECA regulations and fund-raising limits that now apply to hard money activity.

Issue advertising by nonparty ideological groups appears to bother politicians. Senator Max Cleland (D-Ga.) called for new regulations after being subjected to a barrage of ads in Georgia urging him to vote for the ban on partial-birth abortions. The problem with regulating such ads as if they were campaign expenditures is that Cleland is only some six months into a six-year term and will not face voters again until 2002. A "Blue Dog Democrat" reform bill would limit such ads because the "candidate risks losing control of the tone, clarity and content of his or her own campaign."

Thus, the real reason for limiting issue advocacy is revealed: politicians do not want to contend with citizens bringing up issues they would rather ignore. In a classic "I'm from the government and I'm here to help you" story, politicians are attempting to use understandable disgust at their own campaign tactics as an excuse to muzzle anyone who dares to criticize them: Republicans are outraged by labor unions' issue ads; Democrats are outraged at Christian Coalition scorecards; both types of ads are paid for with soft money; and politicians from both parties are trying to figure out how to stop them.

Perhaps the most striking expression of this attitude is the declaration by House minority leader Richard Gephardt (D-Mo.) that "what we have is two important values in conflict: freedom of speech and our desire for healthy campaigns in a healthy democracy. You can't have both."[5] The truth, however, is that these values are not in conflict: the

5. Michael Lewis, "A Question of Honor: The Subversive," *New York Times Magazine*, May 25, 1997, p. 32.

First Amendment's guarantee of freedom of speech was designed to ensure a healthy democracy. One cannot exist without the other.

## CAN CONGRESS LIMIT SOFT MONEY DONATIONS?

The courts generally have insisted that Congress can regulate only direct campaign spending that calls explicitly for the election or defeat of a particular politician: what the Supreme Court called "express advocacy" in its landmark 1976 decision in *Buckley v. Valeo.* To do more than this would encroach on the right to free speech. Freewheeling political debate would be impossible if citizens or organizations had to wonder whether every statement was or was not permissible. Therefore, regulations on political discussions require a "bright line" test, with specific words such as *vote for, elect,* or *defeat* required to trigger regulation.

Since 1976, the Supreme Court has referred to the *Buckley* decision more than 100 times in setting limits on the government's authority to regulate political debate. In a 1996 case, *Colorado Republican Committee v. FEC,*[6] the Court stated very clearly that the "FECA permits unregulated 'soft money' contributions to a party for certain activities." In making this ruling, the Court referred not to any specific permission from Congress for soft money but to the act's definition of "contribution," which was circumscribed in *Buckley* to limit only "express advocacy" of the election or defeat of a federal candidate. In other words, the right to soft money contributions rests in the constitutional limitation on Congress's power to regulate speech. Among the implications of this ruling is that Congress has no authority to regulate contributions for or spending on state elections, even when those contributions are made by, to, or through national political parties.

That political parties, or any other group of Americans, have a right to spend unlimited amounts for politically oriented issue advertising has long been clear; now the Supreme Court has clarified that contri-

---

6. *Colorado Republican Federal Campaign Committee v. Federal Election Commission,* No. 95-489, 135 L.Ed. 2nd 795.

butions for such purposes may not be regulated. *Buckley* distinguished between spending by campaigns and political committees, which may not be limited, and contributions to those committees, which may be subject to limits. Some argue by analogy that Congress might limit soft money donations to parties. Even ignoring the Supreme Court's flatly contrary statement in *Colorado*, extending campaign regulation to activities that, by definition, are not campaign activities would be difficult for the following reasons:

1. The Supreme Court consistently has denied efforts to regulate anything other than campaign funds and "express advocacy" for or against a candidate.

2. If groups other than political parties can collect unlimited donations for soft money activities, political parties arguably have that same right under *Colorado*.

3. *Colorado* suggests that it will be difficult to show a potential for corruption (which is necessary to justify donation limits) through donations to political parties.

*Buckley* specifically rejected an intent test in defining spending to influence a federal election. To claim that soft money, which by definition avoids express advocacy, influences elections in ways that justify regulation flatly contradicts *Buckley*. The Court even anticipated use of the express advocacy loophole exactly as now objected to:

> It would naively underestimate the ingenuity and resourcefulness of . . . groups desiring to buy influence to believe that they would have much difficulty devising expenditures that skirted the restriction on express advocacy of election or defeat but nevertheless benefitted the candidate's campaign.

*Colorado* suggests that the Supreme Court will not buy the argument that there is something unique about political parties that legitimizes restrictions not imposed on other groups: "We do not see how a Constitution that grants to individuals, candidates and ordinary political committees the right to make unlimited independent expenditures could deny the same right to political parties." By similar reasoning, the ability of nonpartisan organizations to collect unlimited donations for issue advocacy would be extended to political parties.

If the Supreme Court did agree to revise its express advocacy rulings, it would still require a showing of potential corruption to legitimize limits on soft money donations. Again, the *Colorado* ruling presents a roadblock: "If anything, an independent expenditure made possible by a $20,000 donation, but controlled and directed by a party rather than the donor, would seem less likely to corrupt than the same (or a much larger) independent expenditure made directly by that donor."

By extension, the Court would find less danger of corruption in soft money donations to parties than in direct (and undisclosed) spending by individuals, unions, or corporations.

Despite the Supreme Court's clarity, regulators and attorneys continue to advance theories to explain why it is acceptable to bend the Constitution to stop some practice they consider objectionable. Some argue that everything a political party does must be related to electing candidates, so it might be acceptable to limit party soft money. But even limits on soft money (well short of a ban) appear to be off the table in the *Colorado* ruling: "We do not see how a Constitution that grants to individuals, candidates and ordinary political committees the right to make unlimited independent expenditures could deny the same right to political parties."

The right to make independent expenditures was established by the same 1976 *Buckley* decision that declared soft money beyond the power of government to regulate. Taken together, the *Buckley* and *Colorado* decisions point inescapably to the conclusion that political parties have a right to spend whatever they wish on activities not directly related to federal elections.

CAN CONGRESS REGULATE ISSUE ADVERTISING?

Limiting or requiring disclosure of soft money issue advertising by political parties and other groups will prove nearly impossible under *Buckley* and other First Amendment rulings.

### Express Advocacy

As *Buckley* makes clear, the Supreme Court requires "express advocacy" to trigger federal regulation of political advertising. The fact that issue discussions "tend naturally and inexorably to exert some influence on voting at elections" makes no difference. Noting that candidates "are intimately tied to public issues," the Court acknowledges that "the distinction between discussion of issues and advocacy of election or defeat of candidates may often dissolve in practical application." It is for this very reason that it crafted the express advocacy standard; thus, arguing that certain issue ads are practically the same as election advocacy is unlikely to strike the Court as convincing.

One Ninth Circuit case, *FEC v. Furgatch*,[7] is slightly broader than *Buckley* in its definition of express advocacy. The Supreme Court did not review *Furgatch*, however, partly because the FEC argued that it was based on a unique set of facts and unlikely to be more broadly applicable. In addition, the Court had reaffirmed its original *Buckley* express advocacy standard only a month before, in *FEC v. Massachusetts Citizens for Life*.[8]

Even if one accepts *Furgatch*, it provides little additional room for regulation, requiring that a communication be "unmistakable and unambiguous" and present a "clear plea for action" (to vote) about which there can be no reasonable doubt. "We emphasize," the Court notes in *Furgatch*, "that if any reasonable alternative reading of speech can be suggested, it cannot be express advocacy subject to the [FECA's] disclo-

---

7. *Federal Election Commission v. Harvey Furgatch*, No. 88-6047, 869 F. 2nd 1256.

8. *Federal Election Commission v. Massachusetts Citizens for Life, Inc.*, No. 85-701, 479 U.S. 238 (1986).

sure requirements." Illustrating the difficulty of attempting to regulate in this area, most issue ads already contain appeals to take some action other than voting, such as writing an officeholder or letting a nonincumbent candidate "know what you think." Any such appeal would make a *Furgatch* standard inapplicable. Any slight expansion of "express advocacy" would cause interested groups merely to recast their ads to avoid whatever bright line test the courts approved.

## Intent, Timing, and Identification of Candidates

Both *Buckley* and other cases explicitly reject any sort of intent test for regulating speech. As *Buckley* again makes clear, such tests put a speaker "wholly at the mercy of the varied understanding of his hearers, and consequently of whatever inference may be drawn as to his intent and meaning." A speaker or an ad may well mean to support or oppose a candidate; but as long as explicit appeals to vote are avoided, such speech may not be regulated.

Many proposals to regulate (or require disclosure of) issue advertising focus on their identification of a candidate in a time period before an election. This standard, however, reaches only half of the express advocacy requirement. Blanket regulation of ads simply because they contain a politician's name or image is clearly unconstitutional. A specific election-related appeal would be required to trigger regulation. Requiring advance notice of such ads would excite particular scrutiny as a form of prior restraint on free speech.

## Lobbying and Broadcasting

Attempting to regulate issue ads as lobbying would prove even more difficult than arguing that they were election-related. In its 1995 decision in *McIntyre v. Ohio Elections Commission*,[9] the Supreme Court defined a right to anonymous pamphleteering even when the subject of the

---

9. Joseph McIntyre, *Executor of Estate of Margaret McIntyre, Deceased, Petitioner v. Ohio Elections Commission*, No. 93-986, 514 U.S. 334.

advertising was an election referendum. Describing efforts to influence public opinion as "core First Amendment activities," the Court specified that regulation of such activities is subject to "exacting scrutiny" and must be "narrowly tailored to meet a compelling state interest."

In *McIntyre*, the Ohio agency argued that a law requiring disclosure of the author's name and address was needed to discourage fraud or libel and to provide voters with a way to evaluate materials. The Court ruled that a blanket disclosure requirement was overly broad as a protection against potentially misleading statements and that the "informational interest" of voters was "plainly insufficient" to justify mandatory disclosure. The *Federalist Papers* arguing for the adoption of the Constitution were printed anonymously, the Court pointed out. Issue advertising unrelated to an election referendum would receive even more protection than the *McIntyre* statements.

The practical limit on the number of broadcast licenses has been advanced as an excuse for requiring mandatory disclosures regarding issue ads on television. The Supreme Court has said that the scarcity of broadcast licenses can justify a requirement that broadcasters provide equal time for opposing viewpoints and that they be fair in their public affairs programming. But a requirement that broadcasters be fair or balanced cannot be stretched to justify regulating those who buy time from broadcasters. The fact that statements are paid advertising rather than a publisher's (or station owner's) own opinions makes no difference from a constitutional standpoint. Congress may promote opportunities for a variety of viewpoints to be heard, but it may not regulate groups simply because they take advantage of those opportunities.

CONCLUSION

Political parties enjoy the same rights as other groups to participate in political debates. Party spending cannot be limited except for direct election spending coordinated with candidates and possibly not even then. Further, Congress cannot limit donations to parties for activities that it cannot regulate directly, including activities protected by the First

Amendment and state elections. Limits on spending or donations for activities other than federal campaigns are beyond the power of Congress. Congress can address divisions between regulated and unregulated activities of political parties, but it cannot arbitrarily define issue discussions, including advertising, as campaign related.

Even if the Supreme Court allowed Congress to change the law to limit political party soft money, we would be far worse off than we are today. Once again, political activity would follow the line of least resistance. Since the right of unions, business groups, and others to conduct unlimited, unregulated, and unreported issue advertising is clear, donors would turn to those groups, which are far less accountable than political parties, to run the same sort of ads we see today.

Politicians are aware of this dynamic, which is why they always couple proposals to limit political party fund-raising with efforts to regulate public affairs discussions by labor unions, business organizations, citizen groups, and even individuals. Rather than just clean up their own campaign practices, President Clinton and many members of Congress want to regulate what everyone else has to say about them. In other words, when politicians say "reform," citizens should run for cover.

Policymakers are struggling with the consequences of constitutionally protected efforts to avoid regulation of political activity. Adding new regulations and limits to the extent permitted by the courts will serve only to add complexity and spur further avoidance of regulated activities. Instead of adding new rules, lawmakers should consider relaxing current rules to encourage political activity to flow through minimally regulated and disclosed channels.

# Campaign Finance Reforms and the Presidential Campaign Contributions of Wealthy Capitalist Families

## Michael Patrick Allen and Philip Broyles

This article first appeared in *Social Science Quarterly* 72, no. 4 (December 1991): 738–50. In this article Allen and Broyles consider the presidential campaign contributions of 590 members of one hundred families with extensive stock ownership. Their contributions are compared for 1972, when full disclosure was required but individual contributions were not constrained by law, and 1984, when contributions were capped; in both years a Republican president was running for reelection against a liberal Democrat.

   The authors find that in 1984 fewer members of wealthy capitalist families contributed, and, when they did contribute, contributed far less, even though the percentage of the total population contributing to presidential campaigns increased and total funds contributed did not decline. Thus, contributions were raised from more people in smaller amounts, a finding consistent with the complaints of politicians about the perpetual fund-raising treadmill.

This research assesses the impact of the Federal Election Campaign Act on the contributions of 590 individuals from one hundred wealthy capitalist families to the 1972 and 1984 presidential campaigns. The analysis reveals that both the magnitude and the frequency of contributions to presidential campaigns by wealthy capitalists declined substantially during this period. Some wealthy capitalists circumvented the limitations on direct contributions to presidential candidates, however, by contributing to both the national party organizations and political

A preliminary version of this paper was presented at the annual meeting of the Pacific Sociological Association, Reno, Nevada, April 1989. The authors are indebted to G. William Domhoff, Alan Neustadt, Dan Clawson, and several anonymous reviewers for their comments and suggestions. Editor's note: Reviewers were David Adamany, Thomas Dye, J. Craig Jenkins, and Thomas Koenig.

action committees. The wealthy capitalists who were most likely to contribute to these presidential campaigns were those who were most visible to the public. Although there was some continuity in the contributions of wealthy capitalists to the two parties, the Democratic Party lost more contributors among wealthy capitalists between 1972 and 1984 than did the Republican Party.

The ability of corporate elites and members of the capitalist class to exercise power through their contributions to political campaigns is a central issue in political sociology (Domhoff 1972; Ferguson and Rogers 1986). For example, in his famous study *The Power Elite* (1956), Mills argued that the members of wealthy families were able, largely as a result of their campaign contributions, to exercise inordinate political power. Specifically, he concluded that "money allows the economic power of its possessor to be translated directly into political party causes" (p. 166). After a series of studies of the governing class in America, Domhoff (1983) reached essentially the same conclusion: "the power elite involves itself in the candidate selection process through the simple, direct, and often very unsubtle means of large campaign donations that far outweigh what other classes and groups can muster" (p. 117). In 1971, however, the Congress passed the Federal Election Campaign Act. This legislation and subsequent amendments were intended to eliminate a number of campaign finance abuses. Indeed, one of the main goals of this legislation was to limit the magnitude of contributions to campaigns for federal office by wealthy individuals. Although this legislation has been in force for over a decade, there has been no empirical research on the effect of these campaign finance limitations on the contributions of wealthy individuals. This research attempts to assess the impact of these reforms on the political power of the capitalist class, at least as it is exercised through campaign finance, by comparing the contributions of the members of one hundred wealthy capitalist families to the presidential campaigns of 1972 and 1984.

PRIOR RESEARCH

Over the past half century there have been a number of empirical studies of the campaign contributions of wealthy individuals. For example, in his celebrated exposé, *America's Sixty Families* (1937), Lundberg argued that sixty wealthy capitalist families effectively dominated American politics. In particular, he provided convincing evidence that members of these families were among the largest contributors to every presidential campaign from 1896 to 1936. Thayer (1973) reached basically the same conclusion in his historical analysis of the involvement of wealthy individuals in the financing of national political campaigns. Using more systematic data, several social scientists interested in campaign finance (Overacker 1937, 1941, 1945; Heard 1960; Alexander 1966, 1971, 1976) have demonstrated that many of the largest contributors to presidential campaigns between 1936 and 1972 were either wealthy entrepreneurs or their descendants. These early studies of campaign finance were largely descriptive and atheoretical. More recent research (Domhoff 1972; Nichols 1974; Allen and Broyles 1989) has used data on campaign contributions to examine specific theoretical hypotheses concerning the relative involvement of various segments of the capitalist class. In general, these studies have established that many of the largest contributors to political campaigns are those members of wealthy capitalist families who serve as officers and directors of major corporations.

Unfortunately, almost all these studies of campaign finance have suffered from a common methodological flaw. Specifically, they have proceeded without an adequate sample of the members of the capitalist class. With only a few exceptions (Domhoff 1972; Alexander 1976), these researchers have inadvertently sampled on the dependent variable of interest by studying only those wealthy individuals who were major contributors to political campaigns. Consequently, these studies have not been able to ascertain the extent to which the members of the capitalist class in general contribute to these political campaigns. Recent research by Allen and Broyles (1989) overcame this limitation by constructing a systematic sample of all of the senior members of the wealthiest capitalist families in America. In their research, they examined the contributions of 629 members of one hundred wealthy capitalist families to the presidential campaign of 1972. They chose to study the 1972 presidential election because it was the first campaign for which there was virtually complete financial disclosure and the last campaign in which there was no limitation on the magnitude of contributions by individuals. Allen and Broyles found that those family members who were visible to the public at large, as a result of serving as directors of corporations, serving as trustees of foundations, or being listed in *Who's Who in America*, were more likely to contribute to the presidential campaign in 1972 than were those family members who were not visible.

This finding—that wealthy capitalists who were visible to the public at large were more likely to contribute to the presidential campaign in 1972 than were those who were not visible—is amenable to at least two distinct interpretations (Allen and Broyles 1989). On the one hand, it can be argued that members of wealthy capitalist families who were visible, as a result of serving as a corporate director, serving as a foundation trustee, or simply being listed in *Who's Who in America*, often became substantial contributors because they were easily identifiable targets for solicitation by presidential candidates and their campaign staffs (Heard 1960, 136). In this view, wealthy capitalists have simply reacted to the "demand" for campaign contributions. On the other hand, it can be argued with equal force that certain members of wealthy capitalist families become visible to the public only because they had assumed public positions of responsibility, such as foundation trustees or corporate directors. Consequently, their involvement as campaign contributors was simply one manifestation of their overall involvement in public affairs (Brown, Hedges, and Powell 1980). In this view, wealthy capitalists have sought, more or less unilaterally, to supply campaign contributions, just as they have voluntarily chosen to serve as foundation trustees or corporate directors. Although both of these interpretations are consistent with the "candidate-selection process" posited by Domhoff (1983), inasmuch as wealthy capitalists are unlikely to contribute to candidates who threaten their economic interests, these interpretations suggest very different patterns of political involvement by members of the capitalist class. An examination of the impact of campaign finance reforms on the presidential campaign contributions by the members of wealthy capitalist families provides a unique opportunity to test these competing interpretations.

The 1972 presidential election was the first campaign in which political campaign committees were required to disclose names of all individuals and groups who contributed in excess of $100. The Federal Election Campaign Act of 1971 went into effect in April 1972. This legislation was intended to replace the largely ineffectual Corrupt Practices Act of 1925. Specifically, the Federal Election Campaign Act of 1971 required all committees that received in excess of $1,000 in the course of any national election cycle to file a report of their receipts, transfers, and expenditures with the newly created Office of Federal Elections. The original legislation, however, did not impose any limits on the campaign contributions of individuals to candidates for federal office. The 1972 presidential election demonstrated both the strengths and weaknesses of the Federal Election Campaign Act of 1971. Although the original act required full disclosure of campaign contributions, it did not impose any limits on the magnitudes of those contributions. Consequently, a number of wealthy individuals contributed large amounts of money to this campaign. Indeed, several wealthy individuals contributed over $1 million to the 1972 presidential campaign (Alexander 1976). Congress amended the Federal Election Campaign Act four times between 1973 and 1983 (Alexander and Haggerty 1987). These amendments established limits on the amount of money that an individual or group could contribute to a political campaign committee on behalf of a candidate for federal office and created an independent Federal Election Commission to administer these regulations. In particular, the Federal Election Campaign Act and its amendments set a limit of $1,000 per individual on contributions to both the primary and general election campaigns. However, individuals were also able to contribute as much as $5,000 to any political action committee or national party organization. Overall, these regulations allowed individuals to contribute a total of $25,000 to all federal elections in any election cycle.

## RESEARCH DESIGN

In order to assess the impact of the Federal Election Campaign Act on the contributions of the members of wealthy capitalist families, this research examines the contributions of the members of one hundred wealthy capitalist families to the presidential campaigns of 1972 and 1984. These two presidential campaigns were selected as the comparison periods for a number of reasons. To begin with, the 1972 presidential campaign was chosen as the baseline period because it was the first year in which there was virtually complete disclosure of major campaign contributions. Of equal importance is the fact that this was also the last year in which there were no limitations on the magnitude of individual contributions to presidential campaigns. The 1984 campaign was selected as the comparison period because it was comparable to 1972 in terms of the essential characteristics of the election: a conservative Republican incumbent, Nixon in 1972 and Reagan in 1984, was opposed by a liberal Democratic challenger, McGovern in 1972 and Mondale in 1984. The similarities between these two elections make them especially suitable for such a comparison. Of course, factors other than campaign finance reforms may have affected the behavior of wealthy capitalists as contributors to these two campaigns. Nevertheless, these two elections provide the best available comparison for examining the effects of campaign finance reforms on the presidential campaign contributions of wealthy capitalist families.

The sample examined in the course of this research represents a subsample of the 629 members of one hundred wealthy capitalist families in 1972 studied by Allen and Broyles (1989). Specifically, it includes the 590 members of these families who were still alive in 1984. (A total of thirty-nine wealthy individuals in the 1972 sample had died without leaving a surviving spouse.) Although it is not exhaustive, this sample is generally representative of the capitalist class inasmuch as it consists of families that were major stockholders in large corporations (Zeitlin 1974). Each of the families in this sample was worth at least $100 million in 1972, and most were worth much more by 1984. In almost every case, one or more members of these families served as officers or directors of family-controlled corporations. These families were identified from earlier studies of family control in large corporations (Lundberg 1968; Burch 1972; Allen 1987). For the purposes of this analysis a family is defined as a descent group consisting of a wealthy entrepreneur and his or her lineal descendants and heirs. Although many members of these families are not listed in various biographical directories (Priest 1982), it is possible to identify the names of the most senior members of these families using biographies, company histories, obituaries, and probate records (Allen 1987). In addition, some of these individuals were identified as officers of large corporations (*Standard & Poor's* 1984), trustees of private foundations (Foundation Center 1983), or individuals listed in *Who's Who in America* (Marquis, *Who's Who*, 1984).

The main variables of interest in this research are the presidential campaign contributions of the members of these wealthy capitalist families in 1972 and 1984. The contributions of wealthy entrepreneurs and their descendants are aggregated with the contributions of their spouses (Tickamyer 1981). Under the Federal Election Campaign Act of 1971 as amended, individuals are able effectively to double their contributions, without exceeding the limitations on individual contributions, by contributing jointly with their spouses. The sample also includes the surviving spouses of deceased family members because these spouses had typically inherited a substantial share of the wealth of that family member. Information on campaign contributions in 1972 was compiled from a variety of sources (Allen and Broyles 1989). The primary source of information, however, was the extensive report prepared by the Office of Federal Elections (U.S. General Accounting Office 1972), which lists all the contributions and loans to presidential and vice-presidential committees in excess of $100. Information on campaign contributions in 1984 was compiled from data obtained from the Federal Election Commission, which list *all* of the contributions and loans to presidential campaign committees in excess of $500.

Moreover, it must be noted that the presidential campaign contributions reported in 1984 represented contributions to the primary election campaigns of these candidates. The general election campaigns were, of course, financed with public funds.

Because of the limitations on campaign contributions to presidential committees imposed by the Federal Election Campaign Act, many contributions to presidential campaigns are now channeled through the national party organizations and various political action committees. Therefore, this analysis includes contributions by the members of wealthy capitalist families to both the Republican National Committee and the Democratic National Committee. In addition, it also includes the contributions of these same individuals to the thirteen independent political action committees with the largest expenditures to the presidential campaign in 1984. These political action committees were independent inasmuch as they were not officially associated with any specific industry, corporation, or union. There were five liberal committees, including the League of Conservation Voters and a number of antinuclear organizations, and eight conservative committees, including the National Conservative Political Action Committee and the Fund for a Conservative Majority. Of course, not all the contributions to the national parties or political action committees were actually expended on the presidential campaigns. The inclusion of these contributions in the analysis, however, provides an estimate of the maximum contribution of these wealthy capitalists to the presidential campaign at the national level. Unfortunately, there are no systematic data on the contributions of these same individuals to the presidential campaign at the state level.

TABLE 1.    Distributions of Contributions by Members of One Hundred Wealthy
                    Capitalist Families to Presidential Campaigns in 1972 and 1984

| Size of Contribution | 1972 (in percent) | 1984 (in percent) |
|---|---|---|
| None | 52.9% | 67.3% |
| Less than $1,000 | 6.8 | 5.1 |
| $1,000 to $1,999 | 9.1 | 11.5 |
| $2,000 to $4,999 | 8.8 | 4.8 |
| $5,000 to $9,999 | 7.3 | 3.2 |
| $10,000 to $24,999 | 5.9 | 6.9 |
| $25,000 to $49,999 | 3.4 | 1.2 |
| $50,000 to $99,999 | 3.4 | 0 |
| More than $100,000 | 2.4 | 0 |
| Number of contributions | 278 | 193 |
| Mean contribution | $29,781 | $5,906 |
| Median contribution | $4,000 | $1,000 |

RESULTS

The first issue to be addressed by this research is the effect of the
campaign finance reforms contained in the Federal Election Campaign
Act on the contributions of the members of wealthy capitalist families
between 1972 and 1984. The distributions of contributions in 1972 and
1984 by the 590 members of the one hundred wealthy capitalist families
are presented in table 1. A comparison of these two distributions indicates that there has been a substantial decline in both the number and
the magnitude of presidential campaign contributions by the members
of wealthy capitalist families since the passage of the Federal Election
Campaign Act. This is also evident in the summary statistics for these
two distributions. In 1972 the mean contribution among the 278
wealthy contributors was $29,781. By 1984 the mean contribution
among the 193 wealthy contributors was only $5,906. Similarly, the
median contribution among wealthy contributors declined from $4,000
in 1972 to only $1,000 in 1984. Overall, 278 wealthy capitalists contrib-
uted a total of $8,279,001 to the presidential campaign in 1972. By 1984,

193 wealthy capitalists contributed a total of $1,139,814. In other words, there was an 86 percent decline in the campaign contributions attributable to the 590 members of one hundred wealthy capitalist families between 1972 and 1984. This decline is especially significant in view of the fact that, despite the introduction of federal funds to finance presidential campaigns, there was no decline in the actual aggregate contributions of individuals and organizations to these campaigns between 1972 and 1984 (Alexander 1976, 78; Alexander and Haggerty 1987, 84–87).

Given the campaign contribution limits imposed by the Federal Election Campaign Act, it is not surprising to find that there has been a dramatic decline in the number and magnitude of large contributions. It must be recalled that, under the limitations imposed by the Federal Election Campaign Act, individuals were entitled to contribute a maximum of $25,000 to federal campaigns in any given election cycle. In addition, spouses were entitled to contribute another $25,000 to these same campaigns. Only 7 of the 590 wealthy capitalists in the sample, however, either individually or with their spouses, contributed as much as $25,000 to the 1984 presidential campaign. By comparison, fifty-four individuals from these one hundred wealthy capitalist families contributed in excess of $25,000 to the presidential campaign in 1972. Although the decline in large contributions in 1984 is not unanticipated, in view of the limitations imposed by the Federal Election Campaign Act, it is somewhat surprising to find that there has been a dramatic decline in the number of wealthy individuals who contributed to the presidential campaign at all. The proportion of wealthy individuals who contributed anything to the presidential campaign declined from just over 47 percent in 1972 to less 34 percent in 1984. Once again, this decline is significant because the proportion of the population contributing to political campaigns actually increased somewhat between 1972 and 1984 (Alexander and Haggerty 1987, 126).

It is apparent from the magnitude of some of the contributions presented in table 1 that many wealthy individuals have been able to circumvent the limitations on direct campaign contributions to presidential candidates by contributing to both national party organizations and political action committees. The frequency distribution of contributions by the members of the one hundred wealthy capitalist families to the presidential candidates, the national party organizations, and the political action committees involved in the presidential campaign is presented in table 2. The magnitude of some of the contributions to presidential candidates indicates that some wealthy capitalists and their spouses contributed to more than one candidate during the primary campaigns. This distribution reveals that 19.8 percent of the sample contributed directly to the presidential candidates. In addition, 18.0 percent of the sample contributed to the national party organizations. However, only 5.3 percent of the sample contributed to the political action committees. Of course, many of those who contributed to the national party organizations and the political action committees also contributed directly to the presidential candidates. Specifically, 51 of the 106 contributors to national party organizations and 19 of the 31 contributors to political action committees were also contributors to presidential candidates. In other words, contributing to a presidential candidate increased the odds of contributing to a national party organization by a factor of 3.99 and increased the odds of contributing to a political action committee by a factor of 2.73.

In view of these changes in the frequency of contributions to presidential campaigns by the members of these wealthy capitalist families, it is important to identify which individuals altered their activities as contributors during this time period. Earlier research has established that those family members who are visible to the public at large as the result of serving as a corporate director, serving as a foundation trustee, or being listed in *Who's Who in America* are more likely to be contributors to presidential campaigns than were those family members who were not visible (Allen and Broyles 1989). In order to examine this relationship over time, it is necessary to compare the campaign contributions of wealthy capitalists to the presidential campaigns in 1972 and

TABLE 2.    Distributions of Contributions by Members of One Hundred Wealthy
Capitalist Families to Presidential Candidates, National Parties, and
Major Political Action Committees in 1984

| Size of Contribution | Candidates | Parties | Committees |
|---|---|---|---|
| $500 to $999 | 23 | 15 | 7 |
| $1,000 to $1,999 | 73 | 23 | 7 |
| $2,000 to $4,999 | 20 | 15 | 7 |
| $5,000 to $9,999 | 1 | 10 | 6 |
| $10,000 to $24,999 | | 36 | 4 |
| $25,000 to $40,000 | | 7 | |
| Total | 117 | 106 | 31 |

1984 in terms of their visibility in those years. Table 3 presents the percentages of capitalists who contributed to the presidential campaigns in 1972 and 1984 in terms of their visibility in those years. To begin with, this analysis reveals that 405 of the 590 wealthy capitalists, fully 68.6 percent, were visible in one or both of these years as a result of serving as a corporate director, serving as a foundation trustee, or being listed in *Who's Who in America*. This same analysis also reveals that there is a modest relationship between being visible in 1972 or 1984 and being a campaign contributor in those same years. This relationship is not as strong in 1984, however, as it was in 1972. Indeed, a comparison of the percentages below the main diagonal with the corresponding percentages above the main diagonal indicates that many wealthy capitalists, even those who were visible to the public, have not been contributors to recent presidential campaigns. In general, many wealthy capitalists have abstained from contributing to presidential campaigns, particularly in recent years.

Given the decline in both the frequency and magnitude of presidential campaign contributions by the members of wealthy capitalist families, the next question is how the limitations imposed by the Federal Election Campaign Act have affected the political finances of the Democratic and Republican Parties and their presidential candidates. Table

TABLE 3.    Members of Wealthy Capitalist Families Contributing to Presidential Campaigns in 1972 or 1984 by Visibility in 1972 or 1984 (in percent)

| | CAMPAIGN CONTRIBUTOR | | | |
|---|---|---|---|---|
| Year Visible | Neither Year | 1972 Only | 1984 Only | Both Years |
| Neither year (N:185) | 68.1 | 14.6 | 10.8 | 6.5 |
| 1972 only (N:115) | 33.0 | 36.5 | 8.7 | 21.7 |
| 1984 only (N:46) | 47.8 | 10.9 | 15.2 | 26.1 |
| Both years (N:244) | 28.7 | 27.0 | 7.8 | 36.5 |
| $x^2 = 103.5 \ (p < .001)$ | | | | |

4 presents the percentages of wealthy capitalists who contributed to the Democratic and Republican Parties and their candidates in 1984 in terms of their contributions in 1972. This analysis reveals that there is some continuity in these contributions over time inasmuch as those who contributed to one party in 1972 are likely to contribute to the same party in 1984. It also shows that many of the wealthy capitalists who were contributors in 1972 were no longer contributors in 1984 and that relatively few capitalists who were not contributors in 1972 became contributors in 1984. Finally, this analysis demonstrates that the Republican Party was less affected by the overall decline in presidential campaign contributions by wealthy capitalists than was the Democratic Party. For example, more wealthy capitalists defected from the Democratic Party to the Republican Party between 1972 and 1984 than defected from the Republican Party to the Democratic Party. Overall, the total contributions of the wealthy capitalists in the sample to the Democratic Party and its presidential candidate declined 92.5 percent, from $2,651,243 in 1972 to $198,587 in 1984. Conversely, the total contributions of these same wealthy capitalists to the Republican Party and its presidential candidate declined only 83.1 percent, from $5,628,098 in 1972 to $952,295 in 1984. In general, both parties lost campaign contributions from the members of wealthy capitalist families as a result of the Federal Election Campaign Act, but the Democratic Party lost more during this period than the Republican Party.

TABLE 4.   Members of Wealthy Capitalist Families Contributing to Presidential
            Campaigns in 1984 by Contributions to Presidential Campaigns in
            1972 (in percent)

| | CONTRIBUTION IN 1984 | | | |
|---|---|---|---|---|
| *Contribution in 1972* | *Neither Party* | *Democratic Party* | *Republican Party* | *Both Parties* |
| Neither party (N:312) | 82.1 | 5.8 | 11.9 | 0.3 |
| Democratic Party (N:42) | 45.2 | 35.7 | 16.7 | 2.4 |
| Republican Party (N:218) | 51.4 | 4.1 | 41.7 | 2.8 |
| Both parties (N:18) | 50.0 | 11.1 | 27.8 | 11.1 |
| $x = 135.7 \ (p < .001)$ | | | | |

CONCLUSIONS

One of the primary goals of the Federal Election Campaign Act was to
limit the magnitude of contributions by wealthy individuals to campaigns for federal office. On the basis of this analysis it must be concluded that this campaign reform legislation was successful in limiting
the magnitude of presidential campaign contributions by the members
of wealthy capitalist families. Contrary to expectations, this legislation
also had the effect of limiting even the frequency of presidential campaign contributions by the members of these families. In 1972 nearly
one out of every two wealthy capitalists contributed to the presidential
campaign. By 1984, only about one in three of these same individuals
were contributors. Overall, these results provide some confirmation of
the "demand" interpretation of the relationship between visibility and
being a campaign contributor. Indeed, it seems entirely possible that
many wealthy capitalists used the limitations on contributions imposed
by the Federal Election Campaign Act as a pretext for refusing solicitations by candidates to contribute to their campaigns. As Alexander
and Haggerty (1987) put it, "many wealthy contributors welcomed the
enactment of contribution limits, which freed them from the impor-
tunity of candidates in search of campaign money" (p. 148). At the
same time, however, a significant number of wealthy capitalists did

exploit the available opportunities to circumvent the campaign limitations by contributing to the national party organizations and to those political action committees that were involved in the presidential campaign. Consequently, the "supply" interpretation of the relationship between visibility and being a campaign contributor may apply to a relatively small but influential group of wealthy capitalists. In particular, the wealthy capitalists who contributed to the presidential campaigns in both years were often those who were already visible to the public at large because they served as corporate directors or foundation trustees.

Finally, it must be noted that the conclusions of this research must be qualified by the limitations of the available data. To begin with, it is possible that factors other than the passage of the Federal Election Campaign Act are responsible for the decline in both the magnitude and the frequency of presidential campaign contributions by the members of wealthy capitalist families. However, this general finding cannot be attributed to any decline in the proportion of the population contributing to political campaigns or even the introduction of federal funds to finance presidential campaigns. In fact, the passage of the Federal Election Campaign Act and its amendments led, almost inadvertently, to the creation of hundreds of political action committees. Some of these committees have become major contributors to campaigns at both the state and national level (Sabato 1985). Of particular importance has been the emergence of corporate political action committees staffed and funded by officers and directors of large corporations. It is quite possible that large corporations, through their political action committees, have largely supplanted wealthy capitalist families as major contributors to political campaigns (Clawson, Neustadt, and Bearden 1986; Burris 1987; Neustadt and Clawson 1988). Moreover, it is also possible that the members of established capitalist families have, to some extent, been supplanted as major campaign contributors by wealthy entrepreneurs who have amassed new fortunes in recent years. Last, but not least, it must be noted that there are several tactics for circumventing the campaign contribution limitations imposed by the Federal Election Campaign Act. For example, some wealthy individuals have contributed "soft money" to political campaigns by contributing to political action committees and party organizations operating at the state level (Alexander and Haggerty 1987, 174–75).

However, it is likely that many of these contributors are the same individuals who have circumvented the restrictions on contributions to presidential candidates by contributing to the national party organizations and various political action committees. In short, although campaign finance reforms have undoubtedly reduced the presidential campaign contributions of many wealthy capitalists, those who wish to influence the political process are probably able to circumvent many of the limitations imposed by these reforms.

REFERENCES

Alexander, Herbert E. 1966. *Financing the 1964 Election.* Princeton, N.J.: Citizens' Research Foundation.

———. 1971. *Financing the 1968 Election.* Lexington, Mass.: Heath.

———. 1976. *Financing the 1972 Election.* Lexington, Mass.: Heath.

Alexander, Herbert E., and Brian A. Haggerty. 1987. *Financing the 1984 Election.* Lexington, Mass.: Heath.

Allen, Michael P. 1987. *The Founding Fortunes: A New Anatomy of the Super-Rich Families in America.* New York: Dutton.

Allen, Michael P., and Philip Broyles. 1989. "Class Hegemony and Political Finance: Presidential Campaign Contributions of Wealthy Capitalist Families." *American Sociological Review* 54: 275–87.

Brown, Clifford W., Jr., Roman B. Hedges, and Lynda W. Powell. 1980. "Modes of Elite Political Participation: Contributors to the 1972 Presidential Campaign." *American Journal of Political Science* 24: 259–70.

Burch, Philip H., Jr. 1972. *The Managerial Revolution Reassessed.* Lexington, Mass.: Heath.

Burris, Val. 1987. "The Political Partisanship of American Business: A Study of Corporate Political Action Committees." *American Sociological Review* 52: 732–44.

Clawson, Dan, Alan Neustadd, and James Bearden. 1986. "The Logic of Business Unity: Corporate Contributions to the 1980 Congressional Elections." *American Sociological Review* 51: 797–811.

Domhoff, G. William. 1972. *Fat Cats and Democrats: The Role of the Big Rich in the Party of the Common Man.* Englewood Cliffs, N.J.: Prentice-Hall.

———. 1983. *Who Rules America Now?* Englewood Cliffs, N.J.: Prentice-Hall.

Ferguson, Thomas, and Joel Rogers. 1986. *Right Turn: The Decline of Democrats and the Future of American Politics.* New York: Hill and Wang.

Foundation Center. 1983. *The Foundation Directory.* New York: Foundation Center.

Heard, Alexander. 1960. *The Costs of Democracy.* Chapel Hill: University of North Carolina Press.

Lundberg, Ferdinand. 1937. *America's Sixty Families.* New York: Vanguard.

———. 1968. *The Rich and the Super-Rich.* New York: Lyle Stuart.

Marquis Who's Who. 1984. *Who's Who in America.* Chicago: Marquis Who's Who.

Mills, C. Wright. 1956. *The Power Elite.* New York: Oxford University Press.

Neustadd, Alan, and Dan Clawson. 1988. "Corporate Political Groupings: Does Ideology Unify Business Political Behavior?" *American Sociological Review* 53: 172–90.

Nichols, David. 1974. *Financing Elections: The Politics of an American Ruling Class.* New York: New Viewpoints.

Overacker, Louise. 1937. "Campaign Funds in the Presidential Election of 1936." *American Political Science Review* 31: 473–98.

———. 1941. "Campaign Finance in the Presidential Election of 1940." *American Political Science Review* 35: 701–27.

———. 1945. "Presidential Campaign Funds, 1944." *American Political Science Review* 39: 899–925.

Priest, T. B. 1982. "A Note on *Who's Who in America* as a Biographical Data Source in Studies of Elites." *Sociological Methods and Research* I.1: 81–88.

Sabato, Larry J. 1985. *PAC Power: Inside the World of Political Action Committees.* New York: Norton.

Standard & Poor's. 1984. *Directory of Corporations: Officers and Directors.* New York: Standard & Poor's.

Thayer, George. 1973. *Who Shakes the Money Tree?* New York: Simon and Schuster.

Tickamyer, Anne R. 1981. "Wealth and Power: A Comparison of Men and Women in the Property Elite." *Social Forces* 60: 463–81.

U.S. General Accounting Office. 1972. *Alphabetical Listing of 1972 Presidential Campaign Receipts.* Washington, D.C.: U.S. Government Printing Office.

Zeitlin, Maurice. 1974. "Corporate Ownership and Control: The Large Corporation and the Capitalist Class." *American Journal of Sociology* 79: 1073–1119.

# Where Are We Now?
# The Current State of Campaign Finance Law

## Trevor Potter

This selection is from *Campaign Finance Reform: A Sourcebook*, ed. Anthony Corrado, Thomas E. Mann, Dan Ortiz, Trevor Potter, and Frank Sorauf (Washington, D.C.: Brookings Institution Press, 1997), pp. 5–24. In this article Trevor Potter, former member and chairman of the Federal Election Commission and now a partner in a Washington law firm, provides a systematic and reliable review of existing campaign finance law—the statutes and the regulations of the Federal Election Commission.

The federal election laws were written broadly by Congress in 1971 and 1974 to cover all money spent "in connection with" or "for the purpose of influencing" federal elections. The intent of Congress was to regulate all funds that might be considered federal election related. However, the Supreme Court in *Buckley v. Valeo*, 424 U.S. 1 (1976), and subsequent cases, has defined these statutory phrases to have a much more limited reach. The Court held that the activity covered by the federal election laws must be narrowly and clearly defined so as not to "chill" speech protected by the First Amendment and to provide notice of regulation to speakers. This chapter describes the regulated portion of the federal campaign finance system (contribution limits) and the use of "soft" and "issue advocacy" money to influence federal elections beyond the reach of the federal election laws. It also describes the many entities engaged in political speech and spending, from party committees to labor unions to 501(c)(3) and (c)(4) organizations.

### DIRECT CONTRIBUTIONS TO FEDERAL CANDIDATES AND NATIONAL COMMITTEES OF POLITICAL PARTIES

The Federal Election Campaign Act (FECA) defines "contribution" to include "anything of value" given to a federal candidate or committee.

TABLE 1.   Campaign Finance Law: A Summary

| Contributors | May contribute to federal candidates | May contribute to party committees | May engage in independent expenditures | May engage in unlimited "issue advocacy" |
|---|---|---|---|---|
| Individuals | Yes—$1,000 per election to candidates | Yes—limited (unlimited soft money) | Yes | Yes |
| Foreign nationals | No | No, except "building funds" | No | Yes |
| Corporations | No | No, except unlimited soft money | No (except to "restricted class") | Yes |
| Unions | No | No, except unlimited soft money | No (except to members) | Yes |
| PACs (including corporate and union) | Yes—generally $5,000 | Yes—unlimited | Yes | Yes |
| Party committees | Yes—variable limits | Unlimited transfers between committees | Yes | Yes |
| 501(c)(4)s | No | No | In some cases | Yes |
| 501(c)(3)s | No | No | No | Some IRS restrictions |

This encompasses not only direct financial contributions, loans, loan guarantees, and the like but also in-kind contributions of office space, equipment, fund-raising expenses, salaries paid to persons who assist a candidate, and the like: 2 U.S.C. § 431(8) (A). The act places limits on the amount individuals and other entities may contribute to candidates and federal committees, whether directly or in kind (see table 1).

## Individuals

The act permits individuals to contribute up to $1,000 to a candidate per election: § 44la(a) (1) (A). The term *election* under the act includes "a general, special, primary, or runoff election": § 431 (1) (A). An individual may therefore contribute up to $1,000 to a candidate's primary and another $1,000 to the general election campaign. Each individual has his or her own limit, so a couple may give $4,000 in total per election cycle to each federal candidate. Additionally, minor children may give if it is their own money, is under their own control, and is voluntarily contributed by them—requirements sometimes ignored by politically active parents of infants and schoolchildren.

Individuals are also limited in the amounts that they can contribute to other political entities. Individuals are limited to $20,000 per year in contributions to the federal accounts of a national party committee, such as the Republican National Committee (RNC) or the Democratic National Committee (DNC): § 44 1 a (a) (1) (B). Additionally, individual contributions are limited to $5,000 a year to any other political committee, including a political action committee (PAC): § 441a(a) (1) (C). Contributions to state party committees are likewise limited to $5,000 a year. Local party committees are considered part of state party committees, so the $5,000 limit is a combined limit on the two.[1]

In addition to these specific limits to various candidates and committees, individuals have an aggregate annual federal contribution limit of $25,000 a year: § 44 1 a (a) (3).[2] Thus, individuals who give to one or more party committees and several candidates may easily reach this limit for a given calendar year. The *Los Angeles Times* routinely runs a

1. In certain circumstances, where a local committee can sufficiently demonstrate its independence, it will not be considered part of a state committee.
2. For purposes of calculating this limitation, a contribution to a candidate for an election in a year other than the year in which the contribution is made is considered to be made during the year in which that election is held. Thus, a $1,000 contribution made in 1997 to a candidate running for office in 1998 will count toward the contributor's annual limit for 1998. Contributions to multicandidate committees are always counted toward the limit of the year in which the contribution is made. 2 U.S.C. § 44la(a) (3).

list of individuals who appear to have violated this limit, based solely on publicly available FEC records. Because of the complex legal and accounting rules involved, there is often a factual dispute whether a violation has occurred. In many cases, however, it appears that the ability to make unlimited "soft money" contributions to nonfederal committees and accounts has resulted in a general case of amnesia about the $25,000 annual federal limit.

The act and FEC regulations contain a host of exceptions from the definition of "contribution" applicable to individuals. Among the principal ones are the donation of personal time to a candidate (unless it is time paid for by someone else, such as an employer), home hospitality up to $1,000 a candidate per election, and costs of personal travel of up to $ 1,000 a candidate per election and up to $2,000 a year for party committees.

## Political Committees

Whether an organization is a "political committee" required to register with the FEC and subject to the federal limitations on amounts and sources of contributions is a crucial question for any entity engaged in political activity. The act defines "political committee" as

(A) any committee, club, association, or other group of persons which receives contributions aggregating in excess of $1,000 during a calendar year or which makes expenditures aggregating in excess of $ 1,000 during a calendar year; or

(B) any separate segregated fund established under [the Federal Election Campaign Act]; or

(C) any local committee of a political party which receives contributions aggregating in excess of $5,000 during a calendar year, or makes payments exempted from the definitions of contribution or expenditure as defined [by the act] aggregating in excess of $5,000 during a calendar year, or makes contributions aggregating in excess of $1,000 during a calendar year or makes expenditures aggregating in excess of $ 1,000 during a calendar year: 2 U.S.C. § 431(4).

Whether an organization (such as GOPAC or the American Israel Public Affairs Committee) is a political committee, and thus subject to all the federal election laws, or is instead an entity completely unregulated by the federal campaign finance laws, has been the subject of much litigation. The question is whether merely spending $1,000 on express advocacy is sufficient to qualify a group as a political committee, or whether its political activity must be significantly more extensive and pervasive.[3] The current legal standard is unclear, as a result of several recent conflicting court decisions. This is a crucial issue for the coverage of the election laws and will likely continue to be hard fought because groups that can successfully avoid qualifying as a federal political committee can spend unlimited sums, raised without restriction or disclosure, for activities often designed to influence federal elections.

Different forms of federal political committees face differing contribution limits. Political action committees are political committees that may qualify for multicandidate committee status. To so qualify, a PAC must demonstrate that it has been registered with the FEC for six months, receive contributions from at least fifty-one persons, and contribute to at least five federal candidates: 11 C.F.R. § 100.5(e)(3). A multicandidate committee may contribute up to $5,000 to a candidate per election and up to $5,000 to other separate PACs each year. Additionally, a multicandidate committee can contribute up to $15,000 a

---

3. The Federal Election Commission has required that a "committee, club, association, or other group of persons" as defined by section A of 2 U.S.C. § 431(4) have the "influencing of federal elections" as a major purpose in order to be considered a "political committee," based on the FEC's reading of Supreme Court rulings. However, the D.C. Circuit recently rejected this criterion, indicating that the $1,000 threshold for contributions is pertinent for evaluating political committee status (but "major purpose" is still the test if the group makes only expenditures). See *Akins v. FEC*, 10 1 F.3d 731 (D.C. Cir. 1996) (*en banc*) (*cert granted*) ~ 65 U.S.L.W. 3825 (U.S. June 16, 1997) (No. 96-1590).

year to a national party committee and has a combined limit of $5,000 a year to local and state party committees.

A PAC that does not qualify for multicandidate committee status is limited to contributions of $1,000 per candidate per election but may still contribute up to $5,000 a year to another PAC. Such PACs may contribute up to $20,000 a year to national party committees (more than multicandidate committees can) and have a combined limit of $5,000 a year to local and state party committees.

There are two types of noncandidate political committees: nonconnected (or independent) committees and corporate or labor PACs, finally called separate segregated funds. Corporations and labor unions may pay all the administrative and solicitation costs of their committees, whereas nonconnected PACs must pay such costs out of the funds they raise. Corporate and labor PACs, however, have strict rules on who they may solicit, while nonconnected committees may solicit the general public.

## Leadership PACs

Beginning in the 1980s, a number of political committees were established that had an "association" with a member of the congressional leadership. These "leadership PACs" usually use the name of a member of Congress in an honorific capacity such as "honorary chair," and the committee treasurer is a close associate of the congressional member (sometimes an employee of the congressional office). Members of Congress often personally solicit contributions to "their" leadership PACs, and the news media report contributions and expenditures by the committees as if they were a component of the member's campaign apparatus.

The advantage of leadership PACs for members of Congress is twofold. Such committees may qualify as "multicandidate" committees and accept contributions of up to $5,000 from individuals (opposed to $1,000 for a candidate's campaign committee). In addition, since leadership PACs are not considered affiliated with their campaign accounts, members of Congress may obtain contributions from the same sources for both committees (so that a single PAC could give $20,000 in an election cycle: $5,000 each for the primary and general elections to the campaign committee and $ 5,000 a year to the leadership PAC). Members of Congress also have in some instances established state leadership PACs, which are not covered by any of the federal contribution limits or disclosure requirements. Such accounts may therefore be considered a new form of soft money. These state PACs may often accept contributions of corporate or labor funds and unlimited personal funds otherwise banned by federal election law.

Leadership PACs have traditionally been used by legislative leaders to contribute to the campaigns of other members of Congress as a way of gaining a party majority and earning the gratitude of their colleagues. Leadership PACs may not expend more than $5,000 to elect or defeat a federal candidate (including their "honorary chair"). However, these committees may not be subject to the FEC's personal use rules (which prohibit the conversion of campaign funds for a candidate's personal expenses) and are now increasingly serving as a source for travel and other expenses of a political nature. Press articles noted that Senator Ted Kennedy's (D-Mass.) leadership PAC spent the vast majority of its funds for such purposes. This development is the latest in the forty-year cycle of regulating "office accounts" (pejoratively known as slush funds). Office accounts have historically allowed supporters of candidates to provide funds that can be used for a candidate's personal expenses related to political activity (member travel and the care and feeding of supporters, potential donors, and constituents). House and Senate rules both now ban "unofficial office accounts" but exempt political committees from that ban.

Various reformers have urged the FEC to find leadership PACs to be under the control of the members of Congress with whom they are associated. The federal election laws state that all contributions made by committees "established," maintained," or "controlled" by any person "shall be considered to have been made by a single political com-

mittee" because the committees are legally affiliated: 2 U.S.C. §
44la(a)(5). Thus, argue reformers, any contribution to a leadership PAC
should also be considered a contribution to the candidate's campaign
committee, subject to a common limit. However, the FEC has declined
to adopt this approach to date.

## Party Committees

FEC regulations define a party committee as "a political committee
which represents a political party and is part of the official party structure at the national, state, or local level": 11 C.F.R. § 100.5 (e) (4). A
party committee's contribution limits are the same as a multicandidate
political committee's, with three major exceptions:

- For federal election law purposes (but not necessarily state law),
  party committees can transfer unlimited funds to other party
  committees, without such transfers being treated as contributions.

- A national party committee and the national senatorial committee may together contribute up to $17,500 to a candidate for
  the U.S. Senate. This $17,500 limit is for the entire election cycle,
  rather than for each separate election within the cycle: 11 C.F.R.
  § 110.2 (e).

- National and state party committees may spend an inflation-
  adjusted amount for coordinated spending supporting the party's House and Senate candidates, which differs by state depending on its voting age population.

In 1979, Congress amended the Federal Election Campaign Act to
exempt from the definition of contribution and expenditure party
spending on certain state party-building or volunteer activity, *provided*
that it was paid for with funds raised under the act ("hard" or "federal"
money) by state parties, and not from soft money or funds transferred
from the national party committees. These exempted activities include

yard signs, bumper stickers and pins, get-out-the-vote programs, and volunteer mailings but not broadcast advertising or certain activities by paid staff. This exemption has generated years of FEC enforcement investigations and litigation—what is "volunteer" activity? what is a "mass mailing?" when is it paid for by a transfer of funds from a national party committee, using which accounting principles?—because such activity provides an important avenue for parties to support their federal candidates in priority races.

EXPENDITURES

The act defines an *expenditure* to include "(i) any purchase, payment, distribution, loan, advance, deposit, or gift of money or anything of value, made by any person for the purpose of influencing any election for Federal office; and (ii) a written contract, promise, or agreement to make an expenditure": 2 U.S.C. § 431(9). "Expenditure" thus encompasses virtually every payment made in connection with the federal election, including contributions. However, expenditures are only considered contributions when there is some connection with the recipient committee. This concept is explained more fully below in the section discussing independent expenditures.

*Party Committee Expenditures*

Under the act, the national and state party committees may expend additional limited amounts for coordinated expenditures on behalf of their federal candidates. The amount is based on the population of the state (or, in the case of House candidates for states with more than one representative, is a fixed dollar amount). These expenditures may be made at any time but only for the benefit of general election candidates: see 2 U.S.C. § 441a(d).

These expenditures can pay for goods and services for candidates, but payments cannot be made directly to the candidates' campaigns— that is, the party committees may not simply give a candidate money. However, it is important to understand that these expenditures are coordinated with the candidate: these are payments candidates can specifically request and direct. Where a committee makes expenditures independent of a candidate, they are not subject to limits, as explained below. The limits on coordinated party expenditures are being challenged in the *Colorado Republican Federal Campaign Committee v. Federal Election Commission* case on constitutional grounds (116 S. Ct. 2309 [19961]).

## Independent Expenditures

*Independent expenditures* are just that—expenditures by individuals and committees involving elections for federal office that are not coordinated with the candidates seeking office. There are now no dollar limitations on independent expenditures, as *Buckley v. Valeo* established that the First Amendment protects the right of individuals and political committees to spend unlimited amounts of their own money on an independent basis to participate in the election process. Independent expenditures, however, must be publicly disclosed through the Federal Election Commission.

At one time, the Federal Election Commission presumed that party committees were incapable of making independent expenditures, reasoning that parties and their candidates were so intertwined that there could be no truly uncoordinated expenditures. In *Colorado Republican*, however, the Supreme Court ruled that party committees had the same right to make independent expenditures as other committees if the factual record demonstrates the actual independence of the activity. The remaining issue in that case (whether party committees may constitutionally be restricted in the amount they may spend on a *coordinated* basis to elect their candidates) is currently on remand to the lower courts.

The definition of what constitutes a "coordinated" expenditure is not clear at this time. The Federal Election Commission is currently in the midst of an administrative rulemaking to define more clearly what coordination means, and when the concept applies. Under current FEC regulations, the commission looks to several criteria in determining coordination. For instance, inside knowledge of a candidate's strategy, plans, or needs, consultation with a candidate or his or her agents about the expenditure, distribution of candidate-prepared material, or using vendors also used by a candidate may be considered by the FEC as evidence of coordination: see 11 C.F.R. § 109.1 (d) (campaign literature); FEC Advisory Opinions 1982-30 and 1979-80 (vendors).

## PROHIBITED CONTRIBUTIONS AND EXPENDITURES

Although most individuals and organizations are limited in their ability to make contributions in connection with federal elections, others are prohibited by law from making such contributions or expenditures. The Federal Election Campaign Act has four such prohibitions.

### *National Banks, Corporations, and Labor Organizations Prohibition*

Section 441b of the act makes it unlawful for any national bank or any corporation organized by authority of any law of Congress, any other corporation, or any labor organization to make contributions in connection with a federal election or for anyone to accept such contributions. Thus, corporations and unions cannot contribute their general treasury funds to a federal candidate (PAC funds, contributed voluntarily by individuals for these purposes, are not covered by this provision). This broad prohibition is subject to three significant exceptions.

Nonprofit issue-advocacy groups exemption.

The Supreme Court has held that certain small, ideologically based nonprofit corporations should be exempt from the prohibition on independent expenditures by corporations in connection with federal elections: Federal Election Commission v. Massachusetts Citizens for Life, Inc., 479 U.S. 238 (1986) (*MCFL*).

The FEC has adopted regulations containing criteria required for a corporation to be exempt under *MCFL*. According to the FEC, such a corporation

1. Must have as its only express purpose the promotion of political ideas[4]

2. Cannot engage in business activities (other than fund-raising expressly describing the intended political use of donations)[5]

3. Can have (i) no shareholders or other persons, other than employees and creditors with no ownership interest, affiliated in any way that could allow them to make a claim on the [corporation's] assets or earnings and (ii) no persons who are offered or who receive any benefit that is a disincentive for them to disassociate themselves with the corporation on the basis of the corporation's position on a political issue

4. Cannot be established by a business corporation or labor organization or accept anything of value from business corporations or labor organizations.[6]

If these criteria are satisfied, the corporation may make unlimited *independent expenditures* in connection with a federal election: 11 C.F.R. § 114.10.

If a qualified *MCFL* corporation makes independent expenditures aggregating more than $250 in a single year, it must report that expenditure to the FEC, as with any other independent expenditure. For *MCFL* corporations, this also involves filing a certification with the FEC that the corporation meets the qualifying criteria for the *MCFL* exemption.

---

4. "Promotion of political ideas" is defined as "issue advocacy, election influencing activity, and research, training or educational activity that is expressly tied to the organization's political goals": 11 C.F.R. § 114.10 M (1).

5. Examples of such benefits are credit cards, insurance policies, savings plans, or training, education, or business information supplied by the corporation: 11 C.F.R. § 114.10(c) (3) (ii) (A) and (B).

6. A nonprofit corporation can show through its accounting records that this criterion is satisfied, or will meet this requirement if it is a qualified 501 (c) (4) corporation and has a written policy against accepting donations from business corporations or labor organizations: 11 C.F.R. § 114. 10 Q (4) (111).

Press exemptions.

The second major exception exempts certain press activities from the act's definition of expenditure: 2 U.S. C. § 431 (9) (B) (I). The section provides that the term *expenditure* does not include "(i) any news story, commentary, or editorial distributed through the facilities of any broadcasting station, newspaper, magazine or other periodical publication, unless such facilities are owned or controlled by any political party, political committee, or candidate." According to the legislative history of this section, Congress included the provision to indicate that it did not intend the act "to limit or burden in any way the first amendment freedoms of the press" and to assure "the unfettered right of the newspapers, TV networks, and other media to cover and comment on political campaigns": H.R. Rep. No. 1239, 93d Cong., 2d Sess., at 4.

Thus, any qualifying media organization can make expenditures in connection with federal elections provided the organization falls within the bounds of the exemption. However, exactly what is within the statute's protection remains unclear. The FEC has indicated that media entities may present debates or cable-cast editorials, but the agency has challenged the distribution of printed materials endorsing a candidate as part of a cable company's billing process. The ultimate determination of that case remains pending: See *Federal Election Commission v. Multimedia CableVision, Inc.*, No. 95-3280 (10th Cir. 1996).

Internal communications exemption.

All corporations are permitted to communicate with their *restricted class* whenever they so choose, and labor unions may likewise communicate with their members. A corporation's restricted class is defined as its stockholders and its executive or administrative personnel and their families: 11 C.F.R. § 114.3 (a). Thus, a corporation can send mailings to its restricted class, endorsing a particular candidate. Similarly, a corporation could invite a candidate to appear before its restricted class and endorse the candidate in connection with the event. However, the corporation must take steps to ensure that only its restricted class receive such communications. Communications with the restricted class are not generally regulated by the FEC, but internal communications of more than $2,000 per election expressly advocating the election or defeat of a candidate must be reported: 2 U.S.C. § 431(9) (B) (iii).

The exemption for communications with members has been used by labor unions for voter registration drives, telephone banks to turn out the vote on election day, and candidate endorsements. Such communications may be completely partisan in nature but can only be made to the union's members or to the corporation's restricted class—not to the general public (see the discussion of general issue advocacy below).

### Foreign Contribution Prohibition

For many years there was no ban on foreign contributions. In 1938, in the face of evidence of Nazi German money spent to influence the U.S. political debate, Congress passed the Foreign Agents Registration Act. This law required agents of foreign entities engaged in publishing political "propaganda" to register and disclose their activities, but it did not regulate political contributions. In 1966, after congressional hearings in 1962–63 revealed campaign contributions to federal candidates by Philippine sugar producers and agents of Nicaraguan president Luis Somoza, Congress moved to prohibit political contributions in *any* U.S. election by any foreign government, political party, corporation, or individual (except foreign nationals who are permanent residents of the United States).[7]

The act now prohibits foreign nationals, either directly or indirectly, from making contributions in connection with any election to political

---

7. Donations to a building fund of a national or state political party committee are specifically excepted from treatment as a "contribution" under the FECA, 2 U.S.C. § 431(8) (B) (viii), and thus seem likely not to be covered by the foreign money prohibition.

The statute states: "any gift, subscription, loan, advance, or deposit of money or anything of value to a national or a State committee of a political party [is not a contribution if it is] specifically designated to defray any cost for construction or purchase of any office facility not acquired for the purpose of influencing the election of any candidate in any particular election for Federal office."

office, including state and local elections as well as federal: 2 U.S.C. § 44 le.[8] The act defines "foreign national" as (1) a foreign principal, as such term is defined by section 611 (b) of title 22, except that the term "foreign national" shall not include any individual who is a citizen of the United States, or (2) an individual who is not a citizen of the United States and who is not lawfully admitted for permanent residence, as defined by section 1101 (a) (20) of title 8.[9]

This prohibition also operates to prevent domestic subsidiaries of foreign corporations from establishing PACs if the foreign parent finances the PAC's establishment, administration, or solicitation costs or if individual foreign nationals within the corporation make decisions for the PAC, participate in its operation, or serve as its officers: 11 C.F.R. § 110.4 (a) (2) and (3). Since federal law prohibits a foreign national from making contributions through another person or entity, a domestic subsidiary of a foreign parent corporation may only make contributions out of domestic profits. It may not make nonfederal contributions out of subsidies received from the foreign parent, nor may it use such funds to pay for the establishment, administration, or solicitation costs of its PAC. Similarly, foreign nationals may not participate in the selection of the individuals who run the PAC.

These provisions are at the heart of much of the controversy about fund-raising activity in the 1996 election. One issue is whether this

8. 22 U.S.C. § 611 (b) provides:

(b) The term "foreign principal" includes (1) a government of a foreign country and a foreign political party; (2) a person outside of the United States, unless it is established that such person is an individual and a citizen of and domiciled within the United States, or that such person is not an individual and is organized under or created by the laws of the United States or of any state or other place subject to the jurisdiction of the United States and has its principal place of business within the United States; and (3) a partnership, association, corporation, organization, or other combination of persons organized under the laws of or having its principal place of business in a foreign country.

9. 8 U.S.C. § 1101 (a) (20) provides: The term "lawfully admitted for permanent residence" means the status of having been lawfully accorded the privilege of residing permanently in the United States as an immigrant in accordance with the immigration laws, such status not having changed.

foreign national prohibition applies to the donation of "soft," or non-federal, money to a national party committee. The Department of Justice's stated view on this question has varied, and the matter is probably fact-specific: Can the funds donated be said to have been used in connection with any election to political office, whether federal, state, or local, or were they only used for nonelection activities?[10]

## Federal Contractors Prohibition

The act prohibits anyone who contracts with the United States or any of its departments or agencies to make any contribution to any political party, committee, or candidate for public office, nor may such a contribution be solicited from any person between the time of the negotiations and completion of the contract. However, federal contractors that are corporations can establish federal PACs: 2 U.S.C. § 441c.

## Contributions in the Name of Another Prohibition

Section 441f of the act provides that "no person shall make a contribution in the name of another person or knowingly permit his name to be used to effect such a contribution, and no person shall knowingly accept a contribution made by one person in the name of another person." This section is often enforced in connection with other prohibitions. For example, where a foreign national gives money to a U.S. citizen to be contributed by such person to a federal candidate, there is

10. Attorney General Janet Reno's testimony before the Senate Judiciary Committee on April 30, 1997, indicates that the Department of Justice may now interpret Section 441e to prohibit soft money contributions to party committees from foreign nationals. See Department of Justice Oversight, *Hearing of the Senate Judiciary Committee*, Federal News Service, April 30, 1997 (responses to questions from Senator Fred Thompson). Senator Thompson asserted in his questioning of Attorney General Reno that her interpretation that "soft money" was never a "contribution" under the act would make acceptance of soft money contributions from foreign sources legal. The attorney general disagreed, stating that "441e prohibits contributions from foreign nationals in connection with all elections, state and federal, and thus they can't use soft money from foreign sources for issue ads by political parties."

both a violation of § 441e (foreign contributions) and § 441f (a contribution in the name of another).

*Major Parties (Democrats and Republicans)*

The contribution and expenditure limits described above apply to all federal elections other than presidential campaigns. Presidential elections are partially publicly funded. That is, once a major party presidential candidate meets certain requirements, the general election campaign may choose to receive full U.S. government funding from the Treasury accounts funded from the $3 voluntary taxpayer checkoff.

Presidential primaries.

Presidential primaries are funded through a combination of public and private funding. The partial public funding is provided in matching funds, public funds matching up to $250 of a single individual's contributions. To qualify for such matching funds, the candidate must demonstrate nationwide support through raising at least $5,000 in individual contributions of up to $250 each in at least twenty separate states. Candidates must also agree, among other things, to

- Limit primary spending to an inflation adjusted amount—approximately $31 million in 1996

- Limit spending in each primary state to a specific amount (which increases with population)

- Limit spending of personal funds to $50,000

Once these requirements are met or agreed to, the candidate can receive matching payments: see generally 11 C.F.R. § 9033. 1.

Private contributions for presidential candidates are still limited as in other federal elections. Individuals may contribute up to $1,000 to a presidential primary campaign committee, and qualified multicandi-date PACs can contribute up to $5,000.

The general election.

Once a candidate becomes the nominee for a major party, he or she becomes eligible for a public grant (which was $61.82 million per can-didate in 1996). To receive these funds, however, the candidate must agree to spend no more than the grant received and must not accept private contributions. Additionally, the two major party national com-mittees may each spend a voting-age population-adjusted amount ($12 million in 1996) in coordination with their presidential candidates: 2 U.S.C. § 441a(d) (2). This amount is separate from any get-out-the-vote or generic party-building activities the parties conduct. As noted below, the Republican and Democratic National Committees do not consider their "issue advocacy" advertising to be subject to this limit (whether or not coordinated with their presidential candidates).

Candidates not accepting public funds.

Candidates are not required to accept public funds in either the primary or general elections. Candidates refusing such funds are permitted to spend as much of their own money in support of their campaigns as they wish. As a result, a candidate refusing public funding would have no per state spending limit or overall spending limit in the primary campaign (Steve Forbes in 1996) and no spending limit in the general election campaign (Ross Perot in 1992). Such a candidate could still accept private contributions in both the primary and general election campaigns, subject to the standard $ 1,000 per election contribution limit for individuals.

Convention funding.

Each of the major parties' nominating conventions may also be paid for, in part, by public funding: see 26 U.S.C. § 9008. Each major party received a grant of $12.36 million in 1996 to finance its nominating convention. Minor parties may qualify for convention funding based on their presidential candidates' share of the popular vote in the preceding election.

Political parties accepting convention funding may spend in connection with the convention only the amount of public funds they receive. However, the host city and other sponsors support conventions in a variety of ways. The city, through its host committee (a federally registered committee created to support convention activities) may spend money promoting itself as a convention location, pay for the convention hall, and provide local transportation and related services to the convention: see 11 C.F.R. § 9008.52. Additionally, the host city itself may directly accept cash and in-kind contributions from local (but not other) businesses, which are often received by a tax-deductible entity. In some circumstances, corporations can also provide goods (such as automobiles) free to the conventions as part of a promotional program. These exemptions, as interpreted by the FEC, have in practice resulted in extensive convention-related fund-raising by the host city and the political parties, usually raising individual, corporate, and labor funds for the convention far greater in total than the federal grant. Conventions now have "official" airlines, computer companies, car rental agencies, and the like, all in addition to the federal grants to the political parties.

## Third- and Minor-Party Presidential Candidates

Minor parties (those that have received at least 5 percent but no more than 25 percent of the popular vote in the preceding presidential election) and new parties (a party that is not a major or minor party) may also receive partial public funding for the general election, in some instances. New- and minor-party candidates may accept private contributions, but only within the general limits on such contributions ($1,000 per election from individuals, and no corporate or labor contributions).

A candidate who agrees to abide by the restrictions applicable to publicly funded presidential candidates (including an FEC audit and a $50,000 limit on the use of personal funds) and who then meets a threshold of 5 percent of the general election vote will receive public funding based on his or her share of the vote but not until after the election: see 11 C.F.R. § 9004.3. Days after the 1980 general election, independent John Anderson became the first such candidate to receive "retroactive" funding, based on unofficial vote totals showing that he had received nearly 7 percent of the popular vote. In subsequent elections, an individual who has received 5 percent or more of the vote in a previous general election may be eligible to receive general election funding before the election: see 11 C.F.R. § 9004.2. The most prominent example is Ross Perot, who ran as an independent in 1992, then appeared on most state ballots as the nominee of the Reform Party in 1996. Even though Perot had not run under the Reform Party banner in 1992, he received public funding in 1996 based on his 1992 general election vote total.

Additionally, minor-party candidates may be eligible for primary funding as well. Examples include Lyndon H. LaRouche, who appeared on the ballot in several states as the candidate of the U.S. Labor Party in 1976 but failed to qualify for public funding in that year's general election. Beginning in 1980, however, LaRouche sought the Democratic Party's nomination for president several times. He secured matching funds for most of those primary campaigns by receiving the necessary individual contributions to meet the statutory criteria for "nationwide support." Similarly, Lenora Fulani received matching funds when she sought the New Alliance Party nomination in 1988 and 1992. Because of the 5 percent threshold, however, she failed to qualify for general election funding in either of those two years.

Once the FEC certifies a minor party or new party as a "national" party, then the party may contribute to its presidential candidate's campaign, subject to the same types of contribution limits that the major parties face. During the 1996 election, the Libertarian, Natural Law, and Taxpayers Parties all had national recognition from the FEC. The Reform Party received no such recognition, in part because Ross Perot argued that the national organization was merely a collection of state parties. Without the national party designation, Perot could avoid federal limits in the personal funding he could provide for the Reform Party's convention. However, he could still only contribute a maximum of $50,000 to his own general election campaign because he accepted federal funding. Before and after the 1996 election, Reform Party members opposed to Perot sought federal recognition of state party organizations they controlled, both to limit Perot's influence and to gain control of the subsequent federal funding guaranteed by Perot's 8 percent showing in 1996. Had Perot not been the Reform Party's nominee in 1996, the party's presidential candidate would have had to meet the 5 percent vote threshold in the 1996 election before receiving any federal funding.

## "SOFT MONEY"

The act prohibits party committees from accepting contributions in excess of individual or PAC limits or from impermissible sources (corporations, unions, foreign nationals). In a series of advisory opinions, the FEC has allowed state and national party committees to accept funds from some sources and in amounts otherwise prohibited by federal election law, provided such funds are placed in separate " nonfederal" accounts and not used for federal election purposes.

The FEC has created a complex system of allocation formulas regulating the proportions of hard and soft money that party committees may use for generic party activity (administrative, overhead, get-out-the-vote, issue ads, and the like). National party committees (but not state or local) are also required to disclose soft money donations to the FEC.

## RESTRICTIONS ON POLITICAL FUND-RAISING BY MEMBERS OF CONGRESS AND EXECUTIVE BRANCH OFFICIALS

There are several statutes that regulate the location and form of political fund-raising. Most of these are designed to protect federal employees from pressure to contribute to federal candidates and parties, but one simply prohibits any solicitation or receipt of a federal contribution in a federal workplace. These statutes carry criminal or civil penalties, and their intricacies have been the focus of much attention as a result of reported fund-raising activities at the White House during the 1996 election.

A series of criminal provisions makes it unlawful to attempt to obtain a political contribution from a government employee by means of threats of firing (18 U.S.C. § 601); for a candidate for Congress or federal employee or officer to solicit a campaign contribution from any other federal employee or officer (18 U.S.C. § 602); for a federal officer or employee to contribute to his or her employer's campaign (18 U.S.C. § 603); for any person to solicit a political contribution from someone known to be entitled to funds for federal "work relief" (18 U.S.C. § 604); or to demote or threaten to demote a federal employee for giving or withholding a political contribution (18 U.S.C. § 606).

Additionally, 18 U.S.C. § 607 makes it a criminal offense (subject to a fine or three years in jail or both) to "solicit or receive any contribution . . . in any room or building occupied in the discharge of official duties" by any federal officer or employee. Congress is specifically exempted from the receipt portion of this provision, provided that any funds received are transferred within seven days to a federal political committee and that the contributors were not told to send or deliver the money to the federal office building.

*"Soft Money"*

The most important limitation on the scope of these solicitation provisions was probably unintentional. In 1979, Congress amended each of these sections to replace language referring to "contributions for any political purpose" or "to be applied to the promotion of any political object" with the more precise "contribution" as "within the meaning of section 301(8) of the Federal Election Campaign Act of 1971." The result is that this new definition only reaches contributions "for the purpose of influencing" federal elections, thereby arguably leaving solicitations for nonfederal ("soft money") donations beyond the reach of the solicitation ban.

Thus, a key question for federal prosecutors becomes whether the money being solicited is hard or soft (a distinction unknown to Congress when the new definition of "contribution" was inserted in these laws in 1979). This in turn raises questions about contributions solicited by federal candidates or their agents explicitly for the purpose of influencing a federal election but deposited in and spent out of a nonfederal account. Common Cause, among others, has argued that such donations should be considered "contributions" under the Federal Election Campaign Act of 1971, as amended.

A seldom-used FEC regulation adopted in 1990 may be relevant to this debate:

> Any party committee solicitation that makes reference to a federal candidate or a federal election shall be presumed to be for the purpose of influencing a federal election, and contributions resulting from that solicitation shall be subject to the prohibitions and limitations of the Act. This presumption may be rebutted by demonstrating to the Commission that the funds were solicited with express notice that they would not be used for federal election purposes. 11 C.F.R. §102.5 (a) (3).

This provision has the potential to bring the solicitation of funds deposited in party soft money accounts within the federal definition of "contribution." Such a result would have significant implications for the interpretation of the criminal statutes banning solicitations of federal employees for campaign contributions or the solicitation or receipt of such contributions in federal buildings.

Additional issues raised by 1996 events include which areas of the White House are exempt from the solicitation ban because they are not used "in the discharge of official duties" (in 1979, the Department of Justice issued an opinion to President Jimmy Carter that a luncheon with Democratic party fund-raisers held in the White House family quarters fell within the "private residence" exemption implicit in the law). Questions have also been raised about whether the prohibition on solicitation applies when the solicitation occurs through a phone call from a federal office but the recipient of the conversation is not in a federal building, and whether there is an exemption from the ban on "receiving" a contribution for "ministerial" acts (such as taking an envelope containing a contribution and delivering it to an authorized representative of a political committee) .

## Congress

As noted above, the prohibition on receiving contributions in a federal building does not apply to Congress, as long as certain conditions are met. However, the ban on solicitations from a federal workplace does apply to Congress.

The Committee on Standards of Official Conduct has recently reminded House members that, entirely aside from the criminal statute, the Rules of the House also regulate political fund-raising and "are quite specific, and quite restrictive" ("April 25, 1997 Memorandum for All Members, Officers and Employees"). Under House rules, *Members and staff may not solicit political contributions in their office or elsewhere in the House buildings, whether in person, over the telephone, or otherwise"* (emphasis in original). Added the committee: "The rule bars *all* political solicitations in these House buildings. Thus, a telephone solicitation would not be permissible merely because, for example, the call is billed to the credit card of a political organization or to an outside telephone number, or it is made using a cellphone in the hallway." Nor may House telephone numbers be left for a return call if the purpose is the solicitation of a political contribution, according to the committee. This advice responds to claims that members of Congress were using cellular telephones in their offices, or fund-raising in the Capitol, instead of using the cubicles set aside for fund-raising telephone calls in office buildings near the Capitol owned by the Democratic and Republican campaign committees.

The Senate also has rules regulating campaign activity in Senate buildings and the Capitol and restricting the number of members of a senator's staff who may handle campaign contributions.

## The Hatch Act

The Hatch Act, first passed by Congress in 1939 during President Franklin Roosevelt's second administration to protect federal employees from political pressure, bans all Executive Branch federal employees from knowingly soliciting, accepting, or receiving a political contribution from any person: 5 U.S.C. § 7322. Although (unlike the criminal provisions) "political contribution" is still broadly defined as "any gift . . . made for any political purpose," the penalty for violations of the Hatch Act is either thirty days suspension without pay or removal of the employee's position. The Hatch Act has no criminal penalties.

### ISSUE ADVOCACY

Issue advocacy is speech that does not "expressly advocate" the election or defeat of a federal candidate and is therefore not subject to any of the limits, prohibitions, or disclosure provisions of the federal election laws. As a result, corporations, unions, advocacy groups, and party committees may raise and spend funds for such speech without limit, and (except for party committees) without disclosure of sources or amounts. Three current issues concerning issue advocacy are the focus of legal attention:

- When does "issue advocacy" become "express advocacy"?

- When is it "coordinated" with a candidate so as to make it a "contribution" subject to all of the federal election laws?

- Is some party committee issue advocacy exempt from the FEC's soft money allocation regulations because it is unrelated to any election?

## OTHER PLAYERS IN THE ARENA

In addition to those who contribute under the laws established by the act, other significant entities play roles in political campaigns.

### Unions

Although the act and FEC regulations treat corporate and union funds similarly, other considerations have made unions unique in the political landscape. Like corporations, they may not contribute directly to federal candidates but may create and administer a PAC, may contribute to the nonfederal accounts of political parties, and may sponsor "issue" advertising to the general public.

As membership organizations, they may also communicate with their members (numbering in the millions) on any subject (including urging them to vote for specific candidates or parties) and may use union treasury funds to do so. In *Communications Workers of America v. Beck*, 487 U.S. 735 (1988), the Supreme Court determined that the National Labor Relations Act limited union uses of money raised from nonunion employees as a condition of employment to support collective bargaining ("agency agreements"). As a result, nonunion employees in closed-shop states cannot be required to fund political spending as a condition of their employment.

This decision potentially reduces the political use of funds paid involuntarily to unions by nonmembers. On April 13, 1992, President George Bush issued Executive Order 12800, which required government contractors to post notices informing their nonunion employees that they could object to use of their union dues for political purposes. On February 1, 1993, however, President Bill Clinton issued Executive Order 12836, rescinding Executive Order 12800, and referred the issue to the National Labor Relations Board for further consideration.

The broader question on the use of dues from union members themselves for political activity was not addressed in *Beck*. Republican Party leaders argue that union members should be given some mechanism for authorizing or restricting the use of their dues for political purposes (perhaps including issue advertising), claiming that a substantial number of union members disagree with the political choices made by union leaders. Democrats and unions respond that union leaders are freely elected by the membership and are thus only exercising their representative authority. Besides, they add, corporate shareholders do not vote whether to approve corporate political spending on issue advocacy either. Member dues in any case provide only a portion of the funds available to unions for such communications, so union leaders could probably use other funds for these activities if necessary.

In 1996 the AFL-CIO announced a $35 million television advertising campaign, which ran in dozens of congressional districts with vulnerable Republican incumbents, attacking the members' congressional voting records on issues such as social security, medicare, and federal funding for education. These "issue" advertisements were paid for with union treasury funds, on the grounds that they did not "expressly advocate" the election or defeat of the member of Congress but instead had endings such as "tell your representatives to stop cutting medicare." This spending was in addition to direct union PAC contributions to Democratic candidates and party committees and the use of union organizers in congressional districts. Additionally, unions engaged in traditional voter registration activity and election day get-out-the-vote telephone banks directed to union members and reportedly assigned paid organizers to some congressional districts to coordinate communications activities.

## Corporations

Corporations have been prohibited from contributing to federal candidates since the beginning of this century, when the first federal campaign finance restrictions were enacted by Congress. However, like unions, corporations still participate in the political process in a variety of ways.

Most visibly, corporations may establish and pay the administrative costs of separate segregated funds, known as PACs, and may encourage employees and stockholders to contribute personal funds to those committees. Additionally, corporations may communicate with their executives and management personnel, urging them to support and contribute to specific parties or candidates, and may host visits by candidates at corporate facilities, subject to FEC rules. The most important aspect of such internal corporate activity is the ability of corporate executives and PACs to raise funds for federal candidates. The FEC has issued complicated new regulations governing such corporate political activity, but fund-raising by corporate executives under these rules remains a substantial source of money for federal candidates.

Corporations may also pay for "issue advocacy" advertising, either directly or through donations to other groups, such as industry associations or issue-oriented 501 (c) (4)s that are engaged in public advertising programs. Because issue advertising is not defined as a campaign "expenditure," it does not need to be disclosed, making it difficult to identify the sources or amounts of such spending. In 1996, "the Coalition" was formed by a group of business associations, including the U.S. Chamber of Commerce, to respond in kind to the labor unions' televised issue advocacy ads. The Coalition is reported to have raised some $3.5 million from corporations for this activity and has announced plans to continue such general public communications in the future. Additionally, corporations contribute substantial sums of "soft money" to the nonfederal accounts of the national party committees and directly to state parties (where permitted by state law).

Finally, the Supreme Court has held that it is unconstitutional to prohibit corporations from spending funds to campaign for and against state ballot measures. (See *First National Bank of Boston v. Bellotti*, 435 U.S. 765 [1978]; document 3.2.) In states such as California, where ballot initiatives are often identified with particular candidates or political parties, this can provide an avenue for a significant direct expenditure of corporate funds that may have the effect of influencing a federal election.

## 501 (c) (4) Organizations

Section 501 (c) (4) of the Tax Code provides for the establishment of "social welfare organizations" exempt from federal income tax. Although these organizations must be operated exclusively for the promotion of the public social welfare and cannot be for profit, they still can engage in political activities, as long as these activities do not become their primary purpose.

The Internal Revenue Service (IRS) interprets this restriction to allow 501 (c) (4) organizations to participate in an election by doing such things as rating candidates on a partisan basis (Rev. Rul. 67-368, 1967-2 *Cumulative Bulletin* 194 July 1967). They also may promote legislation (Rev. Rul. 71-530, 1971-2 *Cumulative Bulletin* 237 July 1971; Rev. Rul. 67-293, 1967-2 *Cumulative Bulletin* 185 July 1967). As long as its political activities do not become an organization's primary activity, a 501 (c) (4) entity can engage in any activity consistent with state and federal laws. Under new FEC regulations, 501 (c) (4)s that qualify as *MCFL* issue advocacy corporations may engage in independent political expenditures.

As the public becomes more aware of politically active 501 (c) (4) organizations, there have been calls for limits on such activities by tax-exempt entities. For instance, the Christian Coalition, designed as a 501 (c) (4) entity, has played a highly visible role in state and national Republican Party politics, going so far as to claim credit for the Republican success in the 1994 elections and to create a multimillion-dollar war room at the 1996 Republican National Convention. The FEC has sued the group, claiming it has made illegal and unreported contributions to federal candidates, largely through its "voter guide" activities. Republicans argue that many other groups engage in similar (if smaller-scale) activities on behalf of Democrats.

Additionally, the IRS appears to be questioning whether some groups can become so partisan in nature or purpose that they advance a narrow private or partisan purpose, rather than the general social welfare, and thus are not entitled to a tax exemption. The IRS challenged the National Policy Forum, headed by former RNC chairman Haley Barbour, on this basis. It may be raising similar objections to the Christian Coalition, which has apparently yet to receive IRS approval of its application for recognition of 501 (c) (4) status after an unprecedented period of review. Both major parties have traditionally benefited from such organizations: the Democratic Leadership Council (DLC) is a 501 (c) (4) organization that obtained its exemption in the 1980s and was once headed by President Clinton.

Another feature of the 1996 election year was the contribution of substantial sums by party committees to 501 (c) (4) organizations, which then reportedly used those funds for issue advocacy activities. The advantage to the party committee is that the contribution can be entirely soft money, whereas if the same activity were done by the party entity, only 35 percent of it can be paid for with soft money, under FEC allocation regulations discussed above.

## 501 (c) (3) Organizations

Section 501 (c) (3) organizations are tax-exempt entities organized for charitable and other similar purposes and are ostensibly prohibited from intervening in any political campaigns: Internal Revenue Code § 501 (c) (3) of the Tax Code. Thus, these organizations cannot endorse candidates, contribute to campaigns, or organize a political action committee. However, they can conduct nonpartisan voter registration and get-out-the-vote efforts in accord with FEC regulations (see 11 C.F.R. § 114.4). Additionally, they may sponsor candidate forums on issues of public concern (Rev. Rul. 86-95, 1986 *Cumulative Bulletin* 73, August 18, 1986). Candidates and party committees can (and do) raise money to enable such organizations to perform their "nonpartisan" tasks.

The FEC has recently gone to court to prevent party committees from funding 501 (c) (3) voter registration activity solely with soft or nonfederal funds (See *Federal Election Commission v. California Dem-*

*ocratic Party* 97-0891 DFL PAN, Eastern Dist. of Cal., filed May 9, 1997). The commission argues that such voter registration activity can only be paid for by party committees pursuant to the FEC's allocation regulations and thus with a proportional use of hard and soft money. The FEC argues that party committees cannot avoid the allocation rules by "subcontracting" the voter registration activity out to a 501 (c) (3) organization, as it alleges was done by the California Democratic Party.

Many well-known think tanks are 501 (c) (3) organizations, including Brookings, the American Enterprise Institute, Heritage, Cato, the Family Research Council (Gary Bauer's group), and the Progressive Policy Institute (associated with the DLC). Some are genuinely nonpartisan, while others appear close to one party or group of candidates. Additionally, many organizations maintain a collection of entities under one umbrella, such as the Sierra Club, which has a 501 (c) (3), a 501 (c) (4), and a PAC. Many of the ethics charges against Newt Gingrich related to his use of just such a collection of organizations, including charitable and educational groups, for political purposes.

ENFORCEMENT

*The Federal Election Commission*

The federal campaign finance laws are enforced by the FEC in the case of civil violations and by the Department of Justice when a criminal violation is charged. The FEC itself has no independent authority to impose penalties. If, after an investigation, the alleged violators are unwilling to sign a settlement agreement and pay a monetary penalty to the U.S. Treasury, then the FEC can vote to sue the offender in federal court, present the evidence to a judge, and ask the court to find a violation and impose a fine.

Penalties sought by the FEC range from a few hundred dollars to many thousands of dollars, depending on the size and nature of the violation. The act restricts penalties to $5,000 per violation, or the amount at issue, whichever is larger (and doubles these sums in the case of knowing and willful violations).

*Standing Issues—What If the FEC Deadlocks or Fails to Act?*

The act contains a provision allowing parties whose complaints have been dismissed or otherwise not acted on by the FEC to file suit against the FEC in federal court alleging that the FEC's failure to act was arbitrary and capricious. If successful, the party can obtain a court order requiring the FEC to act in accord with FECA on the complaint. If the FEC does not follow the court order within thirty days, the party may sue the alleged campaign law violator directly: 2 U.S.C. § 437g(a) (8). This provision of the act has almost never been used. For an example of a recent rare instance, see *Democratic Senatorial Campaign Committee v. Federal Election Commission,* Civil Action No. 96-2184 (JHG), (D.D.C. May 30,1997), where a federal judge held that the FEC had failed in its statutory duty to investigate a Democratic complaint against Republican campaign activity in a number of Senate campaigns in 1992. The judge ruled that the commission's inability to complete its investigative process after four and a half years was an abdication of its enforcement role, and as a result gave the Democratic Senatorial Campaign Committee the right to sue the National Republican Senatorial Committee directly in federal district court over the alleged violations.

The statutory right to challenge FEC action or nonaction is an unusual provision and has served as the basis for a number of successful challenges to FEC enforcement decisions in the past. However, this right to seek judicial review of FEC actions requires a high standard of proof (that the FEC decision was "arbitrary and capricious") and is in any case now being challenged and limited by the federal courts. As recent D.C. Circuit Court decisions make clear, complainants seeking judicial review of FEC action or nonaction must meet federal standing (right to file suit) requirements under Article III of the Constitution. They must suffer an "injury-in-fact" caused by the FEC's action (or failure to act) that may be redressed by the court's order. In what appear to be somewhat conflicting decisions, the D.C. Circuit has held that if complainants, as voters, were deprived of legally required information about contributions and expenditures, this is a sufficient injury to confer standing: *Akins v. Federal Election Commission,* 101 F.3d 731, 737 (D.C. Cir. 1996) (*en banc*) (*cert granted*, 65 U.S.L.W. 3825 [U.S. June 16, 1997] [No. 96-1590]). However, the assertion that the FEC's acts deprived voters of information generally is not sufficient to convey standing: *Common Cause v. Federal Election Commission,* 108 F.3d 413,418 (D.C. Cir. 1997). In that case, Common Cause was denied the right to challenge the FEC's conclusion of an investigation of Republican Party spending in Montana, even though Common Cause had filed the original complaint with the FEC. The court held that Common Cause had not shown that it was injured by the FEC's decision (or that it would benefit from an FEC or judicial finding that the party activity violated the law) and thus could not bring the case. Since Common Cause has historically challenged numerous FEC enforcement decisions, this holding may significantly restrict the ability of such "public interest" organizations to seek court review of FEC decisions in the D.C. Circuit. The Supreme Court has also recently agreed to review the *Akins* decision. That review has the potential to result in the establishment of a clearer (and perhaps narrower) new nationwide standing rule, which could foreclose a significant amount of judicial review of FEC action or inaction.

### The Justice Department—Criminal Prosecutions

The Justice Department pursues criminal violations of the campaign finance laws either after referral from the FEC or upon independent discovery. U.S. attorneys or the department's Public Integrity Section may investigate alleged violations, using FBI assistance and grand juries. Cases are tried in federal court, and allegations may include ancillary mail fraud/wire fraud or conspiracy violations. Penalties may include jail terms and substantial monetary penalties.

Aggravated and intentional campaign finance crimes may be prosecuted either as misdemeanor violations of the act or as felonies under the conspiracy and false statement provisions: 2 U.S.C. § 437g(d); 18 U.S.C. §§ 371 and 100 V1. Prosecution under the mail or wire fraud statutes may also be available in some cases: see 18 U.S.C. §§ 1341 and 1343. The Department of Justice pursues campaign finance crimes involving $10,000 and under as FECA misdemeanors and considers for felony prosecution only those involving more than $ 10,000.

Criminal prosecution of federal election law violations is pursued in cases demonstrating "willful violation of a core" FECA provision, involving "a substantial sum of money" ($2,000 or more) and resulting "in the reporting of false campaign information to the FEC."[11] The core provisions of FECA include the following:

- Contribution limits[12]

- Ban on corporation and labor contributions[13]

- Ban on contributions from federal contractors[14]

- Ban on contributions from foreign nationals[15]

- Prohibition against making contributions in the name of another[16]

- Avoidance of FEC disclosure requirements

Schemes used to disguise illegal contributions have also been prosecuted as violations of 18 U.S.C. § 371 (conspiracy to obstruct the lawful functioning of a government agency) and § 1001 (submitting false information to a federal agency).

Defendants convicted of FECA misdemeanors may receive sentences of imprisonment: see *United States v. Goland*, 959 F.2d 1449 (9th

11. Individuals may still contribute to a special fund campaign committees may establish under FECA limits/restrictions to pay for legal and accounting compliance expenses.

12. See Select Committee on Ethics, U.S. Senate, *Senate Ethics Manual*, S. Pub. 104-44 (September 1996), pp. 178–88.

13. See generally Laura A. Ingersoll, ed., *Federal Prosecution of Election Offenses*, 6th ed. (Department of Justice, January 1995), pp. 133–35.

14. Ingersoll, *Federal Prosecution of Election Offenses*, p. 115.

15. Ingersoll, *Federal Prosecution of Election Offenses*, p. 93.

16. Ingersoll, *Federal Prosecution of Election Offenses*, p. 109.

Cir. 1992) (ninety days). Corporate defendants may receive large fines for misdemeanor FECA violations: *United States v. Fugi Medical Systems,* C.R. No. 90-288 (S.D.N.Y., sentencing proceedings, August 15, 1990).

Significant sentences have been applied to felony campaign finance crimes prosecuted under §§ 371 (conspiracy) or 1001 (false statements). The theory behind conspiracy prosecutions is explained in the Justice Department's handbook on election law crimes: "A scheme to infuse patently illegal funds into a federal campaign, such as by using conduits or other means calculated to conceal the illegal source of the contribution, thus disrupts and impedes the FEC in the performance of its statutory duties." To obtain a conviction under § 371, the evidence must show that the defendant intended to disrupt and impede the lawful functioning of the FEC (such as by causing false information to be provided to the FEC by the recipient committee, thereby "misleading the public as to the actual source of the contribution"). Causing another person to submit false information to the FEC may be prosecuted as a violation of 18 U.S.C. §§ 1001 and 2, which taken together criminalize acts that cause another person (that is, a campaign treasurer) to submit false information to the FEC: see *United States v. Curran,* 20 F.3d 560 (3d Cir. 1994).

## Statute of Limitations Issues

FECA contains a three-year statute of limitation, which applies to prosecutions for criminal violations of Title 2: 2 U.S.C. § 455 (a). It does not, however, specify the statute of limitations for civil enforcement actions. A number of courts have concluded that the general federal default five-year statute of limitations applies to these civil actions: *Federal Election Commission v. Williams,* 104 F.3d 237, 240 (9th Cir. 1996); *Federal Election Commission v. National Right to Work Committee,* 916 F. Supp. 10 (D.D.C. 1996); and *Federal Election Commission v. National Republican Senatorial Committee,* 877 F. Supp. 15 (D.D.C. 1995). The statute of limitations for campaign finance violations prosecuted under 18 U.S.C. M 371 or 1001 is five years: see 18 U.S.C.

§ 3282. The Justice Department may prosecute under these ancillary criminal provisions (conspiracy, fraud, and so on) even though the three-year FEC statute of limitations has run, if the five-year statute applicable to the federal criminal statutes has not yet passed.

Some courts have found that the statute of limitations period commences when the violation is committed. In *Williams*, the court rejected the FEC's argument that the period should be "tolled" (with the clock not started) until the violation is discovered: *Williams*, 104 F.3d at 240. The FEC also contended that the period should be tolled or frozen under the doctrine of "equitable tolling" for fraudulent concealment. Tolling a limit under this theory requires a showing that the defendant fraudulently concealed operative facts, that the FEC failed to discover the facts in the limitations period, and that the FEC pursued the facts diligently until discovery of the facts. The court rejected this argument also, determining that the FEC had the facts it needed in FECA reports filed by recipient committees to discover the operative facts: *Williams*, 104 F.3d at 241. The practical effect of these decisions is to make it significantly more difficult for the FEC to pursue allegations of campaign finance violations and to cause the commission to close a number of high-profile investigations that were past or near the five-year limit. Especially in the case of presidential campaigns, which undergo a multiyear audit before the commission even authorizes the opening of an enforcement matter, the combination of the FEC's current capabilities and the five-year statute of limitations means that many investigations will as a practical matter be aborted without a resolution.

# Political Money: The New Prohibition

Annelise Anderson

This article first appeared in the Essays in Public Policy series published by the Hoover Institution, Stanford University, in 1997. In *Political Money: The New Prohibition* I address whether or not we are spending too much on political campaigns and whether either expenditure limits or contribution limits are desirable or effective in accomplishing the purposes they supposedly serve. Rather than increase limits on spending and contributions, I recommend abolishing them but strengthening campaign finance reporting requirements and the speed with which data are made available to the public.

EXECUTIVE SUMMARY

Our system of campaign financing fosters subterfuge and corruption, favors wealthy candidates over those not so blessed, puts candidates on a perpetual fund-raising treadmill, and is slanted in favor of incumbents over challengers.

These problems are the direct result of the 1974 Federal Election Campaign Act. Although the Supreme Court has struck down significant portions of this legislation as a violation of freedom of speech, what survives has done significant damage.

The usual prescription is to limit contributions even more than we now do and to put expenditure controls on congressional as well as presidential campaigns.

Such an approach would only make things worse. In 1996 the presidential candidates of the two major parties, both of whom accepted federal funds in return for agreeing to limit direct spending, had $62 million each to spend in the general election, or 31.5 cents per person in the 1996 voting-age population—less than the price of a first-class postage stamp.

The only spending candidates control is that of their own campaigns. When that spending is limited, the spending of other groups who communicate with voters—the media and special interest groups—becomes more important. Funds that cannot be given directly to a candidate are diverted to organizations that can accept them legally and spent indirectly on behalf of the candidate.

Campaign spending in the primaries and the general election in 1995–96 for all federal offices—435 members of the House of Representatives, 33 senators, and the presidency—was about $2 billion. That's only $10 over a two-year period for each person of voting age in the United States in 1996. At the same time, the Federal Election Commission spent less than 5 percent of its funds for public disclosure of campaign contributions.

Instead of further restricting and regulating campaign financing, we should

- Abolish campaign spending limits, so that candidates themselves can communicate effectively with voters

- Abolish campaign contribution limits, so that candidates can raise more money with less time and effort, give challengers the possibility of raising the money they need to compete against incumbents, and reduce the advantage of personally wealthy candidates

- Establish real-time campaign finance reporting requirements, so that we know quickly and effectively—on the Internet in twenty-four hours—who gave what to whom

## INTRODUCTION

The way America finances political campaigns seems to be in serious disarray. Candidates, often officeholders running for reelection, complain about spending more and more time and effort raising money instead of worrying about issues and attending to the jobs we elected them to do. Laws that forbid foreign contributions have been violated. Campaigns seem to be costing more, and the financial advantage of incumbents over challengers has increased. Wealthy candidates can legally spend without limit from their personal resources, but individuals cannot contribute without limit to candidates of their choice, thus handicapping candidates of modest personal means.

Together the Republican and Democratic National Committees raised, in the last election cycle, $262 million in so-called soft money. This money could be spent on party-building activities and uncoordinated candidate support outside the contribution limits on what individuals and political action committees can give to candidates and, for the presidential election, outside the spending limits. In contrast, special interest groups can raise and spend money without limit to advocate their positions on issues; and the media—television, radio, newspapers, and magazines—spend substantial sums covering campaigns.

Current proposals to reform the system are based on the idea that there's too much money involved in politics and that the people and organizations who give that money have too much influence. We would be better off, the argument goes, to limit contributions and spending even more than we now do. Most of the major campaign finance reform legislation introduced in Congress attempts to do so, ostensibly to reduce the influence of money in politics and put candidates, both challengers and incumbents, on a level playing field.

Our current campaign finance problems began in the aftermath of Watergate, when Congress put sharp limits on political activity. The 1974 amendments to the Federal Election Campaign Act limited how much an individual could give to a candidate, a political party, and in total. They also limited candidate expenditures in House, Senate, and presidential races. The 1974 legislation even limited spending by candidates on their own campaigns. Contributions by political action committees were also limited.

Those rules did not last for long. The Supreme Court came to the rescue of free political speech in its 1976 *Buckley v. Valeo* decision. "The First Amendment," the Court said, "denies government the power to determine that spending to promote one's political views is wasteful, excessive, or unwise. In the free society ordained by our Constitution it is not the government, but the people—individually as citizens and candidates and collectively as associations and political committees—who must retain control over the quantity and range of debate on public issues in a political campaign."

The Supreme Court struck down expenditure limits unless those limits were voluntary. The Court has stayed consistent over the past twenty years, and in its most recent case on campaign financing—*Colorado v. Federal Election Commission,* issued in the summer of 1996—it invalidated limits on what a political party could spend to support a candidate if that spending were independent of the candidate. Four members of today's Court—one shy of a majority—went further: they view such limits on spending by political parties as unconstitutional even if that spending is coordinated with the candidate.

In contrast, the Court has left in place contribution limits but not without dissent. In the 1976 *Buckley v. Valeo* case, Chief Justice Warren Burger argued that "limiting contributions, as a practical matter, will limit expenditures and will put an effective ceiling on the amount of political activity and debate that the Government will permit to take place." Burger found it illogical that the Court distinguished between the right of a candidate to spend his own money on his campaign and the right of an individual to contribute unlimited sums to a candidate. In the 1996 Colorado case Judge Clarence Thomas, in a partial dissent, took the position Burger had twenty years earlier, expressing the view that "contribution limits infringe as directly and seriously upon freedom of political expression and association as do expenditure limits."

## ASSAULT ON THE FIRST AMENDMENT

Thirty-eight U.S. senators—thirty-four Democrats and four Republicans—would like to put control over political speech in the hands of Congress rather than the people. On March 18, 1997, they voted to gut the First Amendment to the Constitution by empowering Congress to set limits on contributions and expenditures "by, in support of, or in opposition to" candidates for federal office. That constitutional amendment would have given Congress sweeping authority to limit political speech. It failed by a vote of sixty-one to thirty-eight.

The failure of this ploy leaves only one route open to limiting campaign expenditures: voluntary agreement. And the only route to voluntary agreement is institutional bribery: guaranteed funding in exchange for expenditure limits. This is the ruse under which expenditures of presidential campaigns are controlled. The majority decision in *Buckley v. Valeo* left voluntary expenditure limits in exchange for federal money intact, in spite of Burger's strong dissent that "we are confronted with the Government's actual financing, out of general revenue, a segment of the political debate itself. In my view the inappropriateness of subsidizing, from general revenues, the actual political dialogue of the people—the process which begets the Government itself—is as basic to our national tradition as the separation of church and state also deriving from the First Amendment." He could have quoted Thomas Jefferson: "To compel a man to furnish contributions for the propagation of opinions which he disbelieves and abhors is sinful and tyrannical."

Limiting expenditures is precisely what the most publicized of the campaign reforms bills, the Bipartisan Campaign Reform Act of 1997, introduced by Senators John McCain (R-Ariz.) and Russell Feingold (D-Wisc.), proposes to do. It would limit spending on Senate races ($1.5 million to $8.5 million) and on House races ($600,000). It would also limit the use of funds from political action committees, place geographic requirements on individual contributions, prohibit bundling individual contributions, ban so-called soft money, and regulate "express advocacy" speech by independent groups.

The main bribe in McCain-Feingold is not federal funds but privately owned resources: thirty minutes of free, prime-time television for Senate candidates (House and Senate candidates could also purchase television time at 50 percent of the lowest rate). The secondary bribe is to be paid for by the taxpayers via an appropriation to the Postal Service:

Senate candidates would be able to send two statewide mailings paying only third-class rates; House candidates would get three third-class districtwide mailings.

But Senators McCain and Feingold found that their bill was unpalatable so they scaled it back. Gone are spending limits and the bribes that went with them: free and reduced-rate broadcast time and postal subsidies. But soft money is still banned in federal races, independent advertising is regulated, contribution limits remain in place, and candidates who spend more than $50,000 of their own money are punished: political parties would be forbidden to support their campaigns. The senators have added a provision that would require unions to refund money they spend on political issue ads that has been raised through the dues members are required to pay. Republicans are proposing stronger legislation—a requirement that unions first get a member's permission before spending dues money on issue ads.

## DO WE SPEND TOO MUCH?

The purpose of political campaigns is to communicate with potential voters about the candidates—their policy views, their records, their character, their vision for the future. That is the essence of free speech. In a country the size of the United States, that communication is expensive.

During the 1996 election, the official estimate of the voting-age population in the United States was 196.5 million people. This far-flung population resides in 211 major broadcast television markets; 65 percent of households receive cable television. These people read more than one hundred daily newspapers with circulations of more than 100,000, three major news magazines, and a variety of journals of fact and opinion. They listen to radio in 261 metropolitan markets. They receive millions of pieces of direct mail a year and look at thousands of billboards. They visit an untold number of web sites on the Internet. In a presidential election year, tens of millions of them watch televised debates among the candidates.

Despite this voracious consumption of information, advertising, and opinion, it is not an easy population to reach. The diversity of the media is staggering. Gone are the days of the 1950s, when the average household received three television channels; today the average is forty-five. The available radio spectrum has increased enormously, and cable television and the Internet have come into being.

These 196.5 million potential voters have three basic sources of information in a campaign:

1. The "free" media. Most media coverage is free to the candidates and provides news and opinion on the candidates and the issues. The candidates speak; reporters and editors decide how to cover it. They even decide what questions to ask during presidential debates.

2. The independent spenders. This category includes unions and associations of unions such as the American Federation of Labor and Congress of Industrial Organizations (AFL-CIO) and the National Education Association; corporations and trade associations; and special interest groups such as Common Cause, the National Rifle Association, the Sierra Club, and the Christian Coalition. They communicate with the public in a variety of ways—through the news coverage they get, through paid advertising, through direct mail, through talk shows. To the extent that they spend independently rather than giving to candidates, political action committees and political parties also fall in this category.

3. The candidate's own communications. The most important communication with the voters is paid advertising—television and radio spots, direct mail, brochures passed out at local and national campaign headquarters, billboards, posters, and buttons.

Of the three sources of information, a candidate's own communications are the only ones under his or her direct control and are an important source of information for voters. Not that the information isn't there, in the newspapers and magazines and on the talk shows, but often the news stories, especially on television, are about the horse race—whether it was or was not a good week for this or that candidate. The time television reporting gives to the candidate as a sound bite has gotten briefer; the reporter's commentary has gotten longer. The candidate gets about eight seconds, the reporter, fifty-two. Much of what potential voters read and hear is selected and filtered by strangers.

## A MODEL BUDGET FOR A NATIONAL CAMPAIGN

A candidate must be able to communicate his or her own views—and, in that process, something about character and vision for the future, about an approach to problems and policy as well as stands on specific issues. In the presidential race the time from the nomination to the election is relatively brief. In the approximately sixty-four days between Labor Day and election day, there are about 200 million people to reach. That takes money. In addition to the campaign expenses for renting space, furniture and equipment, travel, telephone, and fax, a reasonable, even modest, communications program—not limited by government regulations—could easily cost hundreds of millions of dollars. A reasonable communications program in a presidential campaign might try to do the following:

- Reach as much of the adult population as possible with television advertising—network, local broadcast, and cable—say, ten times each with thirty-second ads. There's ample proof that repetition is important in communicating a message.

- Present three or four thirty-minute televised "Fireside Chats" with the candidate, possibly on cable television.

- Reach commuters and others by radio in all major markets, with the goal of communicating with 80 percent of listeners at least five times each.

- Take one or two full-page ads in all newspapers with more than 100,000 circulation.

- Send out at least two pieces of direct mail (brochures) to each potential voter.

- Advertise on billboards and produce pins, buttons, bumper stickers, and the like.

- Send all households a videotape about the candidate.

The television advertising and direct mail would cost about $100 million each; we will allow another $400 million for radio, newspapers, billboards, and bumper stickers; possible fireside chats; and all personnel, office, equipment, phone, fax, and travel expenses. That's at least $600 million—or about $3 for each person in the country of voting age. This does not seem to be an unreasonable sum, and yet the amount of money each major presidential candidate could spend for everything except required accounting and legal expenses was $62 million—or 31.5 cents per person, less than the price of a first-class postage stamp, about 10 percent of what a reasonably effective campaign might cost.

If the amount a candidate can spend directly is limited, the relative influence of the free media, the special interest groups, and the national parties themselves increases. It is only the expenditures of the candidate's own campaign organization that are under the direct control of the candidate. With the exception of the presidential debates, other communications are filtered through third parties—through the selective judgment of reporters and editors on a sound bite to use on television or a quote from a speech to print; through independent expenditures; through the focus of a special interest group, whether its concerns are gun control, saving the Northern spotted owl, or abortion policy. Even in debates where candidates obviously speak for themselves, the topic and framing of the questions are determined by others.

Limiting expenditures limits the ability of candidates to communicate with the electorate. As this capability is limited, the free media, special interest groups, and the presidential debates become relatively more important.

## LEVELING THE PLAYING FIELD

Expenditure limitations are sometimes justified on the grounds that having equal monetary resources levels the playing field among candidates. But the playing field is intrinsically impossible to level by controlling expenditures.

First, competing candidates are in different circumstances. One may be more well known to the voters than another. Or one candidate may need to respond to various charges from opponents or the press at a higher cost than another.

Consider the 1996 presidential campaign: President Clinton had no primary opposition and thus no need to answer the kinds of attacks from primary opponents that came Senator Dole's way. Nor was the playing field level during the primaries among the Republican contenders for the nomination. Candidates who accepted federal funds agreed, in doing so, to limitations on state spending during the primaries, whereas candidates who did not do so (Steve Forbes and Morry Taylor) could spend wherever they liked in amounts limited only by their own fortunes and their campaign strategies.

Second, money is only one of the resources important to a campaign. Support from independent groups and volunteers may vary widely among candidates, as may celebrity endorsements. But most important is the free media. As political scientist Larry Sabato notes, studies have repeatedly shown a liberal Democrat tilt in the free media, one acknowledged by members of the press themselves, which shows up in how members of the press register and vote. This bias affects not only the tone of the coverage—favorable or unfavorable—but the selection of the stories themselves.

Equal spending does not and cannot level the playing field. Perhaps the most standard difference in circumstances among candidates is the difference between challengers and incumbents: the incumbents usually have the advantage of being better known to the public. Here spending limits can be decisive. Most successful Senate and House challengers in 1994 and 1996 spent more than the McCain-Feingold limits would allow.

LIMITING CONTRIBUTIONS

The basic argument for limiting contributions is that people with greater financial resources should not have more influence in the political process than those without such resources. But again money is only one resource that gives people the power to influence others. Others include, for example, being a powerful columnist, having celebrity status, or holding a position of leadership in a well-known organization. Except in the voting booth, political influence varies widely.

Given the Supreme Court's affirmation of the right to use one's own funds for political speech, it is not possible to limit the use of individual resources in the political process. A candidate can use his own funds to advocate his own candidacy, as Steve Forbes and Ross Perot have done. And individuals can contribute at will to various special interest groups. What the affluent cannot do, under current law, is contribute unlimited amounts to a particular candidate; the limit is $1,000 per election. Total campaign contributions to all candidates, political action committees, and parties are capped for each individual at $25,000 per election cycle. Nor can political action groups contribute more than $5,000 per election to a candidate.

The Supreme Court's justification, with the exception of the Burger and Thomas dissents, for limiting contributions has been that such limitations are not as restrictive of free political speech as limitations on expenditures and are justified by an intent to reduce the existence and appearance of corruption. Here the Court, in its majority opinion, is most surely wrong. Controlling the use of resources is a fundamental method of censorship in the modern world. The Soviet Union censored the press not with a blue pencil but by controlling access to paper and newsprint. What the censors liked got printed the next day in major newspapers; what they didn't like might get printed in an obscure journal with a small print run sometime in the future.

The U.S. experience with limiting expenditures in presidential campaigns shows what happens when campaign expenditures are capped and direct contributions to candidates are limited: the money flows elsewhere, to places where it can be more freely given and more freely spent, sometimes to organizations that must report receipts, like political parties, and sometimes to organizations that are not required to do so. The Annenberg Center at the University of Pennsylvania estimates that $150 million was spent on issue ads in the 1996 elections, some of it by political parties and some of it by independent groups. The AFL-CIO spent at least $25 million. Independent ads, the Center found, were more likely than other political advertising to be attack ads.

The diversion of funds from candidates themselves makes connections less direct, less obvious. Politicians are less accountable. The candidate's own campaign is starved for funds. Independent organizations and their spending may make the crucial difference.

This approach fosters subterfuge and corruption and a perpetual need to regulate further. Thus even the scaled-back McCain-Feingold bill proposes to give government regulators power over issue advocacy by independent groups if these ads would be understood by "a reasonable person" as advocating the election or defeat of a candidate as shown by "one or more factors," including even where the communication was placed.

## THE CURRENT SITUATION

Our system of financing political campaigns is indeed in need of reform. Candidates spend too much time raising money from too many people. Candidates with their own fortunes have an advantage over those who do not, and wealthy individuals may run for office when they would prefer to support others. Expenditure and contribution limitations push political money underground, into ever more indirect channels where it is hard to follow. The links between political money and the decisions of elected officials become more obscure, and thus those holding office are less obviously accountable. Disclosure requirements do not result in timely, useful data that can be analyzed by the press and anyone else concerned.

Less than 5 percent of the Federal Election Commission's (FEC's) $26.5 million budget is spent on public disclosure; most of it is spent on compliance and litigation. The FEC cannot now require that candidates and political committees submit reports on contributions and expenditures in electronic form, and so it must reenter that data into its own computers. In 1996 it managed to do that within about thirty days, allowing little time for access and analysis during the critical period before an election and leaving the public altogether uninformed about the critical last month before the election. Furthermore, the resulting database can be accessed by the public without charge only from the FEC's office in Washington, D.C. To access the database from a computer outside the FEC office, a prepaid subscription to the service at $20 an hour is required; and only 1,241 people and organizations had such subscriptions during the 1996 election season. Getting the raw data—the reports actually filed by candidates and committees—is not really an option. The FEC replied to a June 30, 1997, inquiry about the reports filed by the Dole campaign by saying that all 27,495 pages of them could be made available in photocopied form in a month at an estimated cost of more than $2,600.

WHAT WE NEED TO DO

*Abolish Campaign Spending Limits*

We need to get rid of expenditure limitations in presidential elections to enable candidates to spend what they need to spend—if they can raise the money—to communicate effectively with potential voters. We need to hear more directly from them and perhaps not so much from special interest groups supporting them. We need to avoid imposing expenditure limits on House and Senate candidates.

The numbers we hear about campaign spending seem large. But the entire amount spent in the 1995–96 elections, including the primaries, by all federal candidates—presidential, House, and Senate—and by national political committees, including so-called soft money, was about $2 billion, or $10 per person of voting age over a two-year period. Compare that with whatever you like—a couple of hamburgers or movie tickets or a paperback book and a magazine or two.

## Abolish Campaign Contribution Limits

We need to get rid of limitations on contributions, so that candidates can raise more money with less time and effort. This will reduce the perpetual fund-raising candidates complain about. It will give challengers the possibility of raising some seed money to make an effective foray against incumbents and reduce the financial advantage of incumbents over challengers. It will give candidates of modest means a fairer shot against personally wealthy rivals. It will help channel the funds of the wealthy to candidates where potential influence will be obvious, rather than to less-accountable special interest groups.

## Establish Real-Time Campaign Finance Reporting Requirements

We need to strengthen reporting requirements to produce timely and useful information. With modern computers and the Internet, there's no reason why campaign contributions and expenditures shouldn't be reported daily and posted on the Internet in a standard format that can be easily accessed and analyzed by the press and the public. Most campaign organizations record receipts and expenditures on computers but print out hard copy to send to the FEC. They could instead simply transmit the electronic file to the FEC over the Internet, so the public can know quickly and easily who is contributing what to whom—not a month after the election takes place but on a daily basis. Full and timely disclosure is the best way to deal with the potentially corrupting effect of political money—and with today's Internet technology, that information should be available to everyone without charge. It is not the job of the FEC to point out patterns of contributions that may suggest undue influence over a candidate. That is the job of a free press and anyone else who wants to take the trouble to access and analyze the information. But it is the job of the FEC to make the information available—and that's a much more important use of its budget and its people than litigating cases about possible violations of the complex web of regulations relating to contributions and expenditures.

There's a bill in Congress that would do these three things—the Citizen Legislature and Political Freedom Act, H.R. 965, introduced by Representative John Doolittle (R-Calif.) and supported most articulately by Senator Mitch McConnell (R-Ky.) It would reverse the attempt to regulate campaign contributions and expenditures—and thus political speech—that has led to the current mess and threatens to involve us in ever more complex limitations on what we can say, when we can say it, and how much we can spend saying it.

That bill should be the top priority of the 105th Congress.

Government regulation is the main culprit distorting and corrupting our campaign finance system. The last thing we need is more of it. It's time to apply the principles of freedom to the elections of a free people.

# PART TWO

# Supreme Court Decisions

This section does not try to be a systematic review of Supreme Court decisions in the field of campaign finance; they have been reviewed in the longer articles in this book.

Most Supreme Court decisions on campaign finance have been split decisions, and the three selections in this section express concerns that did not prevail in the majority opinions or went beyond the majority opinion in their concern about the underlying constitutionality of campaign finance legislation and its threat to free speech and association in the political process.

# Partial Dissent/Partial Concurrence of U.S. Supreme Court Justice Thomas in the Case of the *Colorado Republican Federal Campaign Committee and Douglas Jones, Treasurer, Petitioners v. Federal Election Commission*

Clarence Thomas

Supreme Court Justice Clarence Thomas partially dissented and partially concurred with a campaign finance case decided in the summer of 1996. The Federal Election Commission had brought a case against the Colorado Republican Federal Campaign Committee concerning its support of candidates for office, raising the question whether expenditures of political parties that are coordinated with specific candidates are covered by the legislation limiting contributions and expenditures. The majority opinion in the case was based on the conclusion that the party expenditures were in fact independent of the candidate, and thus not covered by legislative caps, but rather entitled to First Amendment protection. The opinion left uncertain the status of coordinated expenditures.

The chief justice, William Rehnquist, and Justice Scalia joined with Thomas in parts I and III of his opinion, where the distinction between coordinated and independent expenditures is questioned. In part II of the opinion Thomas questions the idea that any meaningful distinction can be made between expenditures and contributions.

I.

The constitutionality of limits on coordinated expenditures by political parties is squarely before us. We should address this important question now, instead of leaving political parties in a state of uncertainty about the types of First Amendment expression in which they are free to engage. . . .

II.

*A.*

. . . Though we said in *Buckley* that controls on spending and giving "operate in an area of the most fundamental First Amendment activities," id., at 14, we invalidated the expenditure limits of FECA and upheld the Act's contribution limits. The justification we gave for the differing results was this: "The expenditure limitations . . . represent substantial rather than merely theoretical restraints on the quantity and diversity of political speech," id., at 19, whereas "limitation[s] upon the amount that any one person or group may contribute to a candidate or political committee entai[l] only a marginal restriction upon the contributor's ability to engage in free communication," id., at 20–21. . . . Since *Buckley*, our campaign finance jurisprudence has been based in large part on this distinction between contributions and expenditures. . . .

In my view, the distinction lacks constitutional significance, and I would not adhere to it. As Chief Justice Burger put it: ". . . contributions and expenditures are two sides of the same First Amendment coin." *Buckley v. Valeo*, supra, 424 U.S., at 241. . . . Contributions and expenditures both involve core First Amendment expression because they further the "[d]iscussion of public issues and debate on the qualifications of candidates . . . integral to the operation of the system of government established by our Constitution." 424 U.S., at 14. When an individual donates money to a candidate or to a partisan organization, he enhances the donee's ability to communicate a message and thereby adds to political debate, just as when that individual communicates the message himself. . . .

Giving and spending in the electoral process also involve basic associational rights under the First Amendment. . . .

Whether an individual donates money to a candidate or group who will use it to promote the candidate or whether the individual spends the money to promote the candidate himself, the individual seeks to engage in political expression and to associate with likeminded persons. A contribution is simply an indirect expenditure; though contributions and expenditures may thus differ in form, they do not differ in substance. . . .

Echoing the suggestion in *Buckley* that contributions have less First Amendment value than expenditures because they do not involve speech by the donor, see 424 U.S., at 21, the Court has sometimes rationalized limitations on contributions by referring to contributions as "speech by proxy." . . . The "speech by proxy" label is, however, an ineffective tool for distinguishing contributions from expenditures. . . .

Moreover, we have recently recognized that where the "proxy" speech is endorsed by those who give, that speech is a fully-protected exercise of the donors' associational rights. . . . To say that their collective action in pooling their resources to amplify their voices is not entitled to full First Amendment protection would subordinate the voices of those of modest means as opposed to those sufficiently wealthy to be able to buy expensive media ads with their own resources." 470 U.S., at 495. . . .

In sum, unlike the *Buckley* Court, I believe that contribution limits infringe as directly and as seriously upon freedom of political expression and association as do expenditure limits.

The protections of the First Amendment do not depend upon so fine a line as that between spending money to support a candidate or group and giving money to the candidate or group to spend for the same purpose. In principle, people and groups give money to candidates and other groups for the same reason that they spend money in support of those candidates and groups: because they share social, economic, and political beliefs and seek to have those beliefs affect governmental policy. I think that the *Buckley* framework for analyzing the constitutionality of campaign finance laws is deeply flawed. Accordingly, I would not employ it, as Justice Breyer and Justice Kennedy do.

## B.

Instead, I begin with the premise that there is no constitutionally significant difference between campaign contributions and expenditures: both forms of speech are central to the First Amendment. . . .

In the context of campaign finance reform, the only governmental interest that we have accepted as compelling is the prevention of corruption or the appearance of corruption, . . . and we have narrowly defined "corruption" as a "financial quid pro quo: dollars for political favors." As for the means-ends fit under strict scrutiny, we have specified that "where at all possible, government must curtail speech only to the degree necessary to meet the particular problem at hand, and must avoid infringing on speech that does not pose the danger that has prompted regulation." . . .

In my opinion, FECA's monetary caps fail the narrow tailoring test. Addressing the constitutionality of FECA's contribution caps, the *Buckley* appellants argued:

"If a small minority of political contributions are given to secure appointments for the donors or some other quid pro quo, that cannot serve to justify prohibiting all large contributions, the vast majority of which are given not for any such purpose but to further the expression of political views which the candidate and donor share. Where First Amendment rights are involved, a blunderbuss approach which prohibits mostly innocent speech cannot be held a means narrowly and precisely directed to the governmental interest in the small minority of contributions that are not innocent." Brief for Appellants in *Buckley v. Valeo*, O. T. 1975, Nos. 75-436 and 75-437, pp. 117–118.

The *Buckley* appellants were, to my mind, correct. Broad prophylactic bans on campaign expenditures and contributions are not designed with the precision required by the First Amendment because they sweep protected speech within their prohibitions. . . .

III.

Were I convinced that the *Buckley* framework rested on a principled distinction between contributions and expenditures, which I am not, I would nevertheless conclude that Section(s) 441a(d)(3)'s limits on political parties violate the First Amendment. Under *Buckley* and its progeny, a substantial threat of corruption must exist before a law purportedly aimed at the prevention of corruption will be sustained against First Amendment attack. . . .

As applied in the specific context of campaign funding by political parties, the anti-corruption rationale loses its force. . . .

In any event, the Government, which bears the burden of "demonstrat[ing] that the recited harms are real, not merely conjectural," Turner Broadcasting System, Inc. v. FCC, 512 U.S. (1994) (slip op., at 41), has identified no more proof of the corrupting dangers of coordinated expenditures than it has of independent expenditures. . . . And insofar as it appears that Congress did not actually enact Section(s) 441a(d)(3) in order to stop corruption by political parties "but rather for the constitutionally insufficient purpose of reducing what it saw as wasteful and excessive campaign spending," ante, at 11 (citing *Buckley v. Valeo*, supra, at 57), the statute's ceilings on coordinated expenditures are as unwarranted as the caps on independent expenditures.

In sum, there is only a minimal threat of "corruption," as we have understood that term, when a political party spends to support its candidate or to oppose his competitor, whether or not that expenditure is made in concert with the candidate. Parties and candidates have traditionally worked together to achieve their common goals, and when they engage in that work, there is no risk to the Republic. To the contrary, the danger to the Republic lies in Government suppression of such activity. Under *Buckley* and our subsequent cases, Section(s) 441a(d)(3)'s heavy burden on First Amendment rights is not justified by the threat of corruption at which it is assertedly aimed.

To conclude, I would find Section(s) 441a(d)(3) unconstitutional not just as applied to petitioners, but also on its face. Accordingly, I concur only in the Court's judgment. . . .

# Partial Dissent/Partial Concurrence of Chief Justice Burger in the Case of *Buckley v. Valeo*

## Warren Burger

In 1976 the Supreme Court rejected major portions of the Federal Election Campaign Act of 1971 and its 1974 amendments with the statement that "the First Amendment requires the invalidation of the Act's independent expenditure ceiling, its limitation on a candidate's expenditures from his own personal funds, and its ceiling on overall campaign expenditures, since those provisions place substantial and direct restrictions on the ability of candidates, citizens, and associations to engage in protected political expression, restrictions that the First Amendment cannot tolerate. . . . The First Amendment denies government the power to determine that spending to promote one's political views is wasteful, excessive, or unwise. In the free society ordained by our Constitution it is not the government, but the people—individually as citizens and candidates and collectively as associations and political committees—who must retain control over the quantity and range of debate on public issues in a political campaign."

The Court found acceptable, however, limits on contributions. Chief Justice Burger, however, disagreed, in what has become a famous and prescient dissent.

For reasons set forth more fully later, I dissent from those parts of the Court's holding sustaining the statutory provisions (a) for disclosure of small contributions, (b) for limitations on contributions, and (c) for public financing of Presidential campaigns. In my view, the Act's disclosure scheme is impermissibly broad and violative of the First Amendment as it relates to reporting contributions in excess of $10 and $100. The contribution limitations infringe on First Amendment liberties and suffer from the same infirmities that the Court correctly sees in the expenditure ceilings. The system for public financing of Presidential campaigns is, in my judgment, an impermissible intrusion by the Government into the traditionally private political process.

More broadly, the Court's result does violence to the intent of

Congress in this comprehensive scheme of campaign finance. By dissecting the Act bit by bit, and casting off vital parts, the Court fails to recognize that the whole of this Act is greater than the sum of its parts. [424 U.S. 1, 236] Congress intended to regulate all aspects of federal campaign finances, but what remains after today's holding leaves no more than a shadow of what Congress contemplated. I question whether the residue leaves a workable program.

DISCLOSURE PROVISIONS

Disclosure is, in principle, the salutary and constitutional remedy for most of the ills Congress was seeking to alleviate. I therefore agree fully with the broad proposition that public disclosure of contributions by individuals and by entities—particularly corporations and labor unions—is an effective means of revealing the type of political support that is sometimes coupled with expectations of special favors or rewards. That disclosure impinges on First Amendment rights is conceded by the Court, ante, at 64–66, but given the objectives to which disclosure is directed, I agree that the need for disclosure outweighs individual constitutional claims.

Disclosure is, however, subject to First Amendment limitations which are to be defined by looking to the relevant public interests. The legitimate public interest is the elimination of the appearance and reality of corrupting influences. Serious dangers to the very processes of government justify disclosure of contributions of such dimensions reasonably thought likely to purchase special favors. These fears have been at the root of the Court's prior decisions upholding disclosure requirements, and I therefore have no disagreement, for example, with *Burroughs v. United States*, 290 U.S. 534 (1934).

The Court's theory, however, goes beyond permissible limits. Under the Court's view, disclosure serves broad informational purposes, enabling the public to be fully informed on matters of acute public interest. Forced disclosure of one aspect of a citizen's political activity [424 U.S. 1, 237], under this analysis, serves the public right to know. This open-ended approach is the only plausible justification for the otherwise irrationally low ceilings of $10 and $100 for anonymous contributions. The burdens of these low ceilings seem to me obvious, and the Court does not try to question this. With commendable candor, the Court acknowledges:

"It is undoubtedly true that public disclosure of contributions to candidates and political parties will deter some individuals who otherwise might contribute." Ante, at 68.

Examples come readily to mind. Rank-and-file union members or rising junior executives may now think twice before making even modest contributions to a candidate who is disfavored by the union or management hierarchy. Similarly, potential contributors may well decline to take the obvious risks entailed in making a reportable contribution to the opponent of a well-entrenched incumbent. This fact of political life did not go unnoticed by the Congress:

"The disclosure provisions really have in fact made it difficult for challengers to challenge incumbents." 120 *Cong. Rec.* 34392 (1974) (remarks of Sen. Long).

See *Pollard v. Roberts*, 283 F. Supp. 248 (ED Ark.), aff'd per curiam, 393 U.S. 14 (1968).

The public right to know ought not be absolute when its exercise reveals private political convictions. Secrecy, like privacy, is not per se criminal. On the contrary, secrecy and privacy as to political preferences and convictions are fundamental in a free society. For example, one of the great political reforms was the advent of the secret ballot as a universal practice. Similarly, the enlightened labor legislation of our time has enshrined the secrecy of choice of a bargaining representative for [424 U.S. 1, 238] workers. In other contexts, this Court has seen to it that governmental power cannot be used to force a citizen to disclose his private affiliations, *NAACP v. Button*, 371 U.S. 415 (1963), even without a record reflecting any systematic harassment or retaliation, as in *Shelton v. Tucker*, 364 U.S. 479 (1960). For me it is far too late in the day to recognize an ill-defined "public interest" to breach the historic safeguards guaranteed by the First Amendment.

We all seem to agree that whatever the legitimate public interest in this area, proper analysis requires us to scrutinize the precise means employed to implement that interest. The balancing test used by the Court requires that fair recognition be given to competing interests. With respect, I suggest the Court has failed to give the traditional standing to some of the First Amendment values at stake here. Specifically, it has failed to confine the particular exercise of governmental power within limits reasonably required.

"In every case the power to regulate must be so exercised as not, in attaining a permissible end, unduly to infringe the protected freedom." *Cantwell v. Connecticut*, 310 U.S. 296, 304 (1940).

"Unduly" must mean not more than necessary, and until today, the Court has recognized this criterion in First Amendment cases:

"In the area of First Amendment freedoms, government has the duty to confine itself to the least intrusive regulations which are adequate for the purpose." *Lamont v. Postmaster General*, 381 U.S. 301, 310 (1965) (BRENNAN, J., concurring).

Similarly, the Court has said:

"[E]ven though the governmental purpose be legitimate [424 U.S. 1, 239] and substantial, that purpose cannot be pursued by means that broadly stifle fundamental personal liberties when the end can be more narrowly achieved. The breadth of legislative abridgment must be viewed in the light of less drastic means for achieving the same basic purpose." *Shelton v. Tucker*, supra, at 488.

In light of these views, it seems to me that the threshold limits fixed at $10 and $100 for anonymous contributions are constitutionally impermissible on their face. As the Court's opinion notes, ante, at 83, Congress gave little or no thought, one way or the other, to these limits, but rather lifted figures out of a 65-year-old statute. As we are all painfully aware, the 1976 dollar is not what it used to be and is surely not the dollar of 1910. Ten dollars in 1976 will, for example, purchase only what $1.68 would buy in 1910. United States Dept. of Labor, *Handbook of Labor Statistics* 1975, p. 313 (Dec. 1975). To argue that a 1976 contribution of $10 or $100 entails a risk of corruption or its appearance is simply too extravagant to be maintained. No public right to know justifies the compelled disclosure of such contributions, at the risk of discouraging them. There is, in short, no relation whatever between the means used and the legitimate goal of ventilating possible undue influence. Congress has used a shotgun to kill wrens as well as hawks. [424 U.S. 1, 240]

In saying that the lines drawn by Congress are "not wholly without rationality," the Court plainly fails to apply the traditional test:

"Precision of regulation must be the touchstone in an area so closely touching on our most precious freedoms." *NAACP v. Button*, 371 U.S. 415, 438 (1938).

See, e. g., *Aptheker v. Secretary of State*, 378 U.S. 500 (1964); *United States v. Robel*, 389 U.S. 258 (1967); *Lamont v. Postmaster General*, supra. The Court's abrupt departure from traditional standards is wrong; surely a greater burden rests on Congress than merely to avoid "irrationality" when regulating in the core area of the First Amendment. Even taking the Court at its word, the particular dollar amounts fixed by Congress that must be reported to the Commission fall short of meeting the test of rationality when measured by the goals sought to be achieved.

Finally, no legitimate public interest has been shown in forcing the disclosure of modest contributions that are the prime support of new, unpopular, or unfashionable political causes. There is no realistic possibility that such modest donations will have a corrupting influence especially on parties that enjoy only "minor" status. Major parties would not notice them; minor parties need them. Furthermore, as the Court candidly recognizes, ante, at 70, minor parties and new parties tend to be sharply ideological in character, and the public can readily discern where such parties stand, without resorting to the indirect device of recording the names of financial supporters. To hold, as the Court has, that privacy must sometimes yield to congressional investigations of alleged subversion, is quite different from making domestic political [424 U.S. 1, 241] partisans give up privacy. Cf. *Eastland v. United States Servicemen's Fund*, 421 U.S. 491 (1975). In any event, the dangers to First Amendment rights here are too great. Flushing out the names of supporters of minority parties will plainly have a deterrent effect on potential contributors, a consequence readily admitted by the Court, ante, at 71, 83, and supported by the record.

I would therefore hold unconstitutional the provisions requiring reporting of contributions of more than $10 and to make a public record of the name, address, and occupation of a contributor of more than $100.

CONTRIBUTION AND EXPENDITURE LIMITS

I agree fully with that part of the Court's opinion that holds unconstitutional the limitations the Act puts on campaign expenditures which "place substantial and direct restrictions on the ability of candidates, citizens, and associations to engage in protected political expression, restrictions that the First Amendment cannot tolerate." Ante, at 58–59. Yet when it approves similarly stringent limitations on contributions, the Court ignores the reasons it finds so persuasive in the context of expenditures. For me contributions and expenditures are two sides of the same First Amendment coin.

By limiting campaign contributions, the Act restricts the amount of money that will be spent on political activity [424 U.S. 1, 242]—and does so directly. Appellees argue, as the Court notes, that these limits will "act as a brake on the skyrocketing cost of political campaigns," ante, at 26. In treating campaign expenditure limitations, the Court says that the "First Amendment denies government the power to determine that spending to promote one's political views is wasteful, excessive, or unwise." Ante, at 57. Limiting contributions, as a practical matter, will limit expenditures and will put an effective ceiling on the amount of political activity and debate that the Government will permit to take place. The argument that the ceiling is not, after all, very low as matters now stand gives little comfort for the future, since the Court elsewhere notes the rapid inflation in the cost of political campaigning. Ante, at 57.

The Court attempts to separate the two communicative aspects of political contributions—the "moral" support that the gift itself conveys, which the Court suggests is the same whether the gift is $10 or $10,000, and the [424 U.S. 1, 243] fact that money translates into communication. The Court dismisses the effect of the limitations on the second aspect of contributions: "[T]he transformation of contributions into political debate involves speech by someone other than the contributor." Ante, at 21. On this premise—that contribution limitations restrict only the speech of "someone other than the contributor"—rests the Court's justification for treating contributions differently from expenditures. The premise is demonstrably flawed; the contribution limitations will, in specific instances, limit exactly the same political activity that the expenditure ceilings limit, and at least one of the "expenditure" [424 U.S. 1, 244] limitations the Court finds objectionable operates precisely like the "contribution" limitations.

The Court's attempt to distinguish the communication inherent in political contributions from the speech aspects of political expenditures simply "will not wash." We do little but engage in word games unless we recognize that people—candidates and contributors—spend money on political activity because they wish to communicate ideas, and their constitutional interest in doing so is precisely the same whether they or someone else utters the words.

The Court attempts to make the Act seem less restrictive by casting the problem as one that goes to freedom of association rather than freedom of speech. I have long thought freedom of association and freedom of expression were two peas from the same pod. The contribution limitations of the Act impose a restriction on certain forms of associational activity that are for the most part, as the Court recognizes, ante, at 29, harmless in fact. And the restrictions are hardly incidental in their effect upon particular campaigns. Judges are ill-equipped to gauge the precise impact of legislation, but a law that impinges upon First Amendment rights requires us to make the attempt. It is not simply speculation to think that the limitations on contributions will foreclose some candidacies. The limitations will also alter the nature of some electoral contests drastically. [424 U.S. 1, 245]

At any rate, the contribution limits are a far more severe restriction on First Amendment activity than the sort of "chilling" legislation for which the Court has shown such extraordinary concern in the past. See, e. g., *Cohen v. California*, 403 U.S. 15 (1971); see also cases reviewed in *Miller v. California*, 413 U.S. 15 (1973); *Redrup v. New York*, 386 U.S. 767 (1967); *Memoirs v. Massachusetts*, 383 U.S. 413 (1966). If such restraints can be justified at all, they must be justified by the very strongest of state interests. With this much the Court clearly agrees; the Court even goes so far as to note that legislation cutting into these important interests must employ "means closely drawn to avoid unnecessary abridgment of associational freedoms." Ante, at 25.

After a bow to the "weighty interests" Congress meant to serve, the Court then forsakes this analysis in one sentence: "Congress was surely entitled to conclude that disclosure was only a partial measure, and that contribution ceilings were a necessary legislative concomitant to deal with the reality or appearance of corruption . . . ." Ante, at 28. In striking down the limitations on campaign expenditures, the Court relies in part on its conclusion that other means—namely, disclosure and contribution ceilings—will adequately serve the statute's aim. It is not clear why the same analysis is not also appropriate in weighing the need for contribution ceilings in addition to disclosure requirements. Congress may well be [424 U.S. 1, 246] entitled to conclude that disclosure was a "partial measure," but I had not thought until today that Congress could enact its conclusions in the First Amendment area into laws immune from the most searching review by this Court.

Finally, it seems clear to me that in approving these limitations on contributions the Court must rest upon the proposition that "pooling" money is fundamentally different from other forms of associational or joint activity. But see ante, at 66. I see only two possible ways in which money differs from volunteer work, endorsements, and the like. Money can be used to buy favors, because an unscrupulous politician can put it to personal use; second, giving money is a less visible form of associational activity. With respect to the first problem, the Act does not attempt to do any more than the bribery laws to combat this sort of corruption. In fact, the Act does not reach at all, and certainly the contribution limits do not reach, forms of "association" that can be fully as corrupt as a contribution intended as a quid pro quo—such as the eleventh-hour endorsement by a former rival, obtained for the promise of a federal appointment. This underinclusiveness is not a constitutional flaw, but it demonstrates that the contribution limits do not clearly focus on this first distinction. To the extent Congress thought that the second problem, the lesser visibility of contributions, required that money be treated differently from other forms of associational activity, disclosure laws are the simple and wholly efficacious answer; they make the invisible apparent.

PUBLIC FINANCING

I dissent from Part III sustaining the constitutionality of the public financing provisions of Subtitle H.

Since the turn of this century when the idea of Government [424 U.S. 1, 247] subsidies for political campaigns first was broached, there has been no lack of realization that the use of funds from the public treasury to subsidize political activity of private individuals would produce substantial and profound questions about the nature of our democratic society. The Majority Leader of the Senate, although supporting such legislation in 1967, said that "the implications of these questions . . . go to the very heart and structure of the Government of the Republic." The Solicitor General in his amicus curiae brief states that "the issues involved here are of indisputable moment." He goes on to express his view that public financing will have "profound effects in the way candidates approach issues and each other." Public financing, he notes, "affects the role of the party in campaigns for office, changes the role of the incumbent government vis-a-vis all parties, and affects the relative strengths and strategies of candidates vis-a-vis each other and their party's leaders."

The Court chooses to treat this novel public financing of political activity as simply another congressional appropriation whose validity is "necessary and proper" to Congress' power to regulate and reform elections and primaries, relying on *United States v. Classic*, 313 U.S. 299 (1941), and *Burroughs v. United States*, 290 U.S. 534 (1934). No holding of this Court is directly in point, because no federal scheme allocating public funds in a comparable manner has ever been before us. The uniqueness of the plan is not relevant, of course, to whether Congress has power to enact it. Indeed, I do not question the power of Congress to regulate elections; nor do I [424 U.S. 1, 248] challenge the broad proposition that the General Welfare Clause is a grant, not a limitation, of power. *M'Culloch v. Maryland*, 4 Wheat. 316, 420 (1819); *United States v. Butler*, 297 U.S. 1, 66 (1936).

I would, however, fault the Court for not adequately analyzing and meeting head on the issue whether public financial assistance to the private political activity of individual citizens and parties is a legitimate expenditure of public funds. The public monies at issue here are not being employed simply to police the integrity of the electoral process or to provide a forum for the use of all participants in the political dialogue, as would, for example, be the case if free broadcast time were granted. Rather, we are confronted with the Government's actual financing, out of general revenues, a segment of the political debate itself. As Senator Howard Baker remarked during the debate on this legislation:

"I think there is something politically incestuous about the Government financing and, I believe, inevitably then regulating, the day-to-day procedures by which the Government is selected . . . .

"I think it is extraordinarily important that the Government not control the machinery by which the public expresses the range of its desires, demands, and dissent." 120 *Cong. Rec.* 8202 (1974).

If this "incest" affected only the issue of the wisdom of the plan, it would be none of the concern of judges. But, in my view, the inappropriateness of subsidizing, from general revenues, the actual political dialogue of the people—the process which begets the Government itself—is as basic to our national tradition as the separation of church and state also deriving from the First Amendment, see *Lemon v. Kurtzman*, 403 U.S. 602, 612 (1971); *Walz v. Tax Comm'n*, 397 U.S. 664, 668-669 (1970), [424 U.S. 1, 249] or the separation of civilian and military authority, see *Orloff v. Willoughby*, 345 U.S. 83, 93-94 (1953), neither of which is explicit in the Constitution but both of which have developed through case-by-case adjudication of express provisions of the Constitution.

Recent history shows dangerous examples of systems with a close, "incestuous" relationship between "government" and "politics"; the Court's opinion simply dismisses possible dangers by noting that:

"Subtitle H is a congressional effort, not to abridge, restrict, or censor speech, but rather to use public money to facilitate and enlarge public discussion and participation in the electoral process, goals vital to a self-governing people." Ante, at 92–93.

Congress, it reassuringly adds by way of a footnote, has expressed its determination to avoid such a possibility. Ante, at 93 n. 126. But the Court points to no basis for predicting that the historical pattern of "varying measures of control and surveillance," *Lemon v. Kurtzman*, supra, at 621, which usually accompany grants from Government will not also follow in this case. Up to now, the Court has always been extraordinarily sensitive, when dealing with First Amendment rights, to the risk that the "flag tends to follow the dollars." Yet, here, where Subtitle H specifically requires the auditing of records of political parties and candidates by Government inspectors, the Court shows [424 U.S. 1, 250] little sensitivity to the danger it has so strongly condemned in other contexts. See, e.g., *Everson v. Board of Education*, 330 U.S. 1 (1947).

Up to now, this Court has scrupulously refrained, absent claims of invidious discrimination, from entering the arena of intraparty disputes concerning the seating of convention delegates. *Graham v. Fong Eu*, 403 F. Supp. 37 (ND Cal. 1975), summarily aff'd, 423 U.S. 1067 (1976); *Cousins v. Wigoda*, 419 U.S. 477 (1975); *O'Brien v. Brown*, 409 U.S. 1 (1972). An obvious underlying basis for this reluctance is that delegate selection and the management of political conventions have been considered a strictly private political matter, not the business of Government inspectors. But once the Government finances these national conventions by the expenditure of millions of dollars from the public treasury, we may be providing a springboard for later attempts to impose a whole range of requirements on delegate selection and convention activities. Does this foreshadow judicial decisions allowing the federal courts to "monitor" these conventions to assure compliance with court orders or regulations?

Assuming, arguendo, that Congress could validly appropriate public money to subsidize private political activity, it has gone about the task in Subtitle H in a manner which is not, in my view, free of constitutional infirmity. I do not question that Congress has "wide discretion in the manner of prescribing details of expenditures" in some contexts, *Cincinnati Soap Co. v. United States*, 301 U.S. 308, 321 (1937). Here, however, Congress has not itself appropriated a specific sum to attain the ends of the Act but has delegated to a limited group [424 U.S. 1, 251] of citizens—those who file tax returns—the power to allocate general revenue for the Act's purposes—and of course only a small percentage of that limited group has exercised the power. There is nothing to assure that the "fund" will actually be adequate for the Act's objectives. Thus, I find it difficult to see a rational basis for concluding that this scheme would, in fact, attain the stated purposes of the Act when its own funding scheme affords no real idea of the amount of the available funding.

I agree with MR. JUSTICE REHNQUIST that the scheme approved by the Court today invidiously discriminates against minor parties. Assuming, arguendo, the constitutionality of the overall scheme, there is a legitimate governmental interest in requiring a group to make a "preliminary showing of a significant modicum of support." *Jenness v. Fortson*, 403 U.S. 431, 442 (1971). But the present system could preclude or severely hamper access to funds before a given election by a group or an individual who might, at the time of the election, reflect the views of a major segment or even a majority of the electorate. The fact that there have been few drastic realignments in our basic two-party structure in 200 years is no constitutional justification for freezing the status quo of the present major parties at the expense of such future political movements. Cf. discussion, ante, at 73. When and if some minority party achieves majority status, Congress can readily deal with any problems that arise. In short, I see grave risks in legislation, enacted by incumbents of the major political parties, which distinctly disadvantages minor parties or independent candidates. This Court has, until today, been particularly cautious when dealing with enactments that tend to perpetuate those who control legislative power. See *Reynolds v. Sims*, 377 U.S. 533, 570 (1964).

I would also find unconstitutional the system of [424 U.S. 1, 252] matching grants which makes a candidate's ability to amass private funds the sole criterion for eligibility for public funds. Such an arrangement can put at serious disadvantage a candidate with a potentially large, widely diffused—but poor—constituency. The ability of a candidate's supporters to help pay for his campaign cannot be equated with their willingness to cast a ballot for him. See *Lubin v. Panish*, 415 U.S. 709 (1974); *Bullock v. Carter*, 405 U.S. 134 (1972).

I cannot join in the attempt to determine which parts of the Act can survive review here. The statute as it now stands is unworkable and inequitable.

I agree with the Court's holding that the Act's restrictions on expenditures made "relative to a clearly identified candidate," independent of any candidate or his committee, are unconstitutional. Ante, at 39-51. Paradoxically the Court upholds the limitations on individual contributions, which embrace precisely the same sort of expenditures "relative to a clearly identified candidate" if those expenditures are "authorized or requested" by the "candidate or his agents." Ante, at 24 n. 25. The Act as cut back by the Court thus places intolerable pressure on the distinction between "authorized" and "unauthorized" expenditures on behalf of a candidate; even those with the most sanguine hopes for the Act might well concede that the distinction cannot be maintained. As the Senate Report on the bill said:

"Whether campaigns are funded privately or publicly . . . controls are imperative if Congress is to enact meaningful limits on direct contributions. Otherwise, wealthy individuals limited to a $3,000 direct contribution [$1,000 in the bill as finally enacted] could also purchase one hundred thousand [424 U.S. 1, 253] dollars' worth of advertisements for a favored candidate. Such a loophole would render direct contribution limits virtually meaningless." S. Rep. No. 93-689, p. 18 (1974).

Given the unfortunate record of past attempts to draw distinctions of this kind, see ante, at 61-62, it is not too much to predict that the Court's holding will invite avoidance, if not evasion, of the intent of the Act, with "independent" committees undertaking "unauthorized" activities in order to escape the limits on contributions. The Court's effort to blend First Amendment principles and practical politics has produced a strange offspring.

Moreover, the Act—or so much as the Court leaves standing—creates significant inequities. A candidate with substantial personal resources is now given by the Court a clear advantage over his less affluent opponents, who are constrained by law in fund-raising, because the Court holds that the "First Amendment cannot tolerate" any restrictions on spending. Ante, at 59. Minority parties, whose situation is difficult enough under an Act that excludes them from public funding, are prevented from accepting large single-donor contributions. At the same time the Court sustains the provision aimed at broadening the base of political support by requiring candidates to seek a greater number of small contributors, it sustains the unrealistic disclosure thresholds of

$10 and $100 that I believe will deter those hoped-for small contributions. Minor parties must now compete for votes against two major
parties whose expenditures will be vast. Finally, the Act's distinction
between contributions in money and contributions in services remains,
with only the former being subject to any limits. As Judge Tamm put it
in dissent from the Court of Appeals' opinion:

"[T]he classification created only regulates certain [424 U.S. 1, 254]
types of disproportional influences. Under section 591 (e) (5), services
are excluded from contributions. This allows the housewife to volunteer
time that might cost well over $1000 to hire on the open market, while
limiting her neighbor who works full-time to a regulated contribution.
It enhances the disproportional influence of groups who command large
quantities of these volunteer services and will continue to magnify this
inequity by not allowing for an inflation adjustment to the contribution
limit. It leads to the absurd result that a lawyer's contribution of services
to aid a candidate in complying with FECA is exempt, but his first
amendment activity is regulated if he falls ill and hires a replacement."
171 U.S. App. D.C. 172, 266, 519 F.2d 821, 915 (1975).

One need not call problems of this order equal protection violations
to recognize that the contribution limitations of the Act create grave
inequities that are aggravated by the Court's interpretation of the Act.

The Court's piecemeal approach fails to give adequate consideration
to the integrated nature of this legislation. A serious question is raised,
which the Court does not consider: when central segments, key operative provisions, of this Act are stricken, can what remains function in
anything like the way Congress intended? The incongruities are obvious.
The Commission is now eliminated, yet its very purpose was to guide
candidates and campaign workers—and their accountants and lawyers—through an intricate statutory maze where a misstep can lead to
imprisonment. All candidates can now spend freely; affluent candidates,
after today, can spend their own money without limit; yet, contributions
for the ordinary [424 U.S. 1, 255] candidate are severely restricted in
amount—and small contributors are deterred. I cannot believe that

Congress would have enacted a statutory scheme containing such incongruous and inequitable provisions.

Although the statute contains a severability clause, 2 U.S.C. 454 (1970 ed., Supp. IV), such a clause is not an "inexorable command." *Dorchy v. Kansas*, 264 U.S. 286, 290 (1924). The clause creates a rebuttable presumption that "'eliminating invalid parts, the legislature would have been satisfied with what remained.'" *Welsh v. United States*, 398 U.S. 333, 364 (1970) (Harlan, J., concurring, quoting from *Champlin Rfg. Co. v. Commission*, 286 U.S. 210, 235 (1932)). Here just as the presumption of constitutionality of a statute has been overcome to the point that major proportions and chapters of the Act have been declared unconstitutional, for me the presumption of severability has been rebutted. To invoke a severability clause to salvage parts of a comprehensive, integrated statutory scheme, which parts, standing alone, are unworkable and in many aspects unfair, exalts a formula at the expense of the broad objectives of Congress.

Finally, I agree with the Court that the members of the Federal Election Commission were unconstitutionally appointed. However, I disagree that we should give blanket de facto validation to all actions of the Commission undertaken until today. The issue is not before us and we cannot know what acts we are ratifying. I would leave this issue to the District Court to resolve if and when any challenges are brought.

In the past two decades the Court has frequently [424 U.S. 1, 256] spoken of the broad coverage of the First Amendment, especially in the area of political dialogue:

"[T]o assure unfettered interchange of ideas for the bringing about of political and social changes desired by the people," *Roth v. United States*, 354 U.S. 476, 484 (1957);

and:

"[T]here is practically universal agreement that a major purpose of [the First] Amendment was to protect the free discussion of governmental affairs . . . [including] discussions of candidates . . .," *Mills v. Alabama*, 384 U.S. 214, 218 (1966);

and again:

"[I]t can hardly be doubted that the constitutional guarantee [of the First Amendment] has its fullest and most urgent application precisely to the conduct of campaigns for political office." *Monitor Patriot Co. v. Roy*, 401 U.S. 265, 272 (1971).

To accept this generalization one need not agree that the Amendment has its "fullest and most urgent application" only in the political area, for others would think religious freedom is on the same or even a higher plane. But I doubt that the Court would tolerate for an instant a limitation on contributions to a church or other religious cause; however grave an "evil" Congress thought the limits would cure, limits on religious expenditures would most certainly fall as well. To limit either contributions or expenditures as to churches would plainly restrict "the free exercise" of religion. In my view Congress can no more ration political expression than it can ration religious expression; and limits on political or religious contributions and expenditures effectively curb expression in both areas. There are many prices we pay for the freedoms secured by the First Amendment; the risk of undue [424 U.S. 1, 257] influence is one of them, confirming what we have long known: Freedom is hazardous, but some restraints are worse.

# Supreme Court Reconsiders Contribution Limits

## Dan Manatt

This selection originally was titled "In Shrink PAC v. Nixon, Supreme Court to Hear Challenge to Contributions Limits," from the "Recent Developments in the Campaign Finance Regulations" section of the Brookings Institution's web site (www.brookings.org). This article addresses the Supreme Court's decision to review *Nixon v. Shrink Missouri Government PAC*, in which the Eighth Circuit Court of Appeals invalidated Missouri's limits on campaign contributions.

The case was heard in the fall of 1999. The article summarizes not only the positions of the two parties to the case but also those of other groups that presented briefs to the Court including the ACLU, Common Cause, various PACs, and academics. It is an important case because in its January 24, 2000, decision, the Court upheld the Court of Appeals, thus validating campaign contribution limits at the state level and implicitly at the federal level.

In fall 1999, the Supreme Court will hear *Nixon v. Shrink Missouri Government PAC*, its first contribution limits case since the landmark 1976 *Buckley v. Valeo*. The Court will review the decision of the U.S. Federal Court of Appeals for the 8th Circuit, which invalidated Missouri's state contribution limits on First Amendment grounds. The Missouri law set limits at $1,075 for statewide office, $525 for state senate, and $275 for state representative.

The Court in *Buckley* upheld the constitutionality of the Federal Election Campaign Act's $1,000 contribution limit applicable to federal candidates, including candidates for president, senator, and representative, despite arguments that they were unconstitutional restrictions on free speech.

Several federal courts have recently invalidated low contribution limits on the basis that they prevent candidates from raising sufficient money to wage an effective campaign for office. These cases have addressed contribution limits of $100 to $200, and the Supreme Court has declined to review those decisions. The 8th Circuit decision marks the first time a contribution limit higher than the current $1,000 federal limit has been ruled unconstitutionally low.

The *Shrink PAC* case will enable the Court to reaffirm or revise its holding in *Buckley* in light of twenty-five years of historical experience, the development of campaign finance case law, and the impact of inflation on the value of campaign contribution limits.

## KEY ISSUES

The parties and friends of the court, with a few exceptions, agree on key parts of Buckley's holdings on contribution limits:

- Contribution limits may be constitutionally justified if they stem corruption or the appearance of corruption.

- Contribution limits may violate the First Amendment if they are so low that candidates are unable to raise enough money to engage in "effective advocacy," i.e., to wage an effective campaign.

The parties and friends of the court disagree, however, on key questions:

1. Are contribution limits unconstitutional not only because they violate candidates' free speech rights, but the free speech rights of contributors?

2. What standard of proof should be required for candidates and contributors to demonstrate that their rights have been unconstitutionally restricted?

3. What standard of proof should be required for states to demonstrate corruption or the appearance of corruption in the

campaign finance system sufficient to justify contribution limits?

4. Who bears the initial burden of proof—i.e., in this case, must the candidate or contributor (plaintiffs Shrink PAC and Zedman) first demonstrate that their free speech has been substantially restricted in order to challenge the Missouri law, or must Missouri first demonstrate that the state has a "real" problem with corruption and the appearance of corruption to justify the contribution limit?

5. What constitutes corruption—only legislative quid pro quos, or other political "favors" such as special access to lawmakers? Can contribution limits be justified by the "appearance of corruption" alone, and if so how can the "appearance of corruption" be demonstrated?

6. Are contribution limits below a certain dollar amount per se unconstitutional? The 1974 *Buckley* opinion summarily stated that there was no evidence that the $1,000 contribution limit was too low. Now, twenty-five years later, some argue both that evidence to the contrary exists since that $1,000 limit approved in *Buckley* is worth only $350 today after inflation.

The Supreme Court's decision could have far-reaching effects. Not only might it invalidate existing limits, it may undercut efforts to enact contribution limits in states through the referendum process. In addition, although the issues are not raised in this case, *Shrink PAC* may affect other campaign finance limitations, including contribution limits to PACs and the current federal aggregate $25,000 limit applicable to individuals.

BRIEFS

*Briefs of the Parties*

Jeremiah (Jay) Nixon, attorney general of Missouri (Petitioner), argues that, before a court closely scrutinizes a contribution limit, a party such as Shrink PAC has the burden of proof to show that its free speech rights have been unconstitutionally restricted, and that the standard of proof required of Missouri to demonstrate that contribution limits are justified by corruption or the appearance of corruption is an intermediate, not strict, standard of scrutiny. Missouri also notes that political candidates in the state have raised more money since enactment of the state's contribution limits laws, suggesting the contribution limits have not severely restricted fund-raising efforts.

Shrink Missouri Government PAC (Respondent) argues that Missouri has the burden of proof to show corruption constitutes a "real harm" to Missouri, not merely that there is an "appearance of corruption." Shrink PAC argues that the evidence offered in the trial and appeals court, including the affidavit of a key sponsor of the legislation and newspaper articles documenting possible (but unproven) quid pro quos by lawmakers, is insufficient.

Joan Bray (Intervenor-Respondent in Support of Missouri's position), a Missouri state representative whose brief was prepared by the Brennan Center for Justice, argues that litigants challenging contribution limits not only have the burden of proof but must prove that their speech rights have been substantially limited—i.e., that contribution limits "severely interfere with the ability of candidates" to "conduct effective advocacy" in order to trigger strict scrutiny. More generally, Bray's brief argues such a standard is consistent with what it views as the Court's "flexible" approach to campaign finance law, including a "pragmatic" evidentiary standard. Under this standard, the brief says, anecdotal evidence sufficed in *Buckley* to demonstrate "corruption." The brief says legislators and the public, when voting for legislative referenda, are owed substantial deference by the courts.

*Amicus (Friends-of-the-Court) Briefs*

United States Solicitor General's Office asserts that upholding the 8th Circuit's opinion would not merely invalidate the Missouri law but would necessarily overrule *Buckley v. Valeo*'s contribution limits framework. The brief argues that Missouri offered hard evidence of corruption, even though, the brief argues, the state was not required to do so.

Mitch McConnell, Missouri Republican Party, Republican National Committee, and National Republican Senatorial Committee, urges the Court to consider ruling that contribution limits are "per se" unconstitutional. The brief argues that limits have had a "severe adverse effect" on the ability of candidates to fund their campaigns. The brief also argues that contribution limits have not succeeded in stemming corruption or the appearance of corruption. Finally, the McConnell brief says that contribution limit cannot be justified by an "appearance of corruption" alone and that the granting of "access" to contributors does not constitute corruption or the appearance of corruption.

The brief on behalf of Senators Jack Reed, John McCain, Russ Feingold, Congressmen Christopher Shays, Marty Meehan, and other members of Congress, like the McConnell brief, urges the Supreme Court to "reexamine its campaign finance jurisprudence," which it says has "become a straitjacket" limiting reform efforts. However, the members of Congress urge the Court to be more deferential, rather than more strict, in reviewing campaign finance legislation. Specifically, they urge the court to use an intermediate standard of review when ruling on finance legislation and generally give substantial deference to legislative enactments in the area.

The brief of Secretaries of State of Arkansas, Connecticut, Iowa, Massachusetts, Mississippi, Missouri, Montana, New Hampshire, New Mexico, Rhode Island, Tennessee, West Virginia, and Wisconsin, and Election Officials from Hawaii and Kentucky, drafted by the National Voting Rights Institute, argues that the contribution limits are justified by "the pervasive appearance of corruption in electoral politics not only [arising] from the legion historical examples of influence peddling but also from the simple fact that the vast majority of Americans cannot afford to contribute substantial money to campaigns as their wealthy counterparts do." The brief says that the Court's analysis "must be informed by this reality," despite the fact that *Buckley* squarely rejected the so-called "level playing field" rationale for limits.

American Civil Liberties Union (ACLU), which argued unsuccessfully that contribution limits were unconstitutional in the original *Buckley* decision, argues that, in light of twenty-five years of historical experience, contribution limits are "clearly unconstitutional" because in its view contribution limits have done nothing to "provide a meaningful check on the corrupting influence of money in the electoral system." The ACLU continues: "The First Amendment bargain that *Buckley* struck in upholding contribution limits simply has not paid off. It is time to consider a different approach."

Common Cause, Democracy 21, League of Women Voters, Public Campaign, et al. argue that Missouri has a low standard of proof to demonstrate corruption or the appearance of corruption—in fact, they argue corruption is "inherent" where campaign contributions are unlimited and that courts should not require evidence or proof of corruption. The brief also includes a lengthy section on incidents of corruption, including recent controversies arising out of the 1996 presidential election.

The brief of the National Right to Life PAC, National Rifle Association Political Victory Fund, and National Right to Work Committee PAC (State Employee Rights Campaign Committee) argues that contribution limits should be subject to a strict scrutiny standard of proof because of how contribution limits restrict the rights of contributors, not just candidates. The brief further argues that the Court defines "corruption" narrowly, to include only money exchanges for political favors—i.e., quid pro quos. It states that "empirical studies demonstrate that there is no causal connection between campaign contributions and legislative behavior."

The brief of William J. Olson, P.C., for Gun Owners of America, Inc., et al., challenges the entire scheme of campaign finance regulation as an impermissible restraint on free speech, designed to protect incumbents from challenges and to preserve the media's powerful voice as the only entities able to spend an unlimited amount of money on elections.

Public Citizen urges the Court to rule for the petitioner based on "the basic rule that laws passed by democratically elected legislatures are presumed constitutionally valid and that the burden is on those challenging a law to establish their invalidity." In addition, the brief says courts should not "second-guess elected representatives" on the proper level of contribution limits, unless a candidate offers evidence that the limits interfere with the candidate's ability to run for office.

U.S. Term Limits makes the most strongly libertarian argument against contribution limits, saying that "any campaign finance regulation has the undeniable effect of limiting the very speech that this Court has ruled is at the 'zenith' of First Amendment protection." The brief generally argues that contribution limits necessarily favor incumbents and that the wise course is to deregulate campaign finance.

The James Madison Center argues that Missouri has the burden of proof—and the high standard of strict scrutiny—to demonstrate corruption or the appearance of corruption. The center says contribution limits are invalid unless justified by substantial record evidence rather than "unreasonable and manipulated public perceptions of an appearance of corruption." In addition, the center says "contribution limits can be so low that they are themselves a cause of corruption."

The amicus brief by fourteen political scientists—Professors Paul Allen Beck, Thad Beyle, Janet M. Box-Steffensmeier, Leon D. Epstein, Donald P. Green, Ruth S. Jones, Ira Katznelson, Jonathan S. Krasno, David B. Magleby, Michael J. Malbin, Thomas E. Mann, Burke Marshall, Frank J. Sorauf, Raymond E. Wolfinger—offers empirical analyses of the effect of contribution limits, and concludes that the Missouri limits as well as federal contribution limits do not severely restrict candidates. Specifically, the brief argues many challengers raise money in amounts rivaling or exceeding the amounts raised by opposing incumbents and that the growth in campaign spending has outpaced inflation. It also notes that the average spending per candidate in Missouri's statewide races in 1996 increased for all but one candidate, despite the new contribution limits.

The brief of Pacific Legal Foundation and Lincoln Club of Orange County, California, argues that legislatures do not enact contribution limits for the legitimate purpose of combating financial quid pro quos—which the brief argues are very rare in any case. Rather, it argues the anticorruption rationale is a subterfuge for constitutionally illegitimate policy objectives of "leveling the playing field" and enabling "legislatures to set the rules of the electoral game so as to keep themselves in power." The brief argues—as Justice Clarence Thomas has—that contribution limits are unnecessary in light of bribery and disclosure statutes, and press scrutiny.

# PART THREE

# Regulation and Proposed Legislation

The documents in this section include a defeated amendment to the Constitution to give Congress the power to regulate campaign spending and contributions, an announcement from the Federal Election Commission on permitted spending in the 1996 presidential campaign, and two documents on the major proposed legislation on campaign finance: the text of the deregulatory and relatively brief Doolittle bill and a summary of the very different McCain-Feingold legislation, calling for greater controls on campaign contributions and expenditures.

# Attempt to Amend the Constitution

Supreme Court decisions on campaign finance reaffirm that the First Amendment to the Constitution protects freedom of speech, and above all political speech. The Court concludes that Congress thus lacks the power to limit campaign expenditures except through voluntary restraints.

The idea that Congress ought to be able to legislate expenditure controls is in fact popular with the public, at least on first blush. Bills to amend the Constitution to allow such legislation have been introduced in the Congress, most recently as S.J. RES. 18, which was resoundingly defeated in the Senate March 18, 1997, by a vote of 38 for, 61 against. Of the 38, 4 were Republicans.

Here is the text, the vote, and the floor discussion.

Proposing an amendment to the Constitution of the United States relating to contributions and expenditures intended to affect elections.

Resolved by the Senate and House of Representatives of the United States of America in Congress assembled (two-thirds of each House concurring therein),

That the following article is proposed as an amendment to the Constitution of the United States, to be valid only if ratified by the legislatures of three-fourths of the several States within 7 years after the date of final passage of this joint resolution:

Article

SECTION 1. Congress shall have power to set reasonable limits on the amount of contributions that may be made by, in support of, or in opposition to, a candidate for nomination for election to, or for election to, Federal office.

SECTION 2. A State shall have the power to set reasonable limits on the amount of contributions that may be accepted by, and the amount of expenditures that may be made by, in support of, or in opposition to, a candidate for nomination for election to, or for election to, State or local office.

SECTION 3. Congress shall have power to implement and enforce this article by appropriate legislation.

## Rollcall Vote No. 31 Leg.

YEAS—38

Akaka, Daniel (D, HI)
Baucus, Max (D, MT)
Biden, Joseph (D, DE)
Bingaman, Jeff (D, NM)
Boxer, Barbara (D, CA)
Breaux, John (D, LA)
Bryan, Richard (D, NV)
Byrd, Robert (D, WV)
Cleland, Max (D, GA)
Cochran, Thad (R, MS)
Conrad, Kent (D, ND)
Daschle, Thomas (D, SD)
Dodd, Christopher (D, CT)

Dorgan, Byron (D, ND)
Feinstein, Dianne (D, CA)
Ford, Wendell (D, KY)
Glenn, John (D, OH)
Graham, Robert (D, FL)
Harkin, Thomas (D, IA)
Hollings, Ernest (D, SC)
Inouye, Daniel (D, HI)
Jeffords, James (R, VT)
Johnson, Tim (D, SD)
Kerry, John (D, MA)
Landrieu, Mary (D, LA)
Lautenberg, Frank (D, NJ)

Levin, Carl (D, MI)
Lieberman, Joseph (D, CT)
Mikulski, Barbara (D, MD)
Murray, Patty (D, WA)
Reed, Jack (D, RI)
Reid, Harry (D, NV)
Robb, Charles (D, VA)
Roth, William (D, DE)
Sarbanes, Paul (D, MD)
Specter, Arlen (R, PA)
Wellstone, Paul (D, MN)
Wyden, Ron (D, OR)

NAYS—61

Abraham, Spencer (R, MI)
Allard, Wayne (R, CO)
Ashcroft, John (R, MO)
Bennett, Robert (R, UT)
Bond, Christopher (R, MO)
Brownback, Sam (R, KS)
Bumpers, Dale (D, AR)
Campbell, Ben (R, CO)
Chafee, John (R, RI)
Coats, Daniel (R, IN)
Collins, Susan (R, ME)
Coverdell, Paul (R, GA)
Craig, Larry (D, ID)
D'Amato, Alphonse (R, NY)
DeWine, Michael (R, OH)
Domenici, Pete (R, NM)
Durbin, Richard (D, IL)
Enzi, Michael (R, WY)
Faircloth, D. M. (R, NC)
Feingold, Russell (D, WI)
Frist, Bill (R, TN)

Gorton, Slade (D, WA)
Gramm, Phil (R, TX)
Grams, Rod (R, MN)
Grassley, Charles (R, IA)
Gregg, Judd (R, NH)
Hagel, Chuck (R, NE)
Hatch, Orrin (R, UT)
Helms, Jesse (R, NC)
Hutchinson, Tim (R, AR)
Hutchison, Kay (R, TX)
Inhofe, James (R, OK)
Kempthorne, Dirk (R, ID)
Kennedy, Edward (D, MA)
Kerry, Bob (D, NE)
Kohl, Herbert (D, WI)
Kyl, Jon (R, AZ)
Leahy, Patrick (D, VT)
Lott, Trent (R, MS)
Lugar, Richard (R, IN)
Mack, Connie (D, FL)

McCain, John (R, AZ)
McConnell, Mitch (R, KY)
Moseley-Braun, Carol (D, IL)
Moynihan, Daniel (D, NY)
Murkowski, Frank (R, AK)
Nickles, Donald (R, OK)
Roberts, Pat (R, KS)
Rockefeller, John (D, WV)
Santorum, Rick (R, PA)
Sessions, Jeff (R, AL)
Shelby, Richard (R, AL)
Smith, Bob (R, NH)
Smith, Gordon (R, OK)
Snowe, Olympia (R, ME)
Stevens, Ted (R, AK)
Thomas, Craig (R, WY)
Thompson, Fred (R, TN)
Thurmond, Strom (R, SC)
Torricelli, Robert (D, NJ)
Warner, John (R, VA)

NOT VOTING—1

Burns, Conrad (R, MT)

The PRESIDING OFFICE: On this vote, the yeas are 38, the nays are 61. Two-thirds of the Senate voting, a quorum being present, not having voted in the affirmative, the joint resolution is rejected.

MR. MCCONNELL: Mr. President, just a couple of observations about the vote just completed.

The constitutional amendment to strip political speech out of the first amendment and give the Government the power to control said speech was just defeated 61 to 38. We have had previous votes on the Hollings amendment in other years.

I would just like to mention for the benefit of my colleagues this is the biggest vote against the Hollings amendment yet achieved in the Senate. . . . So I think it was a very encouraging indication of the growing support for protecting the first amendment.

I want to thank my colleagues for this overwhelming vote against the amendment.

# FEC Announces 1996 Presidential Spending Limits, March 15, 1996

## Federal Election Commission

This FEC document, published in the spring of the 1996 general election year, lays out the federal funds available to presidential candidates in the primaries and the general election and the conditions they must meet in order to receive these funds, as well as funding available for the party conventions.

If a candidate does not accept federal funds, his or her spending is not limited, nor is there then any limitation on the use of personal funds or the amounts that can be spent in any particular state.

WASHINGTON—Presidential candidates who accept public funding may spend $37.092 million on their prenomination efforts while each party's nominee will be able to spend $61.82 million during the 1996 general election, according to unofficial calculations released today by the Federal Election Commission (see table 1).

Each of the two major parties will be able to spend up to $11,994,007 on behalf of their presidential nominees and $12,364,000 on their conventions, according to those calculations.

There is an overall spending limit for the entire preconvention period as well as limits for spending in each state (see table 2). The limits apply only to those campaigns choosing to accept federal funds. Campaigns that forgo federal funding may spend unlimited amounts of money.

The overall "base" spending limit for presidential primary campaigns is $10 million, plus a cost-of-living adjustment (over 1974). For the 1996 primary season, the "base" spending limit is $30,910,000. An exemption for 20 percent of a campaign's fund-raising expenses effectively raises the amount primary contenders may spend in the preconvention period to $37,092,000. Candidates may spend unlimited amounts for certain legal and accounting costs.

TABLE 1. Presidential Spending Limits

| | 1996 | 1992 | 1988 | 1984 | 1980 | 1976 |
|---|---|---|---|---|---|---|
| Primary (+20%) | $30,910,000.00 | $27,620,000.00 | $23,050,000.00 | $20,200,000.00 | $14,720,000.00 | $10,910,000.00 |
| | $37,092,000.00 | $33,144,000.00 | $27,660,000.00 | $24,240,000.00 | $17,664,000.00 | $13,092,000.00 |
| Maximum Entitlement | $15,455,000.00 | $13,810,000.00 | $11,525,000.00 | $10,100,000.00 | $7,360,000.00 | $5,455,000.00 |
| Convention | $12,364,000.00 | $11,048,000.00 | $9,220,000.00 | $8,080,000.00 | $4,416,000.00 | $2,182,000.00 |
| General | $61,820,000.00 | $55,240,000.00 | $46,100,000.00 | $40,400,000.00 | $29,440,000.00 | $21,820,000.00 |
| Party 441a(d) | $11,994,007.30 | $10,331,702.92 | $8,291,453.80 | $6,924,802.40 | $4,637,653.76 | $3,203,786.96 |

*Spending Limits per Statute*

Primary  $10,000,00 + COLA base spending limit. Campaigns are also allowed to exempt 20 percent of fund-raising costs from overall limit, which in effect raises their total spending limit by 20 percent. Legal and accounting costs incurred to comply with the law are exempt from the limit.

Convention  $4 million + COLA. Originally, the limit was $2 million + COLA. The base was raised to $3 million for the 1980 convention; then to $4 million for the 1984 convention.

General  $20,000,000 + COLA. Legal and accounting costs incurred to comply with the law are exempt from the limit and may be defrayed from private monies raised in separate compliance funds (subject to contribution limitations and prohibitions.)

Party 441a(d)  $.02 × VAP of U.S. + COLA. Commonly referred to as the coordinated party spending limit, this is the amount that the national party may spend on behalf of its nominee. The party may work in conjunction with the campaign, but the money is raised, spent, and reported by the national party committee. This limit only applies to the general election.

NOTE: COLA is the cost-of-living adjustment [increase] over the base year of 1974.

TABLE 2.    1996 State-by-State Expenditure Limits for Presidential Candidates

| State | Voting-Age Population (in thousands) | Expenditure Limit |
|-------|-------------------------------------|-------------------|
| Alabama | 3,173 | $1,569,239 |
| Alaska | 414 | 618,200 |
| Arizona | 3,025 | 1,496,044 |
| Arkansas | 1,834 | 907,023 |
| California | 22,796 | 11,273,990 |
| Colorado | 2,765 | 1,367,458 |
| Connecticut | 2,477 | 1,225,025 |
| Delaware | 538 | 618,200 |
| District of Columbia | 440 | 618,200 |
| Florida | 10,794 | 5,338,281 |
| Georgia | 5,277 | 2,609,793 |
| Hawaii | 878 | 616,200 |
| Idaho | 815 | 618,200 |
| Illinois | 8,704 | 4,394,650 |
| Indiana | 4,316 | 2,134,521 |
| Iowa | 2,117 | 1,046,984 |
| Kansas | 1,873 | 926,311 |
| Kentucky | 2,888 | 1,428,289 |
| Louisiana | 3,103 | 1,534,620 |
| Maine | 936 | 618,200 |
| Maryland | 3,770 | 1,864,491 |
| Massachusetts | 4,642 | 2,295,748 |
| Michigan | 7,030 | 3,476,757 |
| Minnesota | 3,364 | 1,663,700 |
| Mississippi | 1,935 | 956,974 |
| Missouri | 3,942 | 1,949,556 |
| Montana | 834 | 618,200 |
| Nebraska | 1,194 | 618,200 |
| Nevada | 1,132 | 618,200 |
| New Hampshire | 853 | 618,200 |
| New Jersey | 5,982 | 2,958,458 |
| New Mexico | 1,185 | 618,200 |
| New York | 13,599 | 6,725,521 |
| North Carolina | 5,396 | 2,658,646 |
| North Dakota | 471 | 618,200 |
| Ohio | 8,291 | 4,100,397 |
| Oklahoma | 2,400 | 1,186,944 |
| Oregon | 2,344 | 1,159,249 |
| Pennsylvania | 9,163 | 4,531,653 |
| Rhode Island | 752 | 618,200 |

TABLE 2.  (*continued*)

| State | Voting-Age Population (in thousands) | Expenditure Limit |
|---|---|---|
| South Carolina | 2,729 | 1,349,654 |
| South Dakota | 523 | 618,200 |
| Tennessee | 3,946 | 1,951,534 |
| Texas | 13,324 | 6,589,517 |
| Utah | 1,277 | 631,553 |
| Vermont | 438 | 618,200 |
| Virginia | 5,006 | 2,475,767 |
| Washington | 4,013 | 1,984,669 |
| West Virginia | 1,406 | 695,351 |
| Wisconsin | 3,770 | 1,864,491 |
| Wyoming | 344 | 618,200 |
| U.S. Territories | | |
| American Samoa | | 618,200 |
| Guam | | 618,200 |
| Puerto Rico | | 618,200 |
| Virgin Islands | | 618,200 |

State spending limits are keyed to the voting age population (VAP) of each state, with a minimum of at least $200,000 plus a cost-of-living adjustment for those states with a low VAP. The formula for setting state limits is 16 percent VAP + cost of living. A less populated state, such as New Hampshire, would have a limit of $200,000, plus cost of living, or $618,200. A larger state, such as California, would have a limit of 16 × 22,796,000 (VAP), plus cost of living, or $11,273,990.

The two major party nominees will be given $61,820,000 each for the general election campaign. Candidates opting for general election funding have a spending limit of $20 million plus a cost-of-living adjustment (over 1974). They receive all of their funds from the U.S. Treasury and may not raise private contributions for the campaign, other than for legal and accounting costs, which are not subject to the spending limit.

# The Doolittle Bill:
# Citizen Legislature and Political Freedom Act

## 105th Congress

The legislation introduced by Congressman John T. Doolittle (R-Calif.) provides for deregulating campaign finance, eliminating both contribution and expenditure limitations. It also provides for ending federal financing of presidential campaigns. Its emphasis is on improved disclosure of campaign finance information primarily through electronic filing.

To amend the Federal Election Campaign Act of 1971 to reform the financing of campaigns for election for Federal office.

IN THE HOUSE OF REPRESENTATIVES

March 6, 1997

MR. DOOLITTLE (for himself, MR. DELAY, MR. SAM JOHNSON of Texas, MR. YOUNG of Alaska, MR. BALLENGER, MRS. CHENOWETH, MR. MCKEON, MR. RADANOVICH, MR. LEWIS of California, MR. LEWIS of Kentucky, MR. MCINNIS, MR. HUNTER, and MR. ROHRABACHER) introduced the following bill, which was referred to the Committee on House Oversight, and in addition to the Committee on Ways and Means, for a period to be subsequently determined by the Speaker, in each case for consideration of such provisions as fall within the jurisdiction of the committee concerned.

A BILL

To amend the Federal Election Campaign Act of 1971 to reform the financing of campaigns for election for Federal office.

Be it enacted by the Senate and House of Representatives of the United States of America in Congress assembled,

SECTION 1. SHORT TITLE.

This Act may be cited as the 'Citizen Legislature and Political Freedom Act.'

SEC. 2. REMOVAL OF LIMITATIONS ON FEDERAL ELECTION CAMPAIGN CONTRIBUTIONS.

Section 315(a) of the Federal Election Campaign Act of 1971 (2 U.S.C. 441a(a)) is amended by adding at the end the following new paragraph:

'(9) The limitations established under this subsection shall not apply to contributions made during calendar years beginning after 1998.'

SEC. 3. TERMINATION OF TAXPAYER FINANCING OF PRESIDENTIAL ELECTION CAMPAIGNS.

(a) TERMINATION OF DESIGNATION OF INCOME TAX PAYMENTS— Section 6096 of the Internal Revenue Code of 1986 is amended by adding at the end the following new subsection:

'(d) TERMINATION—This section shall not apply to taxable years beginning after December 31, 1997.'

(b) TERMINATION OF FUND AND ACCOUNT—

(1) TERMINATION OF PRESIDENTIAL ELECTION CAMPAIGN FUND—

(A) IN GENERAL—Chapter 95 of subtitle H of such Code is amended by adding at the end the following new section:

'SEC. 9014. TERMINATION.

The provisions of this chapter shall not apply with respect to any presidential election (or any presidential nominating convention) after December 31, 1998, or to any candidate in such an election.'

(B) TRANSFER OF EXCESS FUNDS TO GENERAL FUND—Section 9006 of such Code is amended by adding at the end the following new subsection:

'(d) TRANSFER OF FUNDS REMAINING AFTER 1998—The Secretary shall transfer all amounts in the fund after December 31, 1998, to the general fund of the Treasury.'

(2) TERMINATION OF ACCOUNT—Chapter 96 of subtitle H of such Code is amended by adding at the end the following new section:

'SEC. 9043. TERMINATION.

The provisions of this chapter shall not apply to any candidate with respect to any presidential election after December 31, 1998.'

(c) CLERICAL AMENDMENTS—

(1) The table of sections for chapter 95 of subtitle H of such Code is amended by adding at the end the following new item:

'Sec. 9014. Termination.'

(2) The table of sections for chapter 96 of subtitle H of such Code is amended by adding at the end the following new item:

'Sec. 9043. Termination.'

SEC. 4. DISCLOSURE REQUIREMENTS FOR CERTAIN SOFT MONEY EX-
PENDITURES OF POLITICAL PARTIES.

(a) TRANSFERS OF FUNDS BY NATIONAL POLITICAL PARTIES—Section 304(b)(4) of the Federal Election Campaign Act of 1971 (2 U.S.C. 434(b)(4)) is amended—

(1) by striking 'and' at the end of subparagraph (H);

(2) by adding 'and' at the end of subparagraph (I); and

(3) by adding at the end the following new subparagraph:

'(J) in the case of a political committee of a national political party, all funds transferred to any political committee of a State or local political party, without regard to whether or not the funds are otherwise treated as contributions or expenditures under this title;'.

(b) DISCLOSURE BY STATE AND LOCAL POLITICAL PARTIES OF INFORMATION REPORTED UNDER STATE LAW—Section 304 of such Act (2 U.S.C. 434) is amended by adding at the end the following new subsection:

'(d) If a political committee of a State or local political party is required under a State or local law, rule, or regulation to submit a report on its disbursements to an entity of the State or local government, the committee shall file a copy of the report with the Commission at the time it submits the report to such an entity.'.

(c) EFFECTIVE DATE—The amendments made by this section shall apply with respect to elections occurring after January 1999.

SEC. 5. PROMOTING EXPEDITED AVAILABILITY OF FEC REPORTS.

(a) MANDATORY ELECTRONIC FILING—Section 304(a)(11)(A) of the Federal Election Campaign Act of 1971 (2 U.S.C. 434(a)(11)(A)) is amended by striking 'permit reports required by' and inserting 'require reports under'.

(b) REQUIRING REPORTS FOR ALL CONTRIBUTIONS MADE TO ANY POLITICAL COMMITTEE WITHIN 90 DAYS OF ELECTION; REQUIRING REPORTS TO BE MADE WITHIN 24 HOURS—Section 304(a)(6) of such Act (2 U.S.C. 434(a)(6)) is amended to read as follows:

'(6)(A) Each political committee shall notify the Secretary or the Commission, and the Secretary of State, as appropriate, in writing, of any contribution received by the committee during the period which begins on the 90th day before an election and ends at the time the polls close for such election. This notification shall be made within 24 hours (or, if earlier, by midnight of the day on which the contribution is deposited) after the receipt of such contribution and shall include the name of the candidate involved (as appropriate) and the office sought by the candidate, the identification of the contributor, and the date of receipt and amount of the contribution.

'(B) The notification required under this paragraph shall be in addition to all other reporting requirements under this Act.'.

(c) INCREASING ELECTRONIC DISCLOSURE—Section 304 of such Act (2 U.S.C. 434(a)), as amended by section 4(b), is further amended by adding at the end the following new subsection:

'(e)(1) The Commission shall make the information contained in the reports submitted under this section available on the Internet and publicly available at the offices of the Commission as soon as practicable (but in no case later than 24 hours) after the information is received by the Commission.

'(2) In this subsection, the term 'Internet' means the international computer network of both Federal and non-Federal interoperable packet-switched data networks.'.

(d) EFFECTIVE DATE—The amendment made by this section shall apply with respect to reports for periods beginning on or after January 1, 1999.

SEC. 6. WAIVER OF 'BEST EFFORTS' EXCEPTION FOR INFORMATION ON IDENTIFICATION OF CONTRIBUTORS.

(a) IN GENERAL—Section 302(i) of the Federal Election Campaign Act of 1971 (2 U.S.C. 432(i)) is amended—

(1) by striking '(i) When the treasurer' and inserting '(i)(1) Except as provided in paragraph (2), when the treasurer'; and

(2) by adding at the end the following new paragraph:

'(2) Paragraph (1) shall not apply with respect to information regarding the identification of any person who makes a contribution or contributions aggregating more than $200 during a calendar year (as required to be provided under subsection (c)(3)).'.

(b) EFFECTIVE DATE—The amendment made by subsection (a) shall apply with respect to persons making contributions for elections occurring after January 1999.

# S. 25: Bipartisan Campaign Reform Act

## John McCain and Russell Feingold

This summary of the McCain-Feingold bill, written by its supporters, Senators McCain (R, Ariz.) and Feingold (D, Wisc.), appears more reasonable and less restrictive of freedom of speech than many commentators consider it to be. It greatly extends the scope of federal limitations on contributions and expenditures and limits extensively political speech outside the confines of federal election law.

Obviously people—an agency of the federal government funded by the U.S. Congress—must be put in charge of making the decisions about what would and would not be permissible under such legislation.

### SOFT MONEY

Federal election law currently allows individuals to contribute $20,000 and PACs to contribute $15,000 to the national parties. These fully disclosed, regulated contributions are referred to as "hard money" contributions.

However, a gaping loophole, known as "soft money," allows corporations, labor unions and wealthy individuals to make unlimited contributions—totaling over $260 million in the 1996 elections—to the national political parties. "Soft money" is then transferred in unlimited amounts to state parties, which are able to make "soft money" expenditures on activities intended to influence the outcome of a federal election. Thus, funds that are barred by federal law from being contributed directly to federal candidates, such as corporate and labor union treasury monies, are nonetheless being raised and spent by the parties on the candidates' behalf and poured into federal elections.

The McCain-Feingold-Thompson proposal bars the national parties, federal officeholders, and candidates from soliciting, receiving, or spending any funds that are not subject to the limitations and reporting requirements in federal election law. This provision would categorically shut down the Washington soft money fund-raising machine. The leg-islation also provides that state and local parties that engage in activities during a federal election year that might affect the outcome of a federal election, such as voter registration and get-out-the-vote efforts, may only do so with funds raised under the federal limits.

## INDEPENDENT EXPENDITURES

An *independent expenditure* is defined as an expenditure expressly ad-vocating the election or defeat of a clearly identified candidate that is made without cooperation or consultation with any candidate. Current law requires independent expenditures to be paid for with federally regulated and fully disclosed hard money dollars. For example, corpo-rations and labor unions may only fund independent expenditures through their PACs and are not permitted to use their treasury monies. Further, any expenditure made by an outside organization in consul-tation with a candidate is considered an in-kind contribution to that candidate.

The legislation requires outside groups to promptly report inde-pendent expenditures aggregating $10,000 or more to the Federal Elec-tion Commission. If the targeted candidate of the independent expen-diture is complying with the spending limits, the FEC must transmit a copy of that advance report to the complying candidate and inform such candidates that they are entitled to an increase in their spending limit equal to the amount of the independent expenditure made against them or for their opponent. This will enable complying candidates to respond on a timely basis to such expenditures without the constraint of a spending cap.

In June 1996, the Supreme Court ruled that political parties could make unlimited hard money independent expenditures when certain circumstances apply. Current law establishes population-based limits on how much parties may spend on "coordinated expenditures" with a particular senate campaign in a given state in connection with a general election. S. 25 allows parties to continue to make coordinated expenditures but only if they agree not to make independent expenditures in the same campaign. Simply put, parties will be unable to make both coordinated expenditures and unlimited independent expenditures in the same federal election.

The bill also tightens current statutory language to ensure that independent expenditures made by political parties are truly independent of any coordination with federal candidates.

## "ISSUE ADVOCACY"

Current law and Supreme Court precedent permit the government to regulate campaign expenditures that "expressly advocate" the election or defeat of a candidate but not "issue advocacy" expenditures that only attempt to raise and discuss issues without advocating a particular candidate.

For example, if a corporation or labor union runs a television ad deemed to "expressly advocate" the election or defeat of a candidate, the ad must be funded from their PAC, composed of voluntary and disclosed contributions from their employees or members. If the same entity makes an issue advocacy expenditure, it is permitted to use its treasury monies, usually from shareholder profits or from member dues. These funds are unregulated and undisclosed.

The statutory definition of what constitutes express advocacy has been exploited in recent elections to the point where attack ads disguised as issue advocacy are dominating many federal campaigns. By purposely avoiding the use of such key phrases as "vote for" or "oppose," groups have been able to fund undisclosed, million-dollar electioneering activities completely outside the scope of federal election law.

This proposal includes language that expands the definition of what constitutes express advocacy. True issue ads that do not attempt to advocate the election or defeat of a particular candidate will not be affected by this new law.

The legislation includes a new definition of *express advocacy* to include any general public communication that advocates the election or defeat of a clearly identified candidate for federal office by using such expressions as "vote for," "support," or "defeat." Further, any disbursement aggregating $10,000 or more for any general public communication that is made within thirty days of a primary election or sixty days of a general election shall be considered express advocacy if the communication refers to a clearly identified candidate and if a reasonable person would understand it as advocating the election or defeat of that candidate.

If a disbursement aggregating $10,000 or more for any general public communication is made prior to thirty days before a primary election or prior to sixty days before a general election, it shall be considered express advocacy if a reasonable person would understand it as advocating the election or defeat of a clearly identified candidate and if the communication is made with the purpose of advocating the election or defeat of a candidate as shown by one or more factors including a statement or action by the person making the communication, the targeting or placement of the communication, or the use by the person making the communication of polling or other similar data relating to the candidate's campaign or election.

FRANKED MASS MAILINGS

Mass mailings are often used by incumbents in an election year to improve their name recognition and share their accomplishments with constituents who have not solicited such a response. Current law recognizes this inherent incumbent advantage by barring the use of such mass mailings ninety days before a House election and sixty days before a Senate election. The McCain-Feingold-Thompson proposal extends this prohibition to the entire calendar year of an election.

ENFORCEMENT

Current law provides campaigns with the option of electronically filing their disclosure statements with the FEC, but many campaigns continue to file handwritten reports that are difficult for the FEC to process and

make available to the public. The McCain-Feingold-Thompson proposal grants authority to the FEC to begin requiring all federal candidates to file their reports electronically, thus improving efficiency and
allowing the public greater access to candidate campaign reports.

The McCain-Feingold proposal toughens penalties for "knowing
and willful" violations of federal election law by tripling the amount of
the penalty the FEC is permitted to assess for such violation. The proposal allows the FEC to randomly audit campaigns to ensure violations
have not occurred and to obtain temporary restraining orders or preliminary injunctions for the most flagrant and egregious violations that
may be occurring in the closing days and weeks of a campaign.

FOREIGN CONTRIBUTIONS

This provision would prohibit anyone who is ineligible to vote in a
federal election, including legal permanent resident aliens, from contributing to federal candidates.

# PART FOUR

# Points of View

This section includes short articles from a variety of people who regularly or occasionally write editorials and opinion pieces for newspapers and magazines—economists, political scientists, pundits, politicians, and political consultants. It concludes with three articles by members of the U.S. Congress who have been especially active in the campaign finance debate—Representative John Doolittle and Senators Mitch McConnell and Russell Feingold. Their varying perspectives and analyses show how deeply the campaign finance issue touches on basic political philosophy and values.

# Enemies of the First Amendment

## Bobby R. Burchfield

This article first appeared in the *Weekly Standard*, October 11, 1999, pp. 23–25. Burchfield, a partner in the law firm of Covington & Burling, summarizes the provisions of the campaign finance bill that passed the U.S. House of Representatives in September 1999 (252–177) and its less stringent Senate counterpart, which was filibustered.

Burchfield's main point is that the authors of these bills and their supporters are well aware that the soft money bans they entail conflict with the First Amendment's protection of free speech. The proponents persist, however, because the Supreme Court's decisions doom limits that apply only to candidates and parties, since the funds can so easily flow to constitutionally protected independent individuals and organizations.

For those who decry the amount and role of money in politics, the problem has an obvious solution: simply outlaw certain campaign donations and strictly limit spending. To accomplish this, however, reformers must get around a long line of court decisions holding that restrictions on political giving and spending suppress political dialogue and thus violate the First Amendment's guarantee of free speech.

Fortunately for the country, there is no way around the First Amendment. The essential provisions of all campaign finance proposals—and that includes the Shays-Meehan bill passed by the House on September 14 and the less sweeping McCain-Feingold bill now pending in the Senate—inevitably fetter the political debate that is basic to our system of government.

Both the case for campaign finance regulation and this core obstacle remain essentially what they were when Congress passed the Federal Election Campaign Act of 1971 and extensively revised it in 1974. Congress recognized that the goals of regulation advocates—"leveling the playing field" by equalizing resources available to candidates, reducing the total amount of money in politics, and eliminating the reality or appearance of quid pro quo corruption—could be achieved only through a vast regulatory regime. The post-Watergate reforms attempted to regulate all activity that "influences a federal election" by imposing disclosure requirements, contribution limits on donations to parties and federal candidates, and spending limits on candidates and independent groups.

Even before they were fully implemented, large portions of the 1974 reforms were struck down by the Supreme Court as offensive to the First Amendment. In its landmark *Buckley v. Valeo* decision in 1976, the Supreme Court ruled that restrictions on political giving and spending have the direct effect of limiting core political speech. "The Act's contribution and expenditure limits," the Court held, "operate in an area of the most fundamental First Amendment activities." Since virtually all means of mass communication require money, limits on campaign spending "necessarily" reduce the number of issues discussed and the quality of the debate. The Court found it "beyond dispute" that campaign regulation was motivated at least in part by the desire to limit communication.

*Buckley* made clear that the only governmental interest in campaign finance sufficient to override these First Amendment concerns is the need to prevent "corruption," which the Court defined as the giving of dollars for political favors—essentially bribery. The Court unequivocally rejected efforts to reduce or equalize candidate spending as "wholly foreign" to the First Amendment. *Buckley* also emphasized the critical importance of letting both donors and spenders know what activities are subject to regulation. To provide notice to donors and spenders, the Court crafted the "express-advocacy standard"—that is, only speech that "expressly advocates the election or defeat of a clearly identified candidate" can be regulated.

Specifically, the *Buckley* Court upheld limits on the contributions individuals can make to candidates and parties for express advocacy in federal elections. (Corporations and unions had been barred from making federal political contributions for decades.) The limits—$1,000 in gifts to a candidate each election cycle and $20,000 each year to a political party for federal election activity—were deemed narrowly tailored to serve the compelling government interest of eliminating actual or apparent corruption. Disclosure requirements for giving and spending for express advocacy also withstood challenge.

But perhaps more important is what the Court refused to allow. *Buckley* struck down all efforts to limit the amount candidates, parties, and interest groups can spend.

Since the moment *Buckley* was decided, campaign regulation advocates have attacked it. Common Cause, the Brennan Center for Justice (named, ironically, for the principal author of the *Buckley* opinion), and other proregulation groups unabashedly call for *Buckley* to be overruled. In a case currently pending before the Supreme Court, Senators John McCain and Russell Feingold, joined by other congressional advocates of tighter regulation, have called the constitutional protections elucidated in *Buckley* a "straitjacket" preventing their proposed reforms. They are absolutely right. But it is the reforms that are defective, not the Court's understanding of the First Amendment.

An important by-product of the reforms of the early 1970s is the distinction between "hard" and "soft" money, hard money being money raised subject to the limitations of the Federal Election Campaign Act, soft money being everything else. Under current law, political parties are allowed to accept both soft and hard money, so long as they keep them in separate accounts and do not use soft money for express advocacy. The current wave of reform proposals aims to stamp out soft money—that is, to bring all political party spending under the regulatory net. The central feature of the Shays-Meehan bill, thus, is a ban on the solicitation or acceptance of soft money by national political parties. The bill would allow national parties to accept only fully regulated hard money.

But the Shays-Meehan bill would do much more. It would effectively prohibit preelection political advertising by corporations, unions, and other groups. Under *Buckley*, dozens of courts have rebuffed federal and state efforts to regulate corporate and union advertisements that do not urge the election or defeat of a clearly identified candidate. No problem. The House bill simply redefines express advocacy to encompass any "communication" on radio or television that mentions a candidate within sixty days of an election. Only hard money could be used to fund such advertisements—meaning, in disregard of settled First Amendment law, that corporations, unions, and other interest groups could not fund them. Shays-Meehan, in other words, would make it illegal for Common Cause, which raises all its money outside the Federal Election Campaign Act's restrictions, to pay for a radio advertisement on October 1 in an election year saying "Support the Shays-Meehan Bill." Virtually no one expects this provision to withstand constitutional scrutiny.

But the House bill would impose new restrictions on hard money as well. It would overrule the Supreme Court's 1996 decision in *Colorado Republican Federal Campaign Committee*, under which political parties have a First Amendment right to spend any amount of hard money to advocate the election or defeat of a particular candidate, so long as they do not coordinate that spending with the candidate. The House bill would prohibit such "independent expenditures" favoring a candidate if the political party also engages in any coordinated activity with the candidate—which it always does.

Finally, Shays-Meehan would punish any candidate who spent more than $50,000 of his own money on his campaign by denying him party funds. The Supreme Court held in *Buckley* that a candidate can spend as much of his own money as he likes, since he obviously cannot corrupt himself. Apparently members of Congress, a great many of whom first won election by spending from their personal or family fortunes, are now so secure in their huge fund-raising advantage over challengers that they are willing to impose the $50,000 limit on all who run for office.

Days after the House passed the Shays-Meehan bill, Senators McCain and Feingold introduced a pared-down version in the Senate.

In its present form, the McCain-Feingold legislation would prohibit soft money donations to national political parties and provide some fairly meaningless protection for a small class of workers against use of their union dues for political activities. Commendably, McCain-Feingold abjures many of the offensive features of the House bill. It would not regulate speech by corporations, unions, and other groups; it would not limit independent expenditures by political parties; and it would not bar individuals from financing their own campaigns.

Even without those odious provisions, however, McCain-Feingold flunks the constitutional test. Like the House bill, it would prohibit the Republican and Democratic national committees and their affiliated congressional campaign committees from accepting soft money.

Unable to justify this provision by citing instances of bribery, advocates of the soft money ban must argue that soft money donations create the appearance of corruption. Donors, they say, receive unequal "access" or "influence" in the legislative process. But this argument is specious. The largest soft money donation to the Republican National Committee during the 1998 election cycle was $500,000, a lot of money, to be sure, but only .28 percent of the RNC's total receipts during that cycle. The largest soft money donation to the Democratic National Committee during the same cycle was $250,000, or .21 percent of its receipts. These donations cannot legally be earmarked to aid any specific candidate. Can anyone credibly argue that the RNC or DNC pressures its officeholders to change positions on issues—inevitably alienating other donors—to increase its receipts by a few tenths of a percent?

The tobacco companies, reformers cry, use soft money to buy influence. But during the 1998 cycle, while Congress was considering legislation that would have imposed hundreds of billions of dollars in additional taxes on the tobacco industry, the tobacco companies' donations to Republican Party committees declined by almost 20 percent, from $5,232,789 during the 1996 cycle to $4,225,611. It is lobbying expenditures by tobacco companies that rose, reaching $77,474,400 in the 1998 cycle, eighteen times their soft money donations.

The fact is that special interests rely on lobbying, not soft money donations, to obtain influence. During the 1998 cycle, the top ten corporate soft money donors gave the national parties $12,002,390—and spent $104,176,042 on lobbying. To believe that eliminating soft money donations to political parties would equalize access to legislators is simply naive.

Not only does the soft money ban, then, target a nonexistent problem, it also offends the Constitution in several respects. The Republican and Democratic Parties are national parties. In addition to candidates for federal office, they help candidates for governor, state legislator, and mayor. And when they aid state and local candidates, they must comply with state law. Thirty states currently allow corporate contributions to parties; thirty-seven allow union contributions. Simply put, each of these states has made a sovereign legislative judgment about how campaigns for state office will be financed. Like the House bill, McCain-Feingold would summarily overrule those state judgments. It would impose existing federal contribution limits on national party participation in state and local elections and would create a new federal contribution limit for state political parties. As policy, this is yet another instance of Congress imposing its will on the states. As law, it is an open assault on the Constitution's federal structure and on the powers reserved to the states by the Tenth Amendment.

Finally, the soft money ban would restrict the ability of political parties to engage in pure issue debates—about taxes, health care, gun control, and so on. The Supreme Court made clear in *Buckley* that speakers have an unfettered First Amendment right to discuss issues, using money from any source.

Clearly unconstitutional, a ban on soft money spending by political parties would also be ineffectual: It would simply cause corporations and unions to redirect their soft money resources from donations to parties, which are fully disclosed, to independent issue advertising, which is not. Corporations and unions would remain free to mount blistering attacks on any candidate by name based on his character or voting record. So long as their speech did not expressly advocate the candidate's election or defeat, it would be constitutionally protected.

Senators McCain and Feingold appear to recognize that the restrictions on corporate and union issue speech in the House bill are unconstitutional. They are perfectly willing, however, to place political parties at a severe disadvantage in relation to such special interests. To join the issue debate at all, parties would have to divert their hard money from direct candidate support. The unavoidable effect of a soft money ban for parties would thus be an abridgment of the parties' political speech and a violation of their right to equal protection.

If restricting issue speech by corporations and unions, personal spending by candidates, and independent spending by parties is so clearly offensive to the First Amendment, why do campaign finance reformers keep trying to do it? The short answer is, they have to. Campaign finance regulation that addresses only party and candidate activity is doomed to fail since political donors will inevitably use their resources to engage in independent speech that does not expressly advocate any candidate's election. Such speech is fundamental to our democracy. It encompasses virtually every public policy discussion on the air and in print—and is fully protected by the First Amendment.

The reformers know this. As they recently told the Supreme Court in a brief, the giant free speech "loophole" thwarts all efforts at "meaningful" reform. Why else would reform advocates ranging from House minority leader Dick Gephardt to presidential candidate Bill Bradley advocate amending the Constitution to clear away the First Amendment as an obstacle to increased regulation?

But free speech is not a loophole, it is the oxygen of democracy. Plainly overreaching, the regulatory scheme constructed by the House would certainly fail the test of constitutionality. McCain and Feingold, though intending to be more deferential to the Constitution, would leave open the means of evading their restrictions. Either way, the effort to ban soft money is doomed to fail.

# The Money Chase

Tom Bethell

An earlier version of this article appeared in the *American Spectator*, November 1999, pp. 18–19. Bethell, Washington correspondent for the *American Spectator*, argues that the real hero of campaign finance reform is not Senator John McCain, who reaps continual praise from the press for his stand on this issue, but Senator Mitch McConnell, who has steadfastly opposed it despite continual media criticism and attacks.

Bethell notes that the media has no objections to the limitations on free speech proposed by campaign finance reformers because these limitations do not apply to them.

McConnell, not McCain, is the profile in courage.

The touted advocate of reform, Sen. John McCain of Arizona, isn't really very interested in the details of comparing finance law. But he's good at having it both ways: complaining about the money in the system, even as he milks the contributions that flow to his presidential campaign as a result of his chairmanship of the Senate Commerce Committee, receiving (with Sen. Russell Feingold of Wisconsin), the $25,000 JFK "Profile in Courage Award" for sponsoring reform legislation, even as he rides the wave of media support for doing so. One close observer on Capitol Hill said: McCain doesn't know the law, he doesn't know the jurisprudence, he doesn't know what's in his own bill. But there's one thing he does know. The issue is a top concern of the *New York Times* and the *Washington Post*.

In September, the Shays-Meehan Bipartisan Campaign Reform Act passed the House by a vote of 252-177. It included a ban on unregulated contributions to political parties and severe restrictions on radio and television issue advertising by private groups for two months before elections. The ACLU rightly objects as follows: "Members of Congress need only wait until the last 60 days before an election (as they often do now) to vote for legislation or engage in controversial behavior so that their actions are beyond the reach of public comment and, therefore, effectively immune from citizen criticism."

When the bill was introduced in the Senate, this filibuster-attracting restriction was dropped. No surprise here. McCain has been stripping down his own reform measure for some time. In 1997 he removed a proposed ban on PACs (supported by 86 senators in 1993), and he also removed the limits on overall spending by politicians. "Everything is negotiable," he would tell Senate colleagues. Yet he continues to be praised as a man of principle. The reformers' plan is to reintroduce the advertising restrictions by amendment on the Senate floor.

Campaign finance laws are abridgments of political speech—the kind of speech that the First Amendment was above all meant to protect. Now, reformers want even more restrictions. We should all be grateful to Sen. Mitch McConnell of Kentucky for opposing them so resolutely. It is he who has shown the profile in courage. His twelve-year stand on the issue has brought him a stream of criticism from brain-dead editorial writers in the *Louisville Courier-Journal* and the *Lexington Herald-Leader*, not to mention weekly attacks by the *New York Times*. McConnell, fifty-seven, is an unusual figure, a professional politician who understands the Constitution and is not afraid of the media. And he has mastered the complexities of campaign finance law.

His greatest victory came in the fall of 1994, with the Democrats still in control of Congress and President Clinton poised to sign the legislation. McConnell successfully filibustered the appointment of conferees to reconcile different versions of a bill that would have seriously undermined the GOP's ability to compete with union-supported Democrats. Since then, campaign finance reform keeps coming back. It has been defeated mainly thanks to McConnell's efforts and to the Senate rule that sixty votes are needed to cut off debate.

Campaign finance laws are the equivalent of price controls on politics. In their effects they resemble New York City's rent-control laws. They make life more difficult for everyone—except the very rich. They tend to protect incumbents. Perversely, money has become more important, not less. That is not what Common Cause had in mind when it promoted the Federal Election Campaign Act of 1971. This law and its amendments fill a 142-page volume—a paradise for lawyers and a headache for politicians. With the $1,000 limit on an individual's contribution to a candidate unadjusted for inflation since 1974, candidates must now spend an inordinate amount of time seeking campaign funds—the Money Chase.

"This is what we talk about in the cloakrooms, this is what we talk about at our lunches," says former senator Dan Coats of Indiana. "This is what we talk about down in the gym and when we have our private moments—this ever-escalating demand on our time to raise these funds." Many others say the same thing, especially when they retire. Sen. Frank Lautenberg of New Jersey is only the most recent. Behind his decision to retire was "the searing reality that I would have had to spend half of every day between now and the next election fund-raising."

With contribution limits locked in place for a quarter of a century, the population expanding, and the federal government hunting as always for new ways to regulate our lives, the money began flowing into unregulated channels. The Supreme Court had said in 1976 that money that did not expressly advocate voting for or against identified candidates was protected by the First Amendment. These money outlets (to political parties) are what the reformers now want to block. Forever denying the existence of unintended consequences, reformers assume that, when their plans go awry, more regulations are needed.

To the extent that there is a problem, it was caused by the money limits. The cost of a serious campaign has risen by a factor of ten since 1974. Even David Broder of the *Washington Post* has called for an increase in the $1,000 limit, which would "reduce the number of phone calls a candidate has to make." Rep. Chris Sahys of Connecticut and Sen. McCain have made the same argument. Yet neither proposed such an increase in their bills. The reason is that Democrats are bitterly opposed to it, as are Common Cause and whiskey heiress Ellen Miller's Public Campaign (supported by George Soros).

The reality is that both Shays, a McGovern supporter in 1972, and McCain have used their nominal Republican affiliation to lend a bipartisan aura to what is in effect Democratic legislation. The latest reform measure would prevent the GOP from using "soft money" to overcome the built-in advantage that compulsory trade union dues and get-out-the-vote efforts have given the Democrats. A partisan bill has been dressed up as a good government measure.

Conventional wisdom says that "obscene" amounts of cash are flowing into politics. The *Washington Post* says it repeatedly—without evidence. When Bill Bradley claims that there is "way too much money in politics," the press corps nods complacently. The very opposite is the truth. In the latest election cycle, $675 million was spent contesting House and Senate seats. With 196 million eligible votes, this is less than $4 a head, or, as Sen. McConnell likes to say, less than the price of a McDonald's extra value meal. In the presidential election year of 1996, *The Economist* wrote, "spending on political ads amounted to only one percent of all television advertising." Yet Congress disposes of more than 20 percent of GDP. Meanwhile, $8 billion a year is spent on pornography. The *Washington Post* has misplaced the obscenity.

In the 1998 Senate races, Senator Chris Dodd of Connecticut said, "Wining candidates raised a total of $161 million for an average cost of just under $5 million." He thought that was too much. But the Congress spends about $1.7 trillion a year, and a senator will be in office for six years. Thus $5 million "buys" a one-hundredth share of control over the disposition of about ten trillion dollars. Divide through by a million to make these figures more meaningful, and we see that five dollars gives you a one-hundredth share of control over $10 million. If only people realized how much of their money Congress disposes of every year, they would rationally spend a great deal more than they do now to gain control over the massive redistributions that take place in Washington. According to Rep. Kevin Brady of Texas, the average cost of competitive campaign for a House seat "is just a little less than a million dollars." (Thus a House seat is somewhat more expensive because it buys a smaller share and for only two years.)

Why do the news media so eagerly support this assault on political speech? The First Amendment, one thought, was the part of the Constitution they took seriously. Think again. When Sen. Ernest Hollings tried an end run around the Supreme Court in 1997 with a constitutional amendment that would have gutted the First Amendment by giving Congress the power to regulate "the amount of expenditures that may be made by, in support of, or in opposition to, a candidate," there was not a peep from the media. The resolution received thirty-eight votes in the Senate (Sens. Cochran, Jeffords, Roth, and Specter voting aye on the GOP side).

The key to understanding the media's position is their exemption from the law. The term "expenditure" does not include "any news story, commentary or editorial distributed through the facilities of any broadcasting station, newspaper, magazine or other periodical publication, unless such facilities are owned or controlled by any political party, political committee or candidate." A McConnell staffer notes that if the Republican Committee bought NBC, the Federal Election Commission would regulate the evening news and that, under Shays-Meehan, "Tom Brokaw could not mention a candidate's name within sixty days of a general election." The new law would increase the media's power by restricting alternative sources of information. Conservative publications, incidentally, would qualify for the media exemption and might even be flooded with political advertising for two months of the year. That indeed would be a consequence unintended by Common Cause.

Campaign finance reformers are usually portrayed as virtuous seekers after the public interest. The truth is that they are imbued with a profound cynicism. They assume that legislators can be bought with campaign donations that exceed $1,000. Sen. Coats drew attention to the canard of corruption when he testified last March: "Most of us couldn't even go through [contributor lists] and identify exactly who gave what, we are so busy trying to do all that we need to do." Candidates may say, "What is our total? How much do we have?" But they don't examine lists. Sen. McConnell says that although he was chairman of the Ethics Committee for four years, "we never got a single complaint on that issue." He repeatedly urged colleagues who used the corruption argument to give him an example. But he "never got one in ten years of handling that debate."

Notice the undisguised cynicism of Max Frankel, former executive editor of the *New York Times*. In a recent column, he referred to campaign contributions as "bribes that must eventually be repaid with political favor and privilege." He should contact the news desk of his own newspaper with the evidence for this. It would be a front page story. John Lott of Yale Law School points out that if contributions cause politicians to vote in opposition to their own preferences, they should behave differently in their last term, when the loss of future contributions is irrelevant. But his research found no relationship between the reduction in campaign expenditures in politicians' final terms and how they voted. In fact, voting tends to remain stable over an entire career.

Yet McCain says: "The level of cynicism about elected representatives is growing quickly and could lead to alienation. It's gotten to the point where most people figure, 'Look, there's nothing we can do about it. These groups are beholden to special interests and they won't change a lucrative system that keeps them in office.'" He stirs up the pot of cynicism and then says how badly it smells.

In October 1999, the McCain-Feingold measure received fifty-five votes in the Senate, and was once again defeated by a McConnell-led filibuster. But a McConnell staffer on the Senate Rules Committee predicted that campaign finance reform will soon return to the legislative calendar, perhaps in the year 2000.

# Campaign Finance Restrictions Violate the Constitution

## Floyd Abrams

This selection first appeared in the *Wall Street Journal*, April 9, 1998, p. A22. In this op-ed Abrams, a partner in the law firm of Cahill Gordon & Reindel and a contributor to Democrats and the Democratic Party, argues that the free speech guaranteed by the First Amendment is more important than whatever problems (for example, the influence of wealthy contributors) might go with it.

Toward the end of the 1992 presidential campaign, I had "maxed out" in my contributions to the Clinton campaign. A thousand dollars for the primaries, another thousand for the general election, and I had given all that the law allows. So I was surprised to receive a call asking me if I would make an additional contribution to the Democratic National Committee.

Thus did I learn the difference between "hard" money and "soft"— that is, between money to be spent on a political campaign (which could only be given in limited amounts) and money dedicated to building one's political party (which was unlimited). And thus did I learn the lack of difference between the two.

It is understandable that proponents of campaign finance reform in Congress would seek to close the "loophole" through which my solicitor was seeking to move my money. It is more than understandable that they would seek to limit how much soft money individuals or political action committees may give. And it is perfectly understandable that they would object to corporations and unions giving soft money and thus effectively circumventing the laws that prevent them from giving hard money.

All these efforts make a kind of sense, but the legislation aimed at campaign finance reform that was defeated last month in the Senate, and last week failed even to reach the House floor, was at war with freedom of speech.

Return with me for a moment to First Amendment principles—to one of the few principles upon which individuals ranging from Robert Bork to Laurence Tribe agree. It is that political speech is at the apex of First Amendment protection. Was I not engaged in political speech when I contributed to the DNC? And when I contributed to the Clinton campaign itself?

Proponents of campaign finance reform argue that the speech I was engaging in by contributing money was dangerous in the sense that too much of it from too few people could result in wealthier contributors skewing the political system in their favor. That is not a ridiculous argument. But it should not lead to restrictions on speech in the service of "protecting" people who have less money. That would strike at the heart of the First Amendment. The Supreme Court recognized as much in *Buckley v. Valeo* (1976). The court held unconstitutional limits on expenditures that Congress had adopted in the aftermath of Watergate. "The concept that government may restrict the speech of some elements in our society in order to enhance the relative voice of others is wholly foreign to the First Amendment," Justice William Brennan wrote for the court.

But while the ruling barred restrictions on campaign spending, it permitted restrictions on contributions to a campaign. The former, the Court said, jeopardized speech more directly, since expenditures were tantamount to speech itself; the latter merely associated the contributor with speech with which the contributor agreed. And contributions (unlike expenditures) were said to raise more directly the specter of corruption.

Result: Steve Forbes and Ross Perot can spend all they want of their own money on their campaigns. But if my political tastes had led me to wish to contribute to their campaigns, I would have been limited to $1,000 per campaign—or could have made unlimited contributions to the political entities Messrs. Forbes and Perot created to tout their candidates.

It's an odd result, not least because the First Amendment distinction between expenditures and contributions is so intellectually shaky. Most of the opposition to having distinct First Amendment rules for the two categories has come from people and groups that wish to limit both political spending and political contributions. But increasing intellectual firepower has come from people who have concluded that the First Amendment does not allow restrictions on either.

Last summer, Justice Clarence Thomas issued a powerful dissenting opinion rejecting the distinction altogether. "Whether an individual donates money to a candidate or group who will use it to promote the candidate or whether the individual spends the money to promote the candidate himself," Justice Thomas wrote, "the individual seeks to engage in political expression and to associate with like-minded persons. A contribution is simply an indirect expenditure."

Kathleen Sullivan of Stanford Law School is one of an increasingly vocal group of scholars who believe that the First Amendment bars limitations on either expenditures or contributions. To share their views, as I do, is not to doom us to a system in which the views of wealthier interests will always rule. Not, at least, if the public knows who is contributing to whom. Ms. Sullivan has thus proposed that limits on spending and contributions be abandoned so long as "the identity of contributors [is] required to be vigorously and frequently reported." House Speaker Newt Gingrich has taken the same approach.

It is certainly an approach that is consistent with deeply rooted First Amendment principles. If we trust people to make sound judgments when properly informed of the facts, why not seek to assure that there is more speech *and* more information about political candidates?

None of this is fanciful. It is not at all clear that Bob Dole profited more from the contributions of tobacco companies than President Clinton did from criticizing Mr. Dole for taking the money. The same may be true of the National Rifle Association, the American Civil Liberties Union, and other advocacy groups.

First Amendment principles should guide whatever legislative solution we choose. The first principle is that it is not for Congress to decide that political speech is some sort of disease that we must quarantine.

# The King's Protection

Meg Greenfield

This selection first appeared in *Newsweek*, January 12, 1998, p. 72. In this article Greenfield argues that campaign contributions are tribute that attempts to buy safe passage, not bribes. Campaign contributions have grown, in her view, because the powers held by government officials have grown.

Much of 1997 in Washington was spent looking for the elusive *quo*, as in *quid pro quo*, and meaning the payoff. What did all those industries and individuals get or expect to get in return for their hefty campaign contributions to incumbents in both parties? Why, both at home and abroad, did they respond with such alacrity and largesse to the big shots' solicitations? As usual, the search for evidence of specific rewards for the money has been largely unavailing, as has been true in many political bribery criminal cases for years. There have been a few demonstrable examples of particular official favors granted directly for money. But, to the frustration of prosecutors and investigators and media sleuths, there have not been very many—and surely not in numbers commensurate with the widespread suspicions and charges. This is taken as vindication, as evidence of innocence by whichever party is being charged. "You can't prove," they say, "that Old Moneybags got *anything* from the Republican Congress or the Democratic White House in return for his gargantuan contributions to both."

And in this they are, most of the time, right. But they are right because the investigators and accusers so often have a skewed idea of the "system" they deplore and are looking for the wrong thing—a single, identifiable payoff such as one-shot legislative relief of a problem or a personal tax break or something like that, which was given in undeniable return for the money.

If the pervasiveness of the enormous campaign donations by single industries and individuals to incumbents of both parties should tell us anything, however, it is that we are not dealing with a system of old-fashioned bribes here. We are dealing with something else: what has been familiar since ancient times as a tributary system. Those who pay tribute are (or believe they are) buying the right to function as they wish, to be left alone, not to be set upon by those with official power to harm them, a right to be treated with special consideration, to be allowed to cross the king's terrain in peace. They are under the king's protection and marauders and bandits thwart them at their own peril.

In antiquity and also in medieval times this idea was well understood. The patronage and high regard of the potentate were invaluable coin, as useful to commerce as they could be essential to personal security. It struck me as oddly provincial last year, when people were expressing doubts that all those foreigners would pay so much for nothing more than a photograph with the president, that one response was that we didn't understand the importance closeness to the leader had in their cultures. Surely from our own mob protection rackets to the influence-peddling claimers of close association with the powerful to the profit-seeking publicity hound who also benefits from *seeming* to be in special favor with the leader, Americans have not been slow to understand the return they get for the tribute they pay. At the local level in old-style, big-city party patronage politics nothing was more dearly understood. Likewise in gang turf struggles and other unsavory enterprises with which we are familiar. It is security at a price.

Yes, it is true that in the campaign-funding world, the benefits are sometimes identifiable and concrete and that many more of them than we know have always been tucked into obscure legislation and bureaucratic rulings, to become apparent only when, by accident or snitching, one of them drops out. And even if you cannot prove the causal connection between the money given and the business break received or political position changed—and many such pairings have been uncovered—that does not mean there was no causal connection. But even without them our newly enlarged and all-encompassing bipartisan tributary system would continue to exist and flourish. People would persist in trying to buy goodwill or at least an environment that is not hostile from those with the power to grant them.

But, you say, we don't have a king. And you are right. Between the White House and the Congress and all the agencies under their control as incumbents, we have many kings who can grant or deny you safe passage. Campaign contributions in our tributary system are meant to propitiate them all and to discourage attack by those who are beholden to or afraid of them. They do not, of course, have monarchical power. But the reason this particular campaign-contribution form of tribute has burgeoned in recent years is that their powers have grown enormously. Over the past two decades, starting roughly with enactment of the Great Society legislation, the federal government has acquired an ever more expansive role in the affairs of business, industry, professions, and institutions than it began to have before. Its power in these realms is neither monolithic nor unchecked. But it is surely large and potentially very consequential to most of those who make the huge donations.

As in most such systems, the receivers of the tribute are hardly passive or unaware participants in the transactions. They may pretend not to understand how the system works, but they do. And they also, as we know, do their best to see that everyone ponies up the price of safe passage. I know there are other reasons that the size of campaign contributions has increased so much. And I know there are vast numbers of people who give (much more modestly usually) on the basis of wanting to see the party representing their political views prevail. But there is something else at the core of the outpouring of huge sums of money into the parties' coffers from all around the world these days. The Republicans who are beneficiaries of the money have, oddly, left it out of their familiar complaint about the way-too-big size of the federal government. So have the Democrats, whose leader, Bill Clinton, said in 1996 that "the era of big government is over." Not even close. You will know that the era of big government is over in Washington when the campaign-financing tributary system has closed down, and people are no longer proffering their checks with the message, less traditionally defiant than newly defensive, "Don't tread on me—please."

# Making Pols into Crooks

## Robert J. Samuelson

This selection first appeared in *Newsweek*, October 6, 1997. Samuelson's view is that the campaign finance laws are so "arbitrary and complex," and the restrictions so unrealistic, that they make criminals out of virtually all politicians and thus promote public cynicism. He argues that genuine reform of the campaign finance system would mean abandoning limits on contributions but enacting tougher disclosure laws, as Representative John Doolittle recommends.

The prospect that an independent counsel will be named to investigate the alleged campaign-law violations of President Bill Clinton and Vice President Al Gore exposes a central contradiction of "campaign finance reform." The "reformers" claim they're trying to lower public cynicism by cleansing politics of the evils of money. Actually, they're doing the opposite: by putting so many unrealistic restrictions on legitimate political activity, the "reformers" ensure that more people—politicians, campaign workers, advocacy groups—will run afoul of the prohibitions. Public cynicism rises as politics is criminalized.

The distasteful reality is that politics requires money. To compete, candidates must communicate; and to communicate, they need cash. Someone has to pay for all the ads, direct mail, and polls. There is no easy way to curb the role of money in politics without curbing free expression. If I favor larger (smaller) government, I should be able to support like-minded candidates by helping them win. Campaign "reformers"—who would like to replace private contributions with public subsidies and impose strict spending limits—reject this basic principle.

Money, they say, is corrupting politics. It isn't. Campaign spending isn't out of control or outlandish. In the 1996 election, campaign spending at all levels totaled $4 billion, says political scientist Herbert Alexander of the Citizens' Research Foundation. That was one-twentieth of 1 percent of the gross domestic product (GDP) of $7.6 trillion. Americans spend about $20 billion a year on laundry and dry cleaning. Is the price of politics really too steep?

Nor have contributions hijacked legislation. Consider the tax code. It's perforated with tax breaks, many undesirable. Some tax breaks benefit wealthy constituents who sweetened their lobbying with generous campaign contributions. But the largest tax breaks stem mostly from politicians' desire to pander to masses of voters. In the 1997 tax bill, Clinton and Congress provided huge tax breaks for college tuition. Does anyone think these passed because Harvard's president is a big contributor?

The media coverage and congressional hearings of today's alleged campaign-finance "abuses" have, of course, revealed the frenzied and demeaning efforts of politicians of both parties to raise money. But there hasn't been much evidence of serious influence buying. The worst we've heard is of President Clinton's, in effect, subletting the Lincoln Bedroom to big contributors and of businessman Roger Tamraz's giving $300,000 to Democrats in the hope of winning government support for an oil pipeline. All Tamraz got was a brief chat with Clinton and no blessing for the project. This sort of preferential "access" isn't dangerous.

More menacing are all the artificial limits that "reformers" have imposed on political expression. What's been created is a baffling maze of election laws and rules that, once codified, establish new types of criminal or quasi-criminal behavior. Anyone tiptoeing around the rules is said to be "skirting the law." And there are violations. In the futile effort to regulate politics, the "reformers" have manufactured most of the immorality, illegality, and cynicism they deplore.

Today's "abuses" stem mostly from the 1974 "reforms" enacted after Watergate. Congress then limited the amount individuals could give a candidate to $1,000 per election; total giving to all candidates (directly, through parties or committees) was limited to $25,000 a year. What happened? The limits inspired evasions. Suppressing contributions to candidates encouraged new political-action committees. People give to

PACs, which give to candidates. In 1974, there were 608 PACs; now there are nearly 4,000.

Another evasion is "independent spending": groups (the Supreme Court says) can promote a candidate by themselves if they don't "co-ordinate" with a candidate. The present evasion of concern is "soft money": contributions to parties for "party-building" activities like voter registration. Soft money contributions have no limits; so Tamraz could give $300,000. But soft money can also be used for general TV ads that mention candidates as long as they don't use such words as "vote for." Does any of this make sense? Not really. Ordinary people can't grasp all the obscure, illogical distinctions.

No matter. The failure of past "reforms" is no barrier to future "reforms." The latest effort is the McCain-Feingold bill now before the Senate. Named after its sponsors (Republican John McCain of Arizona and Democrat Russell Feingold of Wisconsin), it would outlaw soft money and try to ban "issue advocacy" ads in the sixty days before an election. (*Issue advocacy* ads favor or oppose candidates; the distinction between them and "independent spending" cannot briefly be explained.) Most of the bill flouts the spirit, if not the letter, of the First Amendment: "Congress shall make no law . . . abridging the freedom of speech . . . ; or the right of the people peaceably to assemble, and to petition the Government for a redress of grievances."

The connection between campaign "reform" and the Clinton-Gore predicament has emerged, ironically, in the complaints of some "reformers" that the president and vice president are being unfairly targeted. In the *Washington Post*, Elizabeth Drew says that Gore behaved like a "klutz," but that "klutziness isn't a federal crime." The 1883 law that he and the president may have violated (soliciting contributions from federal property), argues Drew, aimed to protect civil servants from being shaken down by politicians. In the *New York Times*, former deputy attorney general Philip Heymann says the campaign against Gore aims only to "destroy the Democratic front runner for president."

All this is true. But it misses the larger point: the campaign finance laws are so arbitrary and complex that they invite "criminality" or its appearance. Bad laws should be discarded. Rep. John Doolittle of California sensibly suggests abandoning all contribution limits and enacting tougher disclosure laws. The best defense against the undue influence of money is to let candidates raise it from as many sources as possible—and to let the public see who's giving. That would be genuine reform.

# Shut Up, They Explained

## David Frum

This selection first appeared in the *Weekly Standard*, November 17, 1997, pp. 18–19. Frum's point in this article is that so-called campaign finance reform is an effort by politicians to limit criticism from the public. Frum looks at the effect in Canada of a law similar to the provisions of McCain-Feingold in limiting the amount of money individuals can spend to express their own views, concludes that the system allows political parties the right to speak but limits the ability of private citizens to speak out, calling them "third-party intervenors." This article is reprinted with permission of the *Weekly Standard*. For information on subscribing to the *Weekly Standard*, please call 1-800-283-2014 or visit the website http://www.weeklystandard.com.

If you were a politician and wanted to enact a law forbidding private citizens to criticize you, what would you call it? If you possessed any flair for publicity at all, you'd do what nearly half the Senate and almost all of the media have done: You'd call it "campaign finance reform." Proponents of campaign finance reform nearly always declare that they're trying to protect ordinary citizens from the dangerous influence of Big Money in politics. But it would be closer to the truth to say that they're trying to protect ordinary citizens from the even more dangerous influence of ordinary citizens in politics. The campaign finance legislation now temporarily blocked in the Senate—the so-called McCain-Feingold bill—imposes startling new restrictions on the right of private citizens to speak up during an election.

Defenders of campaign finance reform justify these restrictions by promising voters that government supervision of political speech will result in a healthier democracy. The National Right to Life Committee—one of the organizations that would be shut up by McCain-Feingold—observed a remarkable bit of reasoning by a prominent advocate of campaign finance reform, Burt Neuborne, legal director of the Brennan Center for Justice.

At a February 27 hearing before the Constitution subcommittee of the House Judiciary Committee, Neuborne commended the panel's chairman, Charles Canady of Florida, "for the disciplined way the hearing has been run, and how carefully you maintained the ground rules that allowed real free speech to come out here. And I'm really saying that the same idea has to be thought of in the electoral process. . . . In a courtroom, speech is controlled. In this room, speech is controlled, and the net result is good speech."

Is it really? If you look just across the border, you'll see a version of McCain-Feingold in operation in Canada. (Canada is to American liberalism what Cuba is to the American automobile industry: a place where broken-down old jalopies are kept running decades after they should have been scrapped.) Is it promoting free speech and democracy?

Consider the case of Gary Nixon of British Columbia. In the summer of 1996, the socialist government of British Columbia called an election. It argued it deserved to be returned to office because it had balanced the province's budget without harsh cuts in social services. Mr. Nixon, a civic-minded accountant, believed that the government was fudging its figures. He dug into his own pocket and paid $6,300 Canadian (about $4,500) for a series of small newspaper and local radio ads denouncing the province's budget as a sham.

The socialists won the election. But it turned out that Mr. Nixon had been right: The province was running a big deficit, and the government *had* been manipulating the numbers to get itself reelected. Unfortunately being right has not done him any good. The chief electoral officer of the province has hit him with a $13,000 fine—without trial— for violating the campaign finance law by speaking up. He got off lightly. A British Columbian advocacy group, the B.C. Fisheries Survival Coalition, bought ads in the same election accusing the socialist government of mismanaging the province's fish stocks. They have been hit, again without a trial, with a $220,000 Canadian fine.

By Canadian standards, British Columbia runs a fairly tolerant regime. Private citizens are allowed to spend up to $5,000 Canadian of their own money to express themselves during a campaign. That pays for a few minutes of radio or a few square inches of newspaper. In the province of Quebec, by contrast, citizen speech has been virtually outlawed: Until the Canadian Supreme Court struck down Quebec's law in October, Quebeckers were permitted to spend no more than $600. What that meant was that Quebeckers dissatisfied with the left-leaning policies of the province's two main parties were forbidden to use any technological device invented after 1400 to communicate their unhappiness with the choices on offer: no newspaper ads, no radio, no television, no meeting halls large enough to require a microphone, no web pages, pretty much nothing except quiet muttering over the back fence.

The Canadian federal government has been attempting to impose a gag law like British Columbia's and Quebec's since 1983, with the support of the three old-line parties: the Liberals, the Conservatives, and the Socialists. It's lost twice in the intermediate-level courts, but the Supreme Court decision that struck down Quebec's $600 limit indicated pretty strongly that a slightly higher limit—the court proposed the figure of $1,000—would be constitutional for both federal and provincial governments. For politicians who believe, with Neuborne and senators McCain and Feingold, that controlled speech is good speech, it was a welcome green light.

Canadian governments so disdain the right of private citizens to have a say in the elections that choose their rulers that they have invented a marvelous phrase for those who try. The law calls them "third-party intervenors." The political parties, you see, are the principals. Private citizens who try to have an influence on their own with any device more sophisticated than a graffiti spraycan or a sandwich board are interlopers, "third parties," meddling where they do not belong. This is the path down which American campaign reformers would take the United States—a path toward a two-class political system. At the top would be the politicians and the media, who may say whatever they please. At the bottom would be everyone else, whose rights to comment on their electoral choices would be regulated and circumscribed.

Over the years, the right of free speech has taken on a strange and even rococo shape in the United States. But at the very same time that it has been twisted and stretched to cover activities that are only remotely speech-like, its core value—the right of citizens to make their voices heard when it's time to decide who will govern them—has come under assault. What kind of free speech right can be understood as guaranteeing government money for smearing your naked body with chocolate on stage, but not your right to take out an ad in the newspaper saying "Joe Smith says he loves the environment but he voted to pave Yellowstone"?

The senators who support McCain-Feingold profess to care about free speech. They say they are protecting it. But the law they've written frankly jettisons the right to speak during an election, in order to make workable the law's otherwise ramshackle and futile latticework of restrictions, regulations, and general bossiness. If McCain-Feingold should ever pass, the right of Americans to speak their minds about the governance of their country, a bedrock right if there ever was one, will depend on the forbearance and good sense of the regulators of electoral speech. And as Gary Nixon can tell you, that's not a position the citizens of a democracy should ever find themselves in.

# Campaign Solution:
# Lift All Contribution Limits

### George F. Will

This selection first appared in the *Washington Post*, April 3, 1997. Will supports ending restrictions on campaign expenditures and contributions as a simple and radical reform consistent with the First Amendment. In this op-ed he makes the point that attempting to control hard money (that given directly to candidates) requires controlling soft money (that given to parties for party-building activities), which in turn requires that spending by independent groups on issue advocacy also be controlled.

Agreeable and unsurprising reports indicate the campaign to inflame the public against the First Amendment is faltering. The debate about campaign financing may yet move in Rep. John Doolittle's direction. But before that desirable eventuality there may be a disagreeable and unsurprising attempt by "progressives" to circumvent democratic processes that their preferred reforms are supposed to perfect.

The campaign, which recently limped from Boston to Philadelphia, aims to gather, by July 4, 1,776,000 (get it?) signatures in support of the McCain-Feingold bill. The First Amendment says "Congress shall make no law . . . abridging the freedom of speech." McCain-Feingold says stuff like:

> If a disbursement aggregating $10,000 or more for any general public communication is made prior to thirty days before a primary election or prior to sixty days before a general election, it shall be considered express advocacy if a reasonable person would understand it as advocating the election or defeat of a clearly identified candidate and if the communication is made with the objective of advocating the defeat of a candidate as shown by one or more factors including a statement or action by the person making the communication, the targeting or placement of the communication, or the use by the person making the communication of

polling or other similar data relating to the candidate's campaign or election.


People staying away in droves from McCain-Feingold rallies may find that unlyrical. It is a sample of what Jonathan Rauch, writing in *National Journal*, calls "the gobbledygook that interposes gibbering hordes of lawyers and bureaucrats between politicians and voters." And it is the result of redoubling a bet on a lame horse.

The horse is the regulation—rationing, really—of campaign giving and spending, meaning political expression. Rauch notes that since the crusade to legislate political hygiene and equity began in 1974, congressional campaign spending has tripled and so has the financial advantage of House incumbents over their challengers. You would almost suspect that incumbents wrote the rationing laws. As Rauch says, "Participatory spending in politics is not a problem and should not be 'solved.'"

Former Sen. Bill Bradley, an ardent speech rationer, says money in politics is like ants in a kitchen: "You have to block all the holes or some of them are going to find a way in." Rauch responds, "But politics, unlike your kitchen, is designed to be permeable."

Deny that, and you must build an increasingly baroque system of speech regulation: To make controls on hard money (given directly to candidates) meaningful, you must control soft money (given to parties for "party building"), and to make soft money controls meaningful you must regulate political and issue advocacy by interest groups.

Soft money is today's target for speech rationers, and President Clinton reportedly wants the rationing bureaucracy, the Federal Election Commission, to ban soft money without waiting for legislation. Naturally. For decades now, the "progressive" agenda (legalizing pornography and abortion on demand, banning school prayer, busing for racial balance, attacking capital punishment, and on and on) has been advanced more by judicial or executive fiats than by persuasion.

The *New York Times* likes Clinton's idea for the FEC to preempt Congress. The media generally like reforms that enlarge the media's unregulated portion of all political expression. Time flies. Time was when Justice William O. Douglas was one of the *Times*'s judicial pinups. He said: "It usually costs money to communicate an idea to a large audience. But no one would seriously contend that a limitation on the expenditure of money to print a newspaper would not deprive the publisher of freedom of the press. Nor can the fact that it costs money to make a speech—whether it be hiring a hall or purchasing time on the air—make the speech any the less an exercise of First Amendment rights."

Rep. Doolittle (R-Calif.) has eighteen cosponsors for H.R. 965, which would end taxpayer financing of presidential campaigns (Jefferson: "To compel a man to furnish contributions for the propagation of opinions which he disbelieves and abhors is sinful and tyrannical"); would repeal all limits on contributing to candidates for federal offices; and would require full disclosure of contributions within twenty-four hours and prompt posting of them on the Internet. This is simple and radical, like the First Amendment.

# Let the Sun Shine In

## Charles Krauthammer

This selection first appeared in the *Washington Post*, October 17, 1997, p. A29. Krauthammer argues that the changes proposed by the McCain-Feingold legislation—banning soft money—would weaken political parties and limit the political speech of individuals while strengthening the position of the media. He too sees deregulation with full disclosure as the solution to the dilemma created by the fact that political speech is precious and protected by the First Amendment, but political money can be a means of political influence and even corruption. He suggests not only disclosure of contributions but also disclosure of access granted to donors.

The conventional view of the failure of campaign finance reform in the 105th Congress is that politicians are too corrupt and cynical to reform the system. Now, politicians may be corrupt and cynical, but that is not why campaign reform failed.

It failed because campaign reform is confronted with two self-evident yet contradictory propositions:

1. Supporting a political campaign is a way of advancing one's political ideas. For those who don't own a printing press or TV station (or write a syndicated column), campaign contributions are an indispensable form of political speech. And political speech is protected by the First Amendment.

2. On the other hand, political money can very obviously also be an instrument of political corruption.

How to eliminate corruption without curtailing political speech? It cannot be done. The most famous attempt to regulate a squaring of the circle—the 1974 post-Watergate reforms—has proved a spectacular failure: loophole-ridden, massively violated, and now the source of the biggest fund-raising scandal since Watergate.

The 1974 campaign reforms proved pernicious because their individual contribution limit forced politicians to spend their entire waking lives on the phone raising money in little bits. Apart from turning them into full-time hustlers, it spawned another unintended consequence: a whole cohort of rich people who, essentially exempt from the campaign laws, can write their own ticket. Ross Perot and Steve Forbes and a Senate of thirty-nine millionaires are the direct legacy of the 1974 reforms.

McCain-Feingold—dead for now but it will rise again—was supposed to fix the old reform. As Jonathan Rauch has pointed out, however, its main effect would be to weaken political parties—it bans "soft money" contributions to them—and curtail the political speech of individuals.

Unintentionally—these reforms are prodigious producers of unintended effects—McCain-Feingold serves as a media-incumbency preservation act. Current owners of newspapers and electronic media can support or savage any candidate they want right up to election day. But you are legally barred from taking out an ad in your local newspaper sixty days before an election to support a candidate. McCain-Feingold then creates a whole new set of regulations that expand the notion of what kinds of political activity count as campaign contributions—and are thus subject to regulation.

McCain-Feingold has the added distinction of combining this obvious unconstitutionality with a cosmic naivete. Its premise is that by regulation, such as banning soft money, it can take money out of politics.

Politics is power. And late-twentieth-century government, which eats up one-third of gross domestic product and then doles it out, is the seat of power. If Willie Sutton were around today, he'd be breaking into government, not banks.

Under McCain-Feingold, money meant to influence government won't dry up. It simply will be redirected away from political parties. It will find its way into lobbies. It will find its way into corporate and union and "independent" advocacy groups. They will spend the political money and end up controlling political speech. The net effect of Mc-Cain-Feingold will be not on money but on the parties—already weak but desperately needed in a far-flung democracy such as ours to harmonize and mediate between narrow interests. Under McCain-Feingold, the narrow interests, flush with money, will be king.

There is an obvious alternative to this futile regulation of speech: deregulation. Abandon the baroque '74 reforms and all attempts to fix them with even more baroque reforms. Let people give whatever they want to whomever they want. But demand full disclosure.

Now, in most proposals this means only disclosing how much money a Roger Tamraz gives to a president or a party or a campaign. But why not require a second form of disclosure? Not just the quid but the quo: A public accounting of the access granted the donor by the donee.

Just a listing. Let the people draw their own conclusions about favors and corruption. Thus disclose that Roger Tamraz gave the Democrats $300,000 in the '96 campaign and disclose that the campaign gave Tamraz so many meetings (with and without coffee) and so many phone calls with the president or the vice president or other high administration officials.

You cannot reconcile the two aspects of political money—speech and corruption—by such Rube Goldberg confections as McCain-Feingold. They can be reconciled only by a system of transparency. Full disclosure squares the circle: no curtailment of speech, but a bright light shone on money meant for corruption.

# Campaign Finance Reforms Don't Work

## Dane Strother

This selection first appeared in the *New York Times*, February 1, 1997, p. 17. Copyright © 1997 by the New York Times Co. Reprinted by permission. Strother, a Democratic political consultant, argues that limiting the spending of candidates for public office increases the influence of special interest groups. Strother favors increased disclosure and raising the amounts that can be contributed to campaigns by individuals and political action committees.

As good-government groups display indignation that would make a Southern revival preacher proud, Congress is nearly hysterical about reforming campaign finance laws, regardless of the consequences. If lawmakers are not careful, they may get what they're asking for.

Limiting candidates' spending usually succeeds only in giving special interests even more clout. Consider recent "reform" efforts in Kentucky and the District of Columbia.

In 1994, Kentucky limited spending in its gubernatorial race to $1.8 million per candidate ($1.2 million of which came from the state) and set a maximum $500 contribution per donor. The problem was that the Supreme Court has ruled repeatedly that an organization or person cannot be stopped from spending money as long as the donation is not coordinated with a candidate's efforts.

In Kentucky, no other special interest could match the labor union money spent on behalf of Paul Patton in the Democratic primary. In the general election, Mr. Patton's labor supporters triumphed over his opponent's business supporters in a battle of independent campaigns. How can this be considered reform?

In 1993, Washington limited contributions in mayoral races to $100, down from $2,000 per election cycle. Some candidates struggled mightily to raise even $30,000, and couldn't get their messages to the public. I lived in the District then, and didn't receive a single political flier or piece of mail. Some do-gooders would find this an improvement, but information is the basis of an educated vote.

Special interests filled the vacuum. Unions and big business set up independent campaigns to help the candidates of their liking, while politicians were reduced to begging them for support. After the election, the City Council returned to the old system.

Now, in the aftermath of the Democratic National Committee's fiasco with Asian money, Senators Russ Feingold, Democrat of Wisconsin, and John McCain, Republican of Arizona, are getting tremendous support for their legislation calling for voluntary spending limits, bans on so-called soft money, and a requirement that broadcasters provide free air time.

These ideas may sound good. But limiting spending requires candidates to "hope" that outside interest will aid their cause. As for free air time, not many voters are likely to tune in to a TV station at an appointed hour to hear candidates speak. Besides, political professionals know that a voter must see the same 30-second spot some ten times before the message sinks in. Campaigns inundate voters with mail, phone calls, and TV and radio ads because, in an age when the media are increasingly less interested in covering campaign issues, such strategies are often the only reliable ways to inform voters.

Consider last year's Senate Democratic primary in Texas. Partly because of a lack of news coverage, confused voters selected an unknown small-town schoolteacher largely because he had the same surname as the state attorney general. The two Democratic members of the House who ran against him could not raise enough money to reach voters in all of Texas's seventeen media markets.

The current system, which limits individual contributions to $1,000 an election, is a joke. A rich person who wants to gain influence calls other rich friends to send over $1,000 checks and then delivers all the checks to the candidate at once.

So instead of lowering spending caps, we should raise the individual limit to $10,000 but require campaigns and parties to notify the Federal

Election Commission of every contribution the day it is received. Current law requires disclosure only every ninety days until the very end of a campaign. Thus the media and a candidate's opponents would be able to get the word out quickly if a notorious polluter or rich union gave the candidate an enormous sum.

Under the same disclosure rules, we should also allow donations up to $20,000 from political action committees—still the best way for working people to pool together and ensure that their views are heard. Direct corporate contributions to candidates, currently banned, should also be allowed but under the same disclosure rules, so we'll know if a candidate intends to become the senator from Texaco or Microsoft.

George Will recently said that more money is spent annually on antacids in this country than on a presidential race. But judging by the uproar over campaign financing, you would think that our very democracy is at stake. Unfortunately, it just may be the reformers who weaken it.

# Price Controls on Democracy

## Pete du Pont

This selection first appeared in the *Wall Street Journal*, September 24, 1997. Reprinted with permission of the Wall Street Journal © 1997 Dow Jones & Company, Inc. All rights reserved. Du Pont, former governor of Delaware, likens the proposals of the McCain-Feingold legislation to price controls, which have repeatedly failed to accomplish their avowed purposes. Du Pont favors full and fast disclosure of contributions.

Hard cases, it is said, make bad law. The hard cases of Clinton campaign cash corruption are pushing Congress toward very bad law—the McCain-Feingold bill, which would, in effect, impose price controls on political involvement.

The First Continental Congress understood well the consequences of legislated prices, which had been imposed during the Revolutionary War. In June 1778 it concluded that "limitations on the prices of commodities are not only ineffectual for the purposes proposed, but likewise productive of very evil consequences to the great detriment of the public service and grievous oppression of individuals."

But the failure of price controls reaches back to the beginning of government. As Robert L. Scheuttinger and Eamonn F. Butler document in "Forty Centuries of Wage and Price Controls," in 2150 B.C., the kingdom of Babylon adopted the Code of Hammurabi. Among its provisions were wage and price controls. For example, the code said the price to hire a 60-ton boat shall be "a sixth part of a shekel of silver per diem" and the pay of a carpenter "four grains of silver per diem."

### "BOUNDLESS AVARICE"

Twenty-five centuries later, in A.D. 284, the Roman emperor Diocletian, complaining of "raging and boundless avarice," decreed that "maximum [prices] be fixed" for all goods and services. Hoarding, riots, a black market and a failed economy soon followed. Four years later Diocletian abdicated his throne.

Sixteen centuries after that, nations ranging from Lenin's USSR to Hitler's Germany to Richard Nixon and Jimmy Carter's America imposed wage and price controls. All failed to achieve their purpose and caused more problems than they solved.

So it makes perfect sense in the world of Washington to insist that they be imposed again. This time Sens. John McCain (R, Ariz.) and Russ Feingold (D, Wis.), aided and abetted by Common Cause, the *New York Times*, and President Clinton, want to impose price controls on political speech and campaigns. Their legislative proposal contains a wide variety of price controls: on campaigns (an overall spending limit), on private broadcasters (advertising rates), on government (postal rates), and on out-of-state contributors to a candidate (the proportion of contributions they may give is restricted).

The legislation is a mind-numbing example of government by the numbers. The overall spending limit for Senate races "shall not exceed the lesser of $5,500,000, or the greater of $950,000 or $400,000 plus 30 cents multiplied by the voting age population not in excess of 4,000,000 and 25 cents multiplied by the voting age population in excess of 4,000,000." Oh, that is unless the candidate runs in a state that has no more than one VHF TV transmitter licensed for operation, in which case 80 cents is substituted for 30, and 70 cents for 25.

In addition the bill proposes free television time for candidates, Each candidate would be entitled to a total of thirty minutes, to be used Monday through Friday between 6 and 10 P.M., in minimum bites of thirty seconds and a maximum of five minutes; but no more than fifteen minutes on an one station. Breathtaking in its complexity, McCain-Feingold calls to mind a statement attributed to Soviet official Vladimir Kabaidze in 1936: "We cannot tolerate the proliferation of this paperwork any longer. We must kill the people producing it."

Other reformers offer alternative schemes of government control. Max Frankel, writing in the *New York Times* magazine, is for "chasing political commercials off the air and giving ballot-worthy candidates enough free air time to present themselves to the voters." Two think-tankers, Thomas Mann of the Brookings Institution and Norman Ornstein of the American Enterprise Institute, want to eliminate political party "soft money" and narrow the definition of how much an individual or organization can spend advocating or opposing a public policy issue. And House and Senate Minority leaders Richard Gephardt (D, Mo.) and Tom Daschle (D, S.D.) want to amend the Constitution, weakening the First Amendment to permit campaign price controls.

All of these ideas are bad economics, bad politics, and, as forty centuries of experience have proved, very bad public policy.

In addition to the First Amendment problem—the Supreme Court ruled unanimously in *Buckley v. Valeo* that political contributions are protected speech—there are enormous fairness issues. Mr. Frankel's formulation hints at them: giving "ballot-worthy candidates" free air time. So who is "ballot-worthy?" Strom Thurmond and the Dixiecrats in 1948? Eugene McCarthy's challenge to Lyndon Johnson in 1968? Harry Browne or Ralph Nader, last year's Libertarian and Green candidates for president? What impartial arbiter would decide who may or may not run for election in America?

Another affront to liberty is the McCain-Feingold proposal to limit a candidate's out-of-state contributions to 40 percent of all contributions. Under such a provision, non-Louisianans who don't want to see David Duke elected to the Senate might be unable to contribute to his opponent.

Limiting issue advocacy is another clear and present danger to American democracy. McCain-Feingold would permit the federal government to regulate campaign speech that contains "express advocacy" intended to affect an election. But advocacy of issues is what elections are about. There should be more of it, not less.

Any state or local party activity, from voter registration to kaffeeklatsches, that "might affect the outcome of a federal election" would also be covered by national campaign controls, effectively federalizing local elections. All this is Big Brother writ large, a bit of Leninism superimposed on modern America.

Finally comes the question of political action committees. Let's be clear, we are not talking of legalizing illegal acts—foreign contributions to political campaigns, solicitations from government offices or making contributions in the name of another. We are considering whether people of similar beliefs—union members or right-to-life advocates—may contribute to a common organization to increase their political impact.

McCain-Feingold purports to outlaw them all. But under the independent expenditure sections of the bill, a union, for example, could advertise and advocate anything it likes. If it spends $35 million, as the AFL-CIO did in last year's congressional elections, opposing candidates would be allowed to spend a like amount in addition to their legislated spending limit. Which is a loophole big enough to drive a hippo through.

So what is the answer to the dilemma of money and politics in this season of discontent? Disclosure—full, accurate, daily disclosure.

Congress should defeat McCain-Feingold and repeal the arcane existing campaign spending rules (which encourage, for example, presidential campaign staffers to sleep across the river in Vermont to avoid their motel bills counting against New Hampshire spending limits) and take a pledge against price controls.

Then let the sunlight in. The quagmire we are in is the result of the post-Watergate campaign reforms. Is it likely that a new set of government regulations will be any better than the old set?

ELECTRONIC REPORTING

Instead of superregulating an already overregulated activity, require every campaign contribution, hard or soft, direct or indirect, to be reported to the Federal Election Commission electronically the day it arrives. If President Clinton's campaign wants to take $50,000 from John Huang, it can. If the Democratic National Committee wants to accept $300,000 checks from federal employee unions, or the Republican National Committee from Phillip Morris or Archer-Daniels-Midland, that's OK too. But it will be reported in the morning paper. And the people will decide if it is wrong when they vote.

What do you suppose the voters would have decided if what we now know of Al Gore's solicitations from the White House, the Chinese connections, and the cost of nights in the Lincoln Bedroom had been reported nightly on the evening news in the last two weeks before the election? A well-informed electorate will safeguard American campaigns far better than any appointed group of the best and brightest Washington regulators.

# The Case for Campaign Reform

## *New York Times* Editorial

This editorial first appeared in the *New York Times*, August 3, 1997, p. 12. Copyright © 1997 by the New York Times Co. Reprinted by permission. Most of the lurid stories about campaign contributions of the 1995–96 season were stories of foreign intrigue and influence. This editorial calls for campaign finance reform on the grounds that "the only way to shut down foreign money is to shut down soft money." It is indeed a slippery slope, the attempt to control one seeming abuse and the unwillingness to tolerate a little slack leading to ever more far-reaching controls. The *New York Times* is willing to slide down that slope, but there is more mud at the bottom than there is at the top.

The first round of Senate hearings on campaign spending, which ended last week when Congress recessed for August, may have produced no smoking guns or irrefutable evidence of Chinese meddling in American elections. Those may still come. But cumulatively, and in a mere four weeks, these hearings have built a powerful case for fundamental changes in the way America finances its political system.

They have also yielded fresh evidence that the White House and the Democratic National Committee chose to look the other way as funds flowed illegally from foreign sources into the Clinton reelection campaign, greatly strengthening the case for an independent counsel to get to the bottom of the entire mess. Attorney General Janet Reno, who has stubbornly refused to appoint one, simply cannot be expected to carry out a credible inquiry of a scandal that has now arrived at her boss's door.

The committee has so far focused on illegal foreign donations. In September it will turn to the so-called soft money that flowed in tidal proportions to both parties in 1996 from American donors—$250 million in technically legal contributions that nevertheless violated the spirit of the campaign financing laws enacted over the last twenty years. But there really isn't that much difference between the foreign and American soft money. Both were made possible by a loophole in current law that allows unlimited giving to the parties, as opposed to individual candidates. The foreign money came barrelling through that door and will keep doing so unless Congress closes it.

The hearings uncovered appalling negligence by both parties. Funds originating overseas are not easy to trace, but the real problem was that both parties, hungry for dollars whatever their origin, not only made no effort to determine their source but also encouraged their flow. Haley Barbour, when he was Republican chairman, orchestrated a complex scheme that allowed a Hong Kong bank to underwrite key congressional races in 1994. For their part, the Democrats gratefully gathered up more than $1 million that flowed from Indonesia's powerful Riady family to the national committee through various entities, some of them clearly shell companies. They also rewarded the Riady's chief American agent, John Huang, with a senior position on the DNC, where he could continue to tap into Asian and Asian-American sources.

Then there was the remarkable saga of Yah Lin (Charlie) Trie, a nimble colleague of Mr. Huang's who received more than $900,000 in wire transfers between 1994 and 1996 from a shadowy Chinese developer named Ng Lap Seng. Mr. Trie used some of this foreign money to underwrite generous contributions to the Democrats from himself and others, in plain violation of federal law. The Democrats finally got around to returning these and other tainted donations in June. But it took them nearly three years to wise up, and in the meantime the chief proprietors of the funny money laundromat—Mr. Huang, Mr. Trie, and even the mysterious Mr. Ng—traipsed in and out of the White House like visiting royalty.

People like the Riadys were able to abuse the current laws because those laws invite abuse. Although the system limits individual contributions to specific candidates, the soft money loophole allows wealthy individuals and corporations to buy access with unlimited donations to the political parties. These funds are supposed to be used for "party building," but they can easily be diverted to individual campaigns. Last year the system spun totally out of control.

One of the peculiar problems associated with foreign soft money is that there is really no practical way to keep track of it. FBI agents on loan to the Senate committee were able to reconstruct the pipeline between Mr. Ng. and Charlie Trie, but it required a major effort. There are thousands of other individuals and corporate entities in the United States besides John Huang and Charlie Trie that foreign sources can use to funnel money into this country. No investigative apparatus has the resources to cover all the avenues.

Thus the only way to shut down foreign money is to shut down soft money. That is one purpose of a bill sponsored by Senators John McCain and Russ Feingold. Three former presidents—Gerald Ford, Jimmy Carter, and George Bush—have expressed support for the bill, but the Senate majority and minority leaders, the two people who can drive it to passage, are unconscionably dragging their feet.

Trent Lott, the Republican leader, has yet to schedule a vote on the bill because many of his colleagues do not support various provisions, including limits on spending by individual candidates. Mr. McCain would probably accept a stripped-down bill aimed only at banning soft money. But he would then have to contend with Tom Daschle, the Senate minority leader, who says that a ban on soft money alone is not good enough.

The danger in this silly partisan jockeying is that nothing will get done about soft money. After all that we have seen and heard in the last few weeks, that would be a tragedy. The foreign fund-raising schemes were bad enough, but they are merely a window on a much broader corruption. Many committee members know that soft money must be extirpated. Their job now is to keep building the case for reform. The American people seem to have gotten the message already. Mr. Lott and Mr. Daschle ignore it at their own peril.

# The Man Who Ruined Politics

*Wall Street Journal* Editorial

This selection first appeared in the *Wall Street Journal*, November 16, 1995, p. A20. Reprinted with permission of the Wall Street Journal © 1995 Dow Jones & Company, Inc. All rights reserved. It is the do-gooders who want to drive money out of politics who are, says this *Wall Street Journal* editorial, doing the most damage—leaving candidates with huge sums to raise in small amounts and taking away the right of wealthy individuals to finance candidates of their choice instead of their own campaigns. A year before the 1996 general elections, significant participants in the electoral process had already been defeated by fund-raising problems and intricacies.

So Colin Powell is not running for president. Neither is Jack Kemp, Bill Bradley, Dick Cheney, Sam Nunn, or William Bennett. Voters are left with the likely choice between two rather tired war horses, Bill Clinton and Bob Dole. No other Democrat is challenging an obviously vulnerable incumbent, and Republican contenders such as Phil Gramm, Pat Buchanan, and Lamar Alexander hover in single digits. In this second rank we now also have millionaire publisher Steve Forbes, who started from nowhere to grab the first rung on the ladder. And, of course, billionaire Ross Perot still haunts the scene.

If you don't like the remaining field, blame Fred Wertheimer and Common Cause, the organization he until recently ran and still animates, the principal architects of the cockamamie financial gauntlet we inflict on our potential leaders. Common Cause is point-lobby for the goo-goos, that is, the earnest folks always trying to jigger the rules to ensure good government. One of their conceits is that money is the root of all political evil, so they seek salvation in the Sisyphean task of eliminating its influence. The chief result of this is a Fred Wertheimer rule outlawing individual political contributions of more than $1,000 and a bureaucracy called the Federal Election Commission to count angels on pinheads in deciding, for example, what counts as a contribution.

A serious presidential campaign is likely to cost $20 million. This means a potential president has to start by persuading 20,000 different people to pony up a grand. Take an arbitrary but probably generous hit rate of 5 percent, and he (or she) has to pass the tin cup 400,000 times. Admittedly these numbers oversimplify, but they give you the idea. Mr. Wertheimer's brainstorm means fund-raising is so consuming that candidates have no time for anything else. Even more important, it is a process virtually designed to drain a potential president of any residue of self-respect.

This may not be the only thing General Powell means when he says running requires a fire he does not yet feel, but it is certainly a big one. His adviser Richard Armitage explicitly said, "Colin Powell going out and asking people for money and then spending all that money wasn't attractive." Mr. Kemp was similarly explicit in not wanting to undertake the fund-raising exercise, and it no doubt inhibited Mr. Cheney as well. On the Democratic side, finding 20,000 donors to challenge an incumbent is an even more daunting challenge; Senator Bradley and Senator Nunn decided to quit rather than fight.

It is no accident that the dropouts are precisely the types the goo-goo crowd would like to keep in politics, which is to say, those motivated by principle instead of sheer ambition. In 1988, to take an earlier example, the exploratory field included Don Rumsfeld, who had been a congressman, White House chief of staff, defense secretary, and a spectacularly successful corporate chief executive. But he threw in the towel rather than run up possibly unpayable debts—"as a matter of principle, I will not run on a deficit."

The doleful effect of such limitations were entirely predictable; indeed, they were predicted right here. As early as 1976, when the Supreme Court partly upheld the 1974 Federal Election Campaign Act, we wrote that the law "will probably act like the Frankenstein's monster it truly is. It will be awfully hard to kill, and the more you wound it, the more havoc it will create." In the face of hard experience, of course, the goo-goos prescribe more of the same, to the point where "campaign finance reform" has become the Holy Grail.

To be fair, the Wertheimer coven hasn't had its way entirely. The logic of the goo-goo impulse is public financing of political campaigns, an idea mostly hooted down by the same taxpayers who eagerly embrace term limits—though in presidential campaigns public finance serves as the carrot getting candidates to accept the FEC nit-picking. And the Supreme Court, while backing away from the obvious conclusion that limiting political expenditures is *prima facie* an infringement of free speech, couldn't bring itself to say someone can't spend his own money on his own campaign.

Thus the millionaire's loophole. Mr. Perot was able to use his billions to confuse the last presidential elections, going in, out, and back in at will. So long as he doesn't accept public money, he can spend as he likes.

Mr. Forbes is an even more interesting case, since he was chairman of Empower America, the political roost of both Mr. Kemp and Mr. Bennett. Who would have guessed a year ago, the latter asks, that the Empower America candidate would be Steve Forbes. On the issues Mr. Forbes is perhaps an even better candidate than his colleagues—backing term limits where Mr. Kemp opposes them, for example—and without his message his money wouldn't do much good. Still, to have a better chance at ultimately winning, it would have been logical for him to bankroll one of his better-known colleagues. But that's against the law, thanks to Mr. Wertheimer, so Mr. Forbes has to hit the stump himself.

With widespread disaffection with the current field, and especially in the wake of the Powell withdrawal, the lunacy of the current rules is coming to be recognized. The emperor has no clothes, think tank scholars are starting to say—notably Bradley A. Smith of the Cato Institute, whose views were published here October 6. Following Mr. Smith, Newt Gingrich said last weekend we don't spend too much on political campaigns but too little. This heresy was applauded this week by columnist

David Broder, which may herald a breakthrough in goo-goo sentiment itself.

Formidable special interests, of course, remain opposed to change in the current rules. Notably political incumbents, who want campaigns kept as quiet as possible and have learned to milk other special interests who want access. So rather than having some maverick millionaire funding his pet candidate on reasons that might relate to ideas and issues, we have all parties funded by Dwayne Andreas and his sisters and his cousins and his aunts, better to protect ethanol subsidies. Finally, of course, we have Mr. Perot and his United We Stand hell-bent for further restrictions on campaign finance, better to protect the political process for billionaires like himself.

Not so, thankfully, Mr. Forbes, who sees campaign spending limits as an incumbent protection device. He recently told an Iowa audience, "If Congress abolished the franking privilege, then I'd be impressed." Lift the caps on giving and spending, but make sure everything is disclosed, he says. "That's real reform."

# Sin Masquerading As Virtue

### Steve Forbes

This selection first appeared in *Forbes*, October 20, 1997, p. 2. Reprinted by permission of Forbes Magazine © 1999 Forbes 1997. In this brief op-ed comment Steve Forbes, editor in chief of *Forbes* and a presidential candidate in the 1996 race, calls campaign finance "reform" an assault on First Amendment freedoms, advantageous to incumbents, and a boon to the media. Raising or eliminating caps on spending and giving, along with fuller disclosure and the elimination of federal subsidies for presidential candidates, are his recommendations.

Many in Congress want to "reform" campaign financing by giving Washington more regulatory powers in determining who can run, who can give, and who can advocate issues. This assault on our First Amendment freedoms is the equivalent of telling a pneumonia patient to go for a roll in the snow.

The so-called reforms advocated by Democrats and a handful of Republicans would increase the already formidable protections and advantages enjoyed by incumbents, making it more difficult for outsiders to effectively challenge them. The reforms would also increase the power of the media in deciding whose views get disseminated to the voters, and how they get disseminated. Rarely has there been such a flagrant example of self-serving, special-interest legislation.

The McCain-Feingold bill would ban so-called soft money—except from the unions. Advocacy groups would be banned from advancing their views if bureaucrats determined that a political candidate supportive of these views might benefit from such advocacy. This bill, by severely restricting the amounts challengers can spend, gives more power to the press, because challengers won't be able to spend what's needed (on mailings, fliers, etc.) to take their causes directly to the voters.

There is a better way. Caps on individual giving should be either substantially raised or eliminated—as should those on campaign spending. Full and prompt disclosure of all contributions must be required. Contributions to campaigns could be posted every evening on the Internet, in a list of who gave how much that day. The key is to make all the relevant information available to voters in a timely manner. Let the voters determine if a candidate has sold his soul to a special interest group or to a group of individuals.

Federal subsidizing of presidential candidates through tax dollars should end. Why should taxpayers have their money used to support causes or candidates they might deplore?

By the way, there are two other approaches that would enhance campaign finance reform. One, of course, is term limits. Naturally, Belt-way enthusiasm for that is muted. The other is to remove from Washington some of the power and influence that attracts so many petitioners and special interests. Start by scrapping the major source of power—the federal income tax code.

# Deregulating Politics

## George F. Will

This selection first appeared in *Newsweek*, November 10, 1997, p. 94. Will's conclusion about the excesses of financing the 1996 presidential campaign is that there is virtually nothing left that is illegal, a situation that has his approval: this is "as it should be." He too judges that attempts to regulate one kind of political money lead to attempts to regulate other kinds of political money—from hard money to soft money to express advocacy to issue advocacy.

Will recounts that Wisconsin legislation restricting communication that has the purpose of influencing an election has led to suits in which legislators have sued on the grounds that they have been harmed by political messages criticizing their performance, thus demonstrating what Will considers the real motive behind campaign finance reform: "The political class thinks it has a right to ration the permissible amount of political communication because it really thinks it has a property right to the offices it holds."

When Earl Long was Louisiana's governor, he did not think highly of the state's attorney general: "If you want to hide something from Jack Gremillion, put it in a lawbook." Nowadays if you want, as sensible people do, to discredit the drive for campaign finance reform, give the reformers ample opportunities to put forth their arguments. The more they talk, the more wind escapes from their movement's sails.

Although Bill Clinton is almost negligible as a president, he may have one large, and largely wholesome, consequence. Having run his last campaign, he now favors new regulations on giving and spending money to disseminate political advocacy. However, suppose, as seems probable and by and large desirable, the final conclusion about his 1996 campaign-financing activities is that although what he did was often coarse and unseemly, it was nevertheless permitted by existing laws. In that case, his behavior will have produced the de facto deregulation of campaigning. That is, there will be almost nothing significant that the laws regulating campaigns will significantly inhibit. Which is as it should be.

Clinton operated on the ethical principle propounded by George Washington Plunkitt, the philosopher of Tammany Hall: "I seen my opportunities and I took em." Republicans, too, took the same opportunities by the fistful. The opportunities were provided by the silly distinction between "hard" and "soft" money, a distinction almost as impractical as that between "express advocacy" and "issue advocacy."

"Hard" money is given to a particular candidate's campaign. "Soft" money is given to parties for issue advertising and other "party-building" activities. But trying to draw a bright line between the political uses of hard and soft money is like trying to draw a line in a river. The purpose of the hard-soft distinction is to segregate, for the purpose of controlling, hard money, meaning money intended to win elections, to influence voters. But Clinton raised pots of money and caused it to be spent on issue ads intended to get voters to think as the Democratic Party does. And wonder of wonders, he benefited with the voters. How could it be—why should it be—otherwise?

Attempts to regulate some kinds of political money lead inexorably to attempts to regulate all kinds. This produces, as Prohibition did, widespread disregard for the law. Prohibition at least had some measurable public health benefits. Today's prohibitionists—the campaign reformers—have no such partially redeeming effect.

The response of reformers to the demonstrated futility of the distinction between hard and soft money has been to multiply distinctions. They say soft money can be meaningfully regulated only if regulation is extended to "express advocacy"—political communication by independent groups urging voters to support or oppose a particular candidate in a particular election. Then they say that this, too, will be nugatory unless regulation also is extended to any "issue advocacy" that has a political purpose—which of course means virtually any conceivable issue advocacy.

Inevitably, this gets government into the business of assessing the intentions of citizens who participate in politics. The bureaucracy of speech regulators must try to divine this: Do the citizens' intentions make the content of the citizens' political communications subject to government regulation? Thus Sen. Fred Thompson's expiring committee, investigating 1996 campaign activities, has issued a blizzard of snooping subpoenas to private advocacy groups across the political spectrum, from the Sierra Club to the National Right-to-Life Committee. It wants to scrutinize the motives and tactical thinking of private citizens engaging in political advocacy, in order to develop a regulatory response. But many of the subpoenaed groups have been splendidly insubordinate, resisting the subpoenas by simple noncompliance and by threatening to seek relief in court. Where does all this pernicious government desire to regulate political speech lead? To the mess Wisconsin is in.

Wisconsin imposes registration and reporting duties on groups that engage not just in express advocacy but also in any communication that has "the purpose of influencing" an election. In 1996 the group Americans for Limited Terms (ALT) began running a radio ad saying that David Travis, a state assemblyman, opposed term limits. The ad urged voters to call Travis and "tell him to change his mind." ALT had not registered, and Travis got a judge to ban the ad on the weekend before the election. Judges also silenced the Sierra Club and the Wisconsin Manufacturers & Commerce (WMC) organization, which were running issue ads.

Now come David Plombon and Michael Wilder with a lawsuit that should help drive a stake through the heart of campaign finance reform. They are Democrats. They were Wisconsin assemblymen. In 1996 they lost campaigns in which WMC ran ads that characterized them as "voting with the Madison liberals nearly 100 percent of the time," that said they voted against certain tax and spending cuts, and that urged voters to call the two legislators and urge them to mend their ways.

Plombon and Wilder are suing WMC, seeking a "permanent injunction" to prevent WMC from running similar ads in the future. They say they are "members of a protected class under the elections laws," meaning that politicians, not voters, are the intended beneficiaries of those laws. They say WMC violated "their property rights in the rights and responsibilities of state office." They say they "have been damaged in the loss of the value of their campaign expenditures and efforts." And they say they "have suffered damages in the loss of their right to hold office and the payment and benefits" to which officeholders are entitled.

There. Plombon and Wilder have blurted out a usually unexpressed motive of campaign reform: the political class thinks it has a right to ration the permissible amount of political communication because it really thinks it has a property right to the offices it holds. This is the reductio ad tedium of campaign reform.

# Vote against McCain. Wait, Can I Say That?

## Jonathan Rauch

This selection first appeared in the *Wall Street Journal*, October 11, 1997, p. A22. Reprinted with permission of the Wall Street Journal © 1997 Dow Jones & Company, Inc. All rights reserved. A contributing editor of *National Journal*, Rauch considers money in political campaigns inevitable and believes limiting it in one manifestation will simply cause it to be used in a different way. He notes the possibility that McCain-Feingold may in fact forbid the mention of itself in the sixty days before an election. Rauch supports increased disclosure but thinks that public financing would be an improvement over the current system.

The McCain-Feingold bill being debated in the Senate this week has become the default option for campaign finance reformers: If you are an editorialist who needs to suggest something better than today's tumbling system, you press the McCain-Feingold button on your word processor. Well, the system today is rotten, and radical change is needed. But McCain-Feingold, for all its good press and good intentions, is a bad bill. It would do nothing to end the failures of the past twenty years. Indeed, it would unflinchingly compound them.

At the core of today's troubles are two realities that will not yield to any amount of legislative or lawyerly cleverness. The first is that private money—a lot of it—is a fact of life in politics, and if you push it out of one part of the system it tends to reenter somewhere else, usually deeper in shadow. The second is that money spent to communicate with voters cannot be regulated without impinging on the very core of the First Amendment, which was written to protect political discourse above all.

We got into today's mess by defying both of these principles, with predictable results. When reformers placed limits on money spent to support or defeat candidates, lobbies simply shifted to ad campaigns that omitted explicit requests to vote for or against candidates: "issue advocacy," which the courts have ruled is constitutionally protected.

And when reformers placed tight limits on contributions to candidates, donors began giving to political parties instead: "soft money."

The distinctions between "hard" and "soft" money, and between "express advocacy" and "issue advocacy," are grounded in legalistic mumbo-jumbo, and so the attempts to enforce them have made campaign law bewilderingly complex without accomplishing any of the law's goals. Campaigns are neither cheaper nor fairer nor less dependent on private money than, say, thirty years ago—just the opposite, in fact. One conclusion you might draw is that the 1970s-style money-regulating model is bankrupt. Another is that a horsedoctor's dose of the old medicine will finally heal the patient. Enter Sens. John McCain (R, Ariz.) and Russell Feingold (D, Wis.).

Among many things their bill would do: First, it would ban soft money given to political parties. Second, to make the soft money ban work, it would also restrict independent issue advocacy. Voilà—no more money, right?

Wrong. Lots and lots of money, but in different places. Ban soft money, and lobbies would bypass the parties and conduct their own campaign blitzes. Candidates and parties are already losing control of their messages as lobbies—which, unlike candidates and parties, are not accountable to voters—run independent advocacy campaigns. The McCain-Feingold bill would accelerate the alienation of politicians from their own campaigns, and, for good measure, it could also starve the parties of funds.

The sponsors are aware that independent advertising might replace soft money: thus the bill's remarkable new limits on all ads that mention candidates within sixty days of an election. In the words of Sen. McCain: "Ads could run which advocate any number of causes. Pro-life ads, pro-choice ads, antilabor ads, pro-wilderness ads, pro–Republican Party ads, pro–Democrat Party ads—all could be aired in the last sixty days. However, ads mentioning the candidates could not." So, for example, I might commit a federal crime by taking out an ad in this newspaper criticizing Sen. McCain for supporting his bill. The Founders would have run screaming from such a notion, and rightly so: You cannot improve the integrity of any political system by letting politicians restrict political speech.

In real life the courts are likely to strike down McCain-Feingold's speech controls, in which case, of course, the limits would not work. But even if the limits were allowed to stand, they still would not work: Everybody would race to game the system by dressing up political expression in absurd costumes, whose legitimacy would be contested ad nauseam in the courts. Maybe my ad couldn't say "vote against McCain and Feingold," but could it say "show the promoters of the dangerous McCain-Feingold bill how you feel"? Who would decide?

The potential for speech micromanagement is endless. Imagine the fun lawyers could have with the bill's exception for "voter guides"—a permissible voter guide being (hold on tight, now) any printed matter written in an "educational manner" about two or more candidates that (1) is not coordinated with a candidate, (2) gives all candidates an equal opportunity to respond to any questionnaires, (3) gives no candidate any greater prominence than any other, and (4) does not contain a phrase *such as* (my italics) "vote for," "reelect," "support," "defeat," "reject," other words that in context can have no reasonable meaning other than to urge the election or defeat of one or more candidates. Is that clear?

So, after McCain-Feingold, campaign law would become even more complex and mystifying. Politicians would remain mendicants, forced by low contribution limits to beg every day and in every way for donations. Our already weak parties would lose their main source of funds, becoming weaker still. If the speech controls were upheld, political discussion would be both chilled and contorted. And if the speech controls were struck down, political campaigns would be run by lobbies ("independent expenditures") rather than by candidates and parties. Quite a reform.

Even total deregulation would be better than McCain-Feingold, provided disclosure were retained. For that matter, doing nothing would be better. Best by a very long measure, however, would be a combination of deregulation, disclosure, and onerous public financing for candidates who forgo private fund-raising—a plan that, instead of trying to eliminate or micromanage private money, would give voters an alternative to it and make the acceptance of private donations an issue in every campaign.

Alas, all of those admittedly imperfect ideas are bitterly opposed by the antimoney crusaders who gave us the system we have now and who still predominate in the "reform community." To change their minds, campaign finance law will probably have to be made worse before it can be made better. That task, at least, McCain-Feingold would perform admirably.

# Deregulating Campaign Finance: Solution or Chimera?

## Thomas E. Mann

This selection first appeared in the *Brookings Review*, Winter 1998, pp. 18–21. In this article Mann, coeditor of *Campaign Finance Reform: A Sourcebook*, published by the Brookings Institution in 1997, considers the merits of the Doolittle proposal to "remove all existing limits on contributions to federal candidates and national parties, end the public financing of presidential primary and general election campaigns, and mandate electronic filing and timely disclosure." This he calls "a proposal breathtaking in its boldness and contrariness."

Deregulation and disclosure are appealing, he concludes, given the continual oversight and repair of the complex task of regulating federal campaign financing. But ultimately he objects. He claims that "a fundamental objective of campaign finance regulation is to ensure that the inequalities generated by the market economy do not undermine the political equality that is a central feature of our democracy" and asks us to "recall" this, as though it were something that we all know and acknowledge, a fundamental linchpin of our way of life.

But it is not. It is a statement of the underlying principle that the influence of money, of both income and wealth, should be stripped from politics and that individuals who earn paychecks that enable them to support candidates and public causes should be as financially limited in their capacity to communicate as those on the public dole.

Those who have more money than others will unduly influence the voters, Mann says, because voters cannot acquire enough information, cannot distinguish the pattern of campaign contributions received by different candidates, and do not have enough incentive to acquire information and punish candidates too heavily under the influence of special interests. In other words, regulation must protect voters from their own inadequacies.

The reports of widespread fund-raising abuses in the 1996 elections have precipitated another heated debate about whether and how best to alter the rules under which money is raised and spent to influence general elections. Alleged violations of existing laws—fund-raising from

foreign nationals, the use of conduits to mask impermissible contributions, improper use of public property for fund-raising events and
telephone calls, and the use of soft money and issue advocacy to circumvent spending limits on publicly funded presidential candidates—have
led to calls for aggressive criminal prosecution (preferably led by an
independent counsel) and for legislative action to plug the legal loopholes that have encouraged or abetted reprehensible conduct by candidates, parties, and outside groups.

In spite of the colorful (and appalling) new material from 1996,
much of the reform rhetoric is stale, reflecting arguments that have been
marshaled time and again during the futile debates of the past fifteen
years. But there is one decidedly new kid on the reform block, a proposal
breathtaking in its boldness and contrariness. Introduced by Rep. John
Doolittle (R-Calif.) and championed by the estimable columnists
Charles Krauthammer, Robert Samuelson, and George Will, H.R. 905
(the "Citizen Legislature and Political Freedom Act") would remove all
existing limits on contributions to federal candidates and national parties, end the public financing of presidential primary and general election campaigns, and mandate electronic filing and timely disclosure on
the Internet of reports on contributions to candidates for federal office.
Faced with widespread evidence of perverse effects and unanticipated
consequences from previous efforts to regulate the flow of money in
elections, Doolittle and his supporters appear to take a lesson from the
largely successful experience with deregulation of the intercity transportation, energy, and financial services industries. In addition to the
obvious virtue of simplicity, this call to "deregulate and disclose"—and
let the chips fall where they may—offers a vision of a political marketplace disciplined not by a legal thicket of arcane rules and zealous
regulators but by rational citizens exercising their franchise.

Part of the appeal of the Doolittle approach is that it explicitly rejects
a regulatory model that by virtually all accounts has failed utterly to
achieve its objectives. Present law regulating the financing of congressional elections restricts the supply of funds (through contribution

limits whose real value has eroded by two-thirds since enactment in 1974) but not demand (since the mandatory spending limits in the law were declared unconstitutional by the Supreme Court). Is it any surprise that this hybrid system has intensified the money chase and stimulated the development of a black market for raising and spending funds to influence the outcome of House and Senate elections? The rules governing the financing of presidential elections (with voluntary spending limits achieved through the provision of generous, inflation-adjusted public financing) were built on a more plausible regulatory model, and for a while they worked largely in the manner anticipated by their architects. But a series of Federal Election Commission rulings beginning in 1978 created an alternative currency, not subject to federal regulation, that proved irresistible to ambitious politicians and resourceful consultants. By 1996 the scramble for this alternative currency (otherwise known as soft money) and its expenditure for what were ostensibly ads about "issues" and not candidates made a mockery of the legal prohibitions and limits on contributions and the voluntary spending limits.

Patching the holes in this regulatory regime is a daunting task, especially in light of the restrictions on policymakers imposed by the *Buckley* Court's holding that money is speech under the First Amendment and can be regulated only if there is a compelling interest in doing so—and only if the rules are narrowly tailored to advance that interest. Increasing the supply of funds (through higher individual and party contribution limits and tax credits) and subsidies (with free broadcast time and mailings) seems essential, as does an insistence that federal campaign activity be financed exclusively with regulated—that is, "hard" money—funds. But this approach is exceedingly complex, both technically and politically, and the solution will be temporary at best, requiring ongoing oversight and repair. All the more reason, say Doolittle advocates, to rely instead on the invisible hand of the political market to allocate campaign resources by disciplining the candidates who raise and spend those funds.

"Deregulate and disclose" is a seductive slogan. But will it have the desired effects? Recall that a fundamental objective of campaign finance regulation is to ensure that the inequalities generated by the market economy do not undermine the political equality that is a central feature of our democracy. Another key objective is to prevent incumbent officeholders from abusing state power to extract private contributions to undermine the competitiveness of elections. Under the Doolittle plan, would voters be able to limit the extent to which campaign donations and expenditures reinforce or magnify the influence of concentrated economic wealth and state power? To do so, they would need to acquire full information on who was giving what to which candidates and parties; be able to differentiate between the opposing candidates or parties in the pattern of campaign contributions; and have a strong incentive to cast their ballots on a single basis: to punish a candidate or party for accepting funds that they find repugnant. It is hard to see how any one, much less all three, of these conditions could be met in the brave new campaign finance world sketched by Representative Doolittle—given the more realistic world described by Anthony Downs of voters rationally limiting the time they invest in pursuing information about politics.

First, take full information. The Doolittle bill does nothing to require disclosure of campaign activity disguised as issue advocacy—the most rapidly growing, the most negative, and the least accountable form of political communication. Assuming the rest is disclosed on the Internet, how are voters to obtain and absorb copious data on campaign contributions? The press can help, but its voice might easily be drowned out by the political ads financed with the unregulated contributions that are supposed to be disciplined by an informed electorate. The Doolittle proposal also underestimates the extent to which full disclosure itself requires an extensive regulatory apparatus—just the thing Doolittle promises to abolish.

Second, even assuming they garner the necessary information, will voters be presented with a clear difference in fund-raising behavior on which to cast their ballots? What is to prevent large economic interests from investing generously in both parties or contributing to winning candidates after the election, in a quest for better access or in response to heavy-handed requests from those public officials? Each party or pair of candidates might attract campaign contributions, albeit from different sources, that voters find equally offensive.

Finally, why would voters sublimate those forces that now weigh heavily on their vote (party identification, political ideology, positions on key issues, economic performance, and the relative attractiveness of the candidates) in the single-minded pursuit of exercising the moral opprobrium that disciplines the role of money in politics? Experience with campaign finance disclosure over the past two decades suggests that citizens are less likely to vote on the basis of this new information than to conclude that the entire system is corrupt.

A deregulated campaign finance system is less a solution to the clear shortcomings of the existing regulatory model than a fanciful exercise in wishing those problems out of existence. The unrestrained use of economic wealth and state power in the electoral process would so clearly subvert the essential attire of our democracy that it would almost certainly lead to insistent public demands for the deregulation of campaign finance. There may be an alternative to muddling through the complexity of the present system. But if there is, it has yet to be persuasively articulated.

# Campaigns Starved for Money

## Martin Anderson

This selection first aired on the *Nightly Business Report*, January 16, 1997. This 90-second television commentary points out that restricting what candidates can raise and spend will increase the power of incumbent politicians, the media, and special interest groups.

In 1997 we are going to hear a lot of talk about how campaign finance reform that limits spending will make our elections better.

Don't believe it. Virtually every reform now on the table would make things worse.

This may sound like heresy, but today the real problem with our political campaigns is that they are starved for money. Candidates, except those with personal wealth, cannot afford to effectively communicate their policies to the voters.

Remember the Dole presidential campaign? I was traveling with him when he tried and failed to explain his economic program to the voters. A major reason for that failure was lack of money.

How many of you saw the Dole television ads explaining his tax reduction plan? Or the full-page newspaper ads that explained in detail how spending control would pay for those tax cuts?

The reason so few people ever saw the ads is that the campaign did not have enough money to run them nationally and often.

We probably spend more money advertising soap than we do on presidential campaigns.

If we reform campaign financing by restricting the amount of money a candidate can raise and spend, we only increase the power of incumbent politicians, the media, and special interest groups.

But what if we replaced existing campaign finance laws with just one new law that said "Anyone can give anyone any amount of money as long as the amount and who gave it is made public within twenty-four hours by publishing it on the computer Internet."

I think more money in the sunlight, rather than less money in the dark, is the best answer to real reform of our political system.

# The Case for Campaign Finance Reform

John Doolittle

This selection first appeared in *A Journal of Ideas*, U.S. House of Representatives, Office of Congressman Peter Hoekstra, Washington, D.C., pp. 53–57. Here is Congressman Doolittle's support of his legislation, in his own words.

The goal of effective campaign finance reform is to encourage political speech rather than limit it. It is to promote competition, freedom, and a more informed electorate. It is to enable any American citizen to run for office. It is to increase the amount of time candidates spend with constituents and debating issues rather than raising money. It is to make candidates accountable to their constituents for the money they raise and spend.

Why are these goals missing from the current debate over campaign finance reform? To date, the campaign finance reform debate has reminded me of the doctor who diagnoses a patient, prescribes a certain treatment, and upon discovering that the patient has reacted horribly to the treatment, then decides to double the dosage rather than rediagnose the problem.

In 1974, in the wake of Watergate, Congress threw a regulatory web over the campaign finance system, a system that had gone largely unregulated throughout our nation's history.

Within two years of the reform's passage, with the encouragement of conservatives and civil libertarians, the Supreme Court, in *Buckley v. Valeo*, struck down parts of the new regulatory scheme on First Amendment grounds.

Since that time, the campaign finance regulators have blamed every problem involving campaign financing on the *Buckley* decision.

There are those of us, however, who believe the problem is not what the Court struck down but what it left.

The regulators would do well to remember that it was not the

Supreme Court that put unreasonably low limits on how much individuals and groups could contribute to campaigns while failing to index for inflation. It wasn't the Supreme Court that ran roughshod over the First Amendment rights of officeseekers and other citizens. And it wasn't the Supreme Court that stacked the deck against challengers, locking in incumbents at an unprecedented rate.

No, the problem is not that the Court invalidated part of the regulators' grand scheme; it's that too much of their scheme remains intact.

It is time we declare that "the emperor has no clothes." It's time to dispel the myths perpetuated by the architects of today's failed campaign finance scheme. And while the regulators devise new schemes on how to limit participation in elections and eliminate money from campaigns, we should look at the real problems that have been caused by their regulatory approach to reform:

Today's campaign finance system requires current and prospective officeholders to spend too much time raising money and not enough time governing and debating issues.

Today's system has failed to make elections more competitive.

Today's system allows millionaires to purchase congressional seats and inhibits the ability of challengers to raise the funds necessary to be competitive.

Today's system hurts taxpayers by taking nearly $900 million collected in federal taxes and subsidizing the presidential campaigns of all sorts of characters, including convicted felons and billionaires.

Today's system hurts voters in our republic by forcing more contributors and political activists to operate outside of the system where they are unaccountable and, consequently, more irresponsible.

These are the problems we face today. And before we decide what reforms should be implemented, we need to decide where we want to go, what kind of new system we want to create.

Consistent with the definition of "effective reform," I think the answer is simple. Our goal should be a system in which any American citizen can compete for and win elective office. We should demand a system that values political participation and encourages the exercise of our First Amendment rights of speech and association by allowing voters to contribute freely to the candidate of their choice.

A healthy campaign finance system would require that candidates fully disclose the source of their contributions so that voters can make informed decisions about who may be attempting to influence a candidate.

This new system would scare some people in Washington because it will require them to do something very rarely considered around here: trust the American people, once informed, to make good decisions.

How can we erect such a system? We begin by uprooting the tired and failed policies of the past and by opening the process up to more Americans.

Such a proposal would

1. Repeal existing limits on how many individuals and political action committees may contribute to candidates or parties and repeal the limits on how much parties may contribute to candidates.

Why? Both academic research and real-world experience show that challengers need a tremendous amount of money to overcome the advantages of incumbency and to be competitive. Although money helps challengers and incumbents alike, higher spending plainly helps challengers more, while spending limits tend to aid incumbents. (For example, every successful Senate challenger and two-thirds of all successful House challengers in 1994 spent more than the limits proposed in McCain-Feingold and its companion bill in the House.) Today's unreasonable contribution limits make it unnecessarily difficult for challengers to raise the funds they need to be competitive. The answer is to eliminate limits on campaign contributions (as long as they are disclosed) so that challengers can raise the seed money they need to become competitive.

2. We need a system of full and timely disclosure of all campaign

contributions. Full disclosure will enable voters to identify and understand the interests that may affect a certain candidate, and it will then allow voters to vote accordingly.

This can be accomplished with electronic filing of campaign reports, including twenty-four-hour filings during the last three months of a campaign. Since its creation more than twenty-five years ago, the Presidential Election Campaign Fund has spent nearly $900 million in taxpayer dollars to subsidize presidential aspirants. Among the candidates deemed "qualified" to receive federal subsidies is convicted felon and perennial candidate Lyndon LaRouche. LaRouche has raked in more than $2.5 million from taxpayers over the last twenty years, despite the fact that he served a five-year prison term for fraud and tax-law violations and has run on a platform that includes a provision to colonize Mars. Support for public financing is at an all-time low, with less than 15 percent of the American people checking the tax-form box to earmark a few dollars for the presidential fund. At a time when we are attempting to balance the federal budget for the first time in a generation, this subsidy for candidates can no longer be justified.

Some may call this idea radical, but I think we are going to see the momentum for new thinking on the campaign finance issue. We can and must do better than the current system. Instead of repeating the mistakes of the past, we are going to build a coalition of Republicans and Democrats, conservatives and civil libertarians, behind a new and effective approach to campaign finance reform.

As in so many other areas, a bigger government bureaucracy and more red tape are not the solution to our current campaign finance problems. It is time to empower voters, and then trust them. As Thomas Jefferson wrote, "I know of no safe depository of the ultimate powers of the society but the people themselves: and if we think them not enlightened enough to exercise their control with a wholesome discretion, the remedy is not to take it from them, but to inform their discretion."

# The Money Gag

## Mitch McConnell

This selection first appeared in the *National Review*, June 30. 1997, pp. 36–38; © by National Review, Inc., 215 Lexington Avenue, New York, NY 10016. Reprinted by permission. Senator McConnell (R-Ky.) chairs the National Republican Senatorial Committee and is a major supporter of deregulating campaign finance.

Proponents of campaign spending limits are stuck between a rock and a hard place: the Constitution and reality.

It is impossible constitutionally to limit all campaign-related spending. The Supreme Court has been quite clear on this matter, most notably in the 1976 *Buckley v. Valeo* decision: "The First Amendment denies government the power to determine that spending to promote one's political views is wasteful, excessive, or unwise. In the free society ordained by our Constitution it is not the government but the people—individually as citizens and candidates and collectively as associations and political committees—who must retain control over the quantity and range of debate on public issues in a political campaign."

For those who do not at first blush see the link between the First Amendment and campaign spending, the Court elaborates: "A restriction on the amount of money a person or group can spend on political communication during a campaign necessarily reduces the quantity of expression by restricting the number of issues discussed, the depth of their exploration, and the size of the audience reached. This is because virtually every means of communicating ideas in today's mass society requires the expenditure of money."

The reformers do not care or, in some cases, cannot accept that spending limits limit speech. They believe that spending limits are justified and necessary to alleviate perceived or actual corruption. But the Court slapped that argument aside, holding that there is "nothing invidious, improper, or unhealthy" in campaigns spending money to communicate. The reformers contend that spending limits are essential because campaign spending has increased dramatically in the past two decades, a woefully lame premise the Court easily dispatched: "The mere growth in the cost of federal election campaigns in and of itself provides no basis for governmental restrictions on the quantity of campaign spending." Appealing to Americans' instinct for fairness, the reformers passionately plead for spending limits to "level" the political playing field. The Court was utterly contemptuous of this "level playing field" argument: "The concept that government may restrict the speech of some elements of our society in order to enhance the relative voice of others is wholly foreign to the First Amendment."

There you have it. The reformers cannot achieve their objectives statutorily. To realize the reformers' campaign finance nirvana would require essentially repealing the First Amendment—blowing a huge hole in the Bill of Rights via a constitutional amendment. Frightfully undemocratic? Yes. Out of the question? No. Thirty-eight United States senators voted to do just that on March 18, 1997. These thirty-eight senators voted, in the name of "reform," for S.J. Res. 18, a constitutional amendment to empower Congress and the states to limit contributions and spending "by, in support of, or in opposition to, a candidate." Thus would the entire universe of political speech and participation be subjected to limitation by congressional edict and enforcement by government bureaucrats.

This wholesale repeal of core political freedom registered barely a ripple in the nation's media. Perhaps reporters and editorial writers do not appreciate that their campaign coverage could be construed as spending "by, in support of, or in opposition to, a candidate" and, therefore, could be regulated under a Constitution so altered. It is not a stretch. The television networks and most major newspapers are owned by corporate conglomerates (aka "special interests") and the blurred distinction is already acknowledged in federal campaign law, which currently exempts from the definition of expenditure "any news story, commentary, or editorial" unless distributed by a political party, committee, or candidate.

I do not advocate regulating newspaper editorials, articles, and headlines. I do not believe that government should compensate candidates who are harmed by television newscasts or biased anchors. However, the political playing field can never be "level" without such regulation, and it is the only area of political speech upon which the vaunted McCain-Feingold bill is silent. McCain-Feingold has provisions to enable candidates to counteract independent expenditures by every "special interest" in America, except the media industry. This "loophole" is the only one that editorial writers are not advocating be closed by the government.

Such regulation of the media may strike one as an absurd result of the campaign reform movement, but it is a logical extrapolation of McCain-Feingold's regulatory regime. The McCain-Feingold bill's spending limit formula for candidates is itself ludicrous. For Senate general elections: 30 cents times the number of the state's voting-age citizens up to 4 million, plus 25 cents times the number of voting-age citizens over 4 million, plus $400,000. However, if you are running in New Jersey, 80 cents and 70 cents are substituted for 30 and 25 because of the dispersed media markets. Moreover, the formula notwithstanding, for all states the minimum general election limit is $950,000 and the maximum $5,500,000. McCain-Feingold sets the primary election limit at 57 per cent of the general election limit and the runoff limit at 20 per cent of the general election limit.

Reading the Clinton-endorsed McCain-Feingold bill, one can only conclude that the era of big government is just beginning. The courts have repeatedly ruled that communications which do not "expressly advocate" the election or defeat of a candidate (using terms such as "vote for," "defeat," "elect") cannot be regulated, yet McCain-Feingold would have the Federal Election Commission policing such ads if "a reasonable person" would "understand" them to advocate election or defeat. Out of 260 million Americans, just which one is to be this "reasonable person"?

The McCain-Feingold bill seeks to quiet the voices of candidates, private citizens, groups, and parties. Why? Because, it is said, "too much" is spent on American elections. The so-called reformers chafe when I pose the obvious question: "Compared to what?"

In 1996—an extraordinarily high-stakes, competitive election in which there was a fierce ideological battle over the future of the world's only superpower—$3.89 per eligible voter was spent on congressional elections. May I be so bold as to suggest that spending on congressional elections the equivalent of a McDonald's "extra value" meal and a small milkshake is not "too much"?

The reformers are not dissuaded by facts. Their agenda is not advanced by reason. It is propelled by the media, some politicians, and the recent infusion of millions of dollars in foundation grants to "reform" groups. Fortunately, the majority of this Congress is not ideologically predisposed toward the undemocratic, unconstitutional, bureaucratic finance scheme embodied in McCain-Feingold. Further, a powerful and diverse coalition has coalesced to protect American freedom from the McCain-Feingold juggernaut.

Ranging from the American Civil Liberties Union and the National Education Association on the left to the Christian Coalition, the National Right-to-Life Committee, and the National Rifle Association on the right, the individual members of the coalition agree on little except the need for the freedom to participate in American politics. There is perhaps no better illustration of the Supreme Court's observation in 1937 that freedom of speech "is the matrix, the indispensable condition, of nearly every other form of freedom." These groups understand that the First Amendment is America's greatest political reform.

Where do we go from here? After ten years of fighting and filibustering against assaults on the First Amendment advanced under the guise of "reform," I am heartened by the honest debate in this Congress. In the House of Representatives, John T. Doolittle's bold proposal to repeal government-prescribed contribution limits and the taxpayer-financed system of (illusory) presidential spending limits has more cosponsors than McCain-Feingold's companion bill, the Shays-Mechan speech-rationing scheme. In the Senate, McCain-Feingold's fortunes cling pathetically to the specter that the Government Affairs investigation into the Clinton campaign finance scandal will fuel public pressure for reform.

My goal is to redefine "reform," to move the debate away from arbitrary limits and toward expanded citizen participation, electoral competition, and political discourse. McCain-Feingold is a failed approach to campaign finance that has proved a disaster in the presidential system. McCain-Feingold would paper over the fatal flaws in the presidential spending-limit system and extend the disaster to congressional elections. Experience argues for scuttling it entirely.

The best way to diminish the influence of any particular "special interest" is to dilute its impact through the infusion of new donors contributing more money to campaigns and political parties. Those who get off the sidelines and contribute their own money to the candidates and parties of their choice should be lauded, not demonized. The increased campaign spending of the past few elections should be hailed as evidence of a vibrant democracy, not reviled as a "problem" needing to be cured.

My prescription for reform includes contribution limits adjusted, at the least, for inflation.

The $1,000 individual limit was set in 1974, when a new Ford Mustang cost just $2,700. The political parties should be strengthened, the present constraints on what they can do for their nominees, repealed. These would be steps in the right direction.

# Representative Democracy versus Corporate Democracy: How Soft Money Erodes the Principle of "One Person, One Vote"

Russell D. Feingold

This selection first appeared in the *Harvard Journal on Legislation* 35, no. 2 (summer 1988): 377–86. In this article Senator Feingold (D-Wisc.) explains the concern with soft money that motivates the legislation he and Senator John McCain (R-Ariz.) coauthored. The McCain-Feingold bill is not the only bill (in fact, there are many) introduced that would further restrict contributions and expenditures in federal elections, but it has been the major vehicle for debate and amendment.

**A**merica's electoral process is rooted in the principle of "one person, one vote," but that principle is drowning in a flood of unlimited political campaign contributions that are, through their ability to secure privileged access to lawmakers, undermining the integrity of both our elections and the legislative process.[1]

As candidates and parties battle to win elections, they are forced to raise ever-greater sums of money.[2] The current campaign finance system

---

1. The concept of "one person, one vote" has been exhaustively examined both in case law and in scholarly articles. Many commentators trace the phrase to Justice William Douglas's majority opinion in *Gray v. Sanders*. See 372 U.S. 368, 381 (1963) ("The conception of political equality from the Declaration of Independence, to Lincoln's Gettysburg Address, to the Fifteenth, Seventeenth, and Nineteenth Amendments can mean only one thing—one person, one vote.").

2. Congressional candidates raised a total of $790.5 million in the 1996 election cycle, a 20 percent increase from the $659.3 million raised in 1992. See Federal Election Commission, *Congressional Fundraising and Spending Up Again in 1996*, April 4, 1997 (visited Apr. 27, 1998) ⟨http://www.fec.gov/press/canye96.htm⟩. The Democratic and Republican parties raised $638.1 million combined in the 1996 election cycle, increasing party fundraising 43 percent from their total of $445 million in the 1992 cycle. See Federal Election Commission, *FEC Reports Major Increase in Party Activity for 1995–96*, Mar. 19, 1997 (visited Apr. 27, 1998) ⟨http://www.fec.gov/press/plyye1.htm⟩.

has taken on the dynamic of the Cold War arms race, with both sides unwilling to relinquish real or perceived political advantages that come from spending more and more money, particularly on negative campaign advertising. The course that both parties so zealously pursue poses a serious threat to the integrity of our democratic process.

That threat is the transformation of our representative democracy into what I call a corporate democracy, in which the "one person, one vote" principle is supplanted by a system that allocates influence over the political process in proportion to the amount of money an individual or group puts into that process.

In this essay, I will describe the insidious role that so-called "soft money" is playing in the transformation of our representative democracy into a corporate democracy and explain how the campaign finance reform legislation I have introduced with Senator John McCain (R-Ariz.), the McCain-Feingold bill,[3] would end the pernicious influence of soft money. I will also address the argument that a ban on soft money violates the Constitution.

## CORPORATE DEMOCRACY AND SOFT MONEY

I learned about the difference between representative and corporate democracy at an early age. When I was thirteen years old, a relative gave me a gift of one share of stock in the Parker Pen Company, an economic fixture in my hometown of Janesville, Wisconsin. My relative wanted me to learn something about how the stock market worked. My one share was probably worth about $13 then, but my father told me that because I owned a share of stock, I owned a small piece of the company. Therefore, I was entitled to a vote at the company stockholders' meeting.

By that age, I was already excited about the political process, and I thought voting at a shareholders' meeting was like voting in an election. I was anxious to exercise my new power so I asked my father when I could go to the shareholders' meeting to vote.

---

3. See *infra* note 17.

My father explained that I could go to the meeting but my vote would not count for much, because the number of votes you get at a shareholders' meeting depends on how many shares you have. Needless to say, my enthusiasm was somewhat dampened, but I quickly came to understand how power in a corporation is apportioned according to the size of the stake held in that corporation by various investors.[4]

This makes sense in the corporate world because those who have invested the most should have the most say about a corporation's direction. But the model of power in a corporation is antithetical to the democratic process of electing representative lawmakers and, by extension, making public policy. I am deeply disturbed that our representative democracy, while still existing in theory, has been transformed in practice to the corporate model.

Soft money contributions, which can run into the hundreds of thousands of dollars from one donor alone, are the main engine behind this transformation. Soft money is a popular umbrella term describing contributions to political parties from sources that are otherwise prohibited from making contributions in connection with federal elections, such as corporations and labor unions, or by wealthy individuals in amounts greater than the limits allowed by federal law.[5] Because they

---

4. Shareholders in a corporation usually vote *pro rata*, rather than *pro capita*. See, e.g., *Davis v. American Telephone and Telegraph Co.*, 478 F.2d 1375 (2d Cit 1973):
> Even assuming that appellee's public character is sufficient to subject it to Fourteenth Amendment requirements, certainly it does not exercise "normal governmental" authority, and its actions, to the extent they affect stockholders qua stockholders, affecting each stockholder in proportion to the number of shares he owns. . . . Therefore, the strict equal protection standard implicit in the phrase "one man, one vote" does not apply.

5. Corporations and unions are prohibited from making contributions or expenditures "in connection with any election to any political office:" 2 U.S.C. § 441b(a) (1994). Corporations have been barred from making such contributions since the passage of the Tillman Act of 1907, ch. 420, 34 Stat. 846. Labor unions have been similarly barred since 1943, when Congress passed the Smith-Connally Act as part of the War Labor Disputes Act, ch. 144, 57 Stat. 163 (1943). Individuals have been limited to contributing $1,000 to candidates and $20,000 per year to national political parties since passage of amendments to the Federal Election Campaign Act in 1974. See 2 U.S.C. § 441 a(1) (1994). Because it is not subject to

are unlimited, soft money donations have the largest potential to tilt the electoral playing field away from ordinary Americans in favor of very wealthy individuals and organizations.[6]

Soft money was not created by federal law but by the evolution of party fund-raising strategies in response to Federal Election Commission advisory opinions.[7] Originally, soft money was only used for party-building activities such as get-out-the-vote campaigns and voter registration drives. But in the last election cycle, the parties paid for much of their tens of millions of dollars of television advertising supporting candidates with soft money.[8] The soft money channel, deeper than a well and far wider than a church door, has allowed millions upon millions of dollars that would have otherwise been barred by federal law to pour into our political system. And, just as floodwaters can wash away everything in their path, so has the flood of soft money overwhelmed our political process.

It has been widely publicized, for example, that during the 1995–1996 election cycle, the Republican and Democratic parties raised more

---

the restrictions of federal law, soft money is sometimes referred to by the Federal Election Commission as "non-federal money."

6. Philip Morris Companies, Inc., including its executives and subsidiaries, donated slightly more than $1.4 million to the Republican and Democratic parties between January 7, 1997 and December 31, 1997, making it the largest soft money donor last year. See Common Cause, *Party Favors: An Analysis of More Than $67 Million in Soft Money Given to Democratic and Republican National Party Committees in 1997* (Feb. 1997) (visited Apr. 27, 1998) ⟨http://www.commoncause.org/publications/partyfavors6.htm⟩. It also was the biggest soft money contributor in the 1996 cycle, giving over $3 million to the political parties. See Center for Responsive Politics, *1995–96 Soft Money Update* (visited Apr. 27. 1998) ⟨http://www.crp.org/btl/top10soft.htm⟩. The top 10 soft money contributors for 1997 gave over $337,000 each. See Common Cause, *supra.*

7. For a good description of the development of the soft money loophole, see *Campaign Finance Reform: A Sourcebook*, 168–73 (Anthony Corrado et al., ed., 1997). FEC Advisory Opinion 197810 may have opened the soft money door. That opinion, responding to inquiries from Kansas State Republican Party, states: "It is also the Commission's view that with respect to an election in which there are candidates for Federal office, expenditures for registration and get-out-the-vote drives need not be attributed as contributions to such candidates unless the drives are made specifically on their behalf." See *id.* at 191.

8. See *id.* at 175.

than $263 million in soft money, more than a threefold increase over the previous presidential election cycle, 1991–1992.[9]

Despite almost continuous news reporting of fund-raising scandals and several congressional investigations into allegations of illegal fund-raising, and despite the growing public outrage surrounding political fund-raising, the soft money chase continues apace. In fact, the pace is picking up. During calendar year 1997, the FEC reports, the Democratic and Republican parties raised a total of more than $67 million in soft money. This was $8 million more than the parties raised in 1995 and more than double the amount raised in 1993, the analogous year in the previous presidential election cycle.[10]

I believe this huge amount of unregulated money represents a threat to the stability and integrity of our representative political system. That is why soft money should be banned.

I am convinced that large campaign contributions are frequently made with at least the expectation of some kind of benefit returning to the contributor. Consider the results of a *Business Week*/Harris poll, which surveyed 400 senior executives from large public corporations, asking questions regarding their opinions on campaign finance and how best to reform the current system.[11] Half the respondents claimed that securing access to lawmakers "to gain fair consideration on issues affecting our business" constituted the major reason for making political contributions—and an additional 27 percent acknowledged that seeking access was at least part of the reason for making contributions. Fifty-eight percent said fear of losing influence to labor or environmental organizations or being placed in a competitive disadvantage to a rival was at least one reason, if not the major reason, for making contributions. Forty-one percent acknowledged that at least part of the reason

9. See Federal Election Commission, *Political Parties' Fundraising Hits $881 Million*, Jan. 10, 1997, available in LEXIS, CMPGN/ELCT 96 Library.

10. See Common Cause, *supra* note 6.

11. See Amy Bonus and Mary Beth Regan, *The Backlash Against Soft Money*, Bus. Wk., Mar. 31, 1997, at 34.

they made political contributions was the hope of receiving "preferential consideration on regulations or legislation benefiting our business."[12] Potential loss of access to lawmakers and other policy professionals was clearly a concern for the respondents.

Some lawmakers have learned to play on this expectation. On one hand, they extend the offer of special access, as one fund-raising letter, sent out over the signature of Senator Mitch McConnell (R-Ky.), chairman of the National Republican Senatorial Committee, did last year. Senator McConnell promised "the rewards of leadership, friendship, effectiveness and *exclusivity*" to contributors in exchange for a $5,000 contribution that would secure membership in a group called the Presidential Roundtable.[13] On the other hand, lawmakers can make it clear to the representatives of various special interests that their chances of being heard when they drop by to discuss legislation may have a direct relationship to their ability to raise and contribute money to their legislators. In 1995, for example, the *Washington Post* reported that House Majority Whip Tom DeLay of Texas maintained a ledger listing amounts and percentages of money that the 400 largest political action committees contributed to Republicans and Democrats during the previous two years.[14] Large contributors to Republicans were labeled "Friendly," the others "Unfriendly."[15] The *Post* story then recounted a meeting between DeLay and an unnamed corporate lobbyist:

"See, you're in the book," DeLay said to his visitor, leafing through the

---

12. *Id.* at 36. Sixty-eight percent of the business executives polled agreed with the statement, "the system is broken and is in need of fundamental reform." *Id.* When the Harris poll-takers offered a list of possible reforms, 68 percent of the respondents recommended ending unlimited "soft money" contributions. *Id.*

13. Letter from Sen. Mitch McConnell, Chairman of the Nat'l Republican Senatorial Comm. at 4 (Aug. 30, 1997) (emphasis added) (on file with author).

14. See David Maraniss and Michael Weisskopf, *Speaker and His Directors Make the Cash Flow Right*, Wash. Post, Nov. 27, 1995, at A1. This is one of many press reports on the nexus between contributions and political influence. See, e.g., Leslie Wayne, *A Special Deal for Lobbyists: A Getaway with Lawmakers*, N.Y. Times, Jan. 26, 1997, at 1.

15. See Maraniss and Weisskopf, *supra*, note 14, at A1.

list. At first the lobbyist was not sure where his group stood, but DeLay helped clear up his confusion. By the time the lobbyist left the congressman's office, he knew that, to be a friend of the Republican leadership his group would have to give the party a lot more money.[16]

Anecdotes like this illustrate the transformation that is so deeply disturbing to me. With our representative democracy becoming a corporate democracy, the amount of money one can put into the electoral process determines the "voice" one has in the legislative process. This transformation raises fundamental issues about how our democracy is supposed to work, and who it is supposed to serve. In a representative democracy, elected officials are accountable to all people equally, but in a corporate democracy, they become the servants of those who give the most money. Those who have greater wealth can purchase a greater voice in determining the outcome of the public policy debates, for large campaign contributions easily translate into special access to lawmakers.

THE MCCAIN-FEINGOLD BILL:
A FIRST STEP TOWARD RECLAIMING OUR DEMOCRACY

For more than two years, I have worked closely with Senator McCain and several other Senate colleagues on a bipartisan, comprehensive campaign finance reform proposal, which has come to be known as the McCain-Feingold bill.[17] This legislation, which is now supported by a majority of the United States Senate, would take an important first step toward reversing the transformation of our political system to a corporate democracy.

16. *Id.*
17. The first campaign finance legislation that Senator McCain and I introduced died in a filibuster in June 1996. See Senate Campaign Finance Reform Act of 1996, S. 1219, 104th Cong. (1996). We reintroduced the legislation as Senate Bill 25 on January 21, 1997. See Bipartisan Campaign Reform Act of 1997, S. 25, 105th Cong. (1997). A modified version, introduced on September 25, 1997, was considered on the floor of the Senate in September and October 1997, and again in late February of this year.

The centerpiece of the bill is a ban on soft money.[18] It would require all contributions to the national political parties to comply with the restrictions on hard money contributions in current federal election law.[19] In addition, it would bar federal officeholders and candidates for those offices from soliciting, receiving, or spending soft money.[20] Further, to prevent the loophole from simply migrating from national to state party fund-raising, McCain-Feingold would prohibit state and local political parties from spending soft money on any activity that might affect a federal election.[21] It would also prohibit the political parties from fund-raising for, or transferring money to, nonprofit organizations.[22]

18. As amended on the floor in February 1998, the bill contains a number of other important reforms, including restrictions on corporate and union spending on campaign advertisements close to an election, a requirement for disclosure of funding sources for campaign advertisements by outside groups, incentives for candidates to curb the amount of personal wealth they contribute to their campaigns, a ban on fund-raising on federal property, and various provisions designed to improve FEC disclosure and enforcement. See Bipartisan Campaign Reform Act of 1997, S. 25, 105th Cong. (1997).

The September 29, 1997 version of the bill was introduced during the February 1998 campaign finance reform debate as an amendment to S. 1663, the Paycheck Protection Act, introduced by the Majority Leader, Sen. Trent Lott (R-Miss.). See 144 Cong. Rec. S933-38 (daily ed. Feb. 24, 1998). Subsequently, the Senate adopted an amendment proposed by Sen. Olympia Snowe (R-Me.). That amendment replaced § 201 of McCain-Feingold with provisions that define and regulate "electioneering communications," a term referring to radio and television advertisements clearly identifying a candidate for federal office that are made within 60 days before a general election or within 30 days of a primary election, and that are broadcast to an audience that includes the electorate for that election. See *id.* at S938-39.

19. See *id.* at S933-34. Section 101 creates a new section, § 324, of the Federal Election Campaign Act. The requirement that national party committees raise only hard money is contained in § 324(a)(1). See *id.* at S933. The requirement applies to all entities controlled or maintained by the political party committee and its officers and agents. See *id.*

20. See *id.* at S933-34.

21. See *id.* at S933. During the 1996 elections, both political parties frequently transferred soft money to state committees, which under current FEC regulations are permitted to fund a larger percentage of their activities with soft money. See, e.g., Kevin McDermott, 'Soft' Money Sent Through Illinois, St. Louis Post-Dispatch, Oct. 6, 1997, at B1; Jill Abramson and Leslie Wayne, *Democrats Used the State Parties To Bypass Limits*, N.Y. Times, Oct. 2, 1997, at A1.

22. See 144 Cong. Rec. S933-34 (daily ed. Feb. 24, 1998). The most notorious of such

These provisions would bring some sanity back to the federal election laws by closing the most prominent loophole in the system today. Few opponents of reform defend soft money, but some do argue that the ban would run afoul of the Supreme Court's 1976 decision in *Buckley v. Valeo*, the landmark U.S. Supreme Court decision striking down certain parts of the post-Watergate amendments to the Federal Election Campaign Act.[23]

Campaign finance reform bills often raise difficult questions of constitutional law. Whether Congress has the power to ban soft money, however, is not one of them. Last September, 126 constitutional scholars co-signed a letter from the Brennan Center for Justice at the New York University School of Law stating that the soft money ban contained in the McCain-Feingold bill will pass constitutional muster.[24]

In *Buckley v. Valeo*, the Supreme Court held that individual contributions can be limited—the current federal limit, which the Court upheld, is $1,000 per election from an individual to a candidate.[25] The Court found that restrictions on the source and size of contributions to candidates are permissible in order to protect our electoral system from corruption or the appearance of corruption. The Court concluded that unrestricted contributions could undermine the integrity of our elections and our democracy.[26]

---

transfers in the 1996 campaign was the Republican Party's gift of $4.6 million to Americans for Tax Reform to pay for direct mail and phone bank activities in the last weeks before the election. See, e.g., Charles Babcock, *Anti-Tax Group Got Big Boost from RNC as Election Neared*, Wash. Post, Dec. 10, 1996, at A4.

23. 424 U.S. I (1976) (per curiam).

24. Letter from the Brennan Ctr. for Justice to Sens. John McCain and Russell Feingold (Sept. 22, 1997) (reprinted in *Cong. Rec.* at S10104 (daily ed. Sept. 29, 1997)) (hereinafter "Brennan Center Letter").

25. See 424 U.S. at 23–35; 2 U.S.C. § 441a (a)(1)(A) (1994).

26. See 424 U.S. at 26–27. The Court noted:

To the extent that large contributions are given to secure a political *quid pro quo* from current and potential office holders, the integrity of our system of representative democracy is undermined. Although the scope of such pernicious practices can never be reliably ascertained, the deeply disturbing examples surfacing after

This is exactly what is happening with soft money. In recent years, both political parties have collected soft money contributions and used them to benefit federal candidates.[27] The McCain-Feingold bill would enforce the law's current restrictions on the size and sources of contributions that the parties can accept. The suggestion that closing the soft money loophole that currently allows prohibited money to make its way back into the system violates a constitutional right is simply wrong.

As the 126 constitutional scholars stated in their letter:

> [S]oft money has become an end run around the campaign contribution limits, creating a corrupt system in which monied interests appear to buy access to, and inappropriate influence with, elected officials. . . . The soft money loophole has raised the specter of corruption stemming from large contributions (and those from prohibited sources) that led Congress to enact the federal contribution limits in the first place. . . . [C]losing the loophole for soft money contributions is in line with the longstanding and constitutional ban on corporate and union contributions in federal elections and with limits on the size of individuals' contributions to amounts that are not corrupting.[28]

The current campaign finance system is corrupting our democratic

---

the 1972 election demonstrate that the problem is not an illusory one. *Id.* at 26–27 (citation omitted). The scandals of the 1996 election, perhaps best symbolized by Roger Tamraz, who gave hundreds of thousands of dollars in soft money to the Democratic National Committee hoping to obtain the Clinton administration's support for an oil pipeline deal, demonstrate that the problem still exists. See David Rosenbaum, *Oilman Says He Paid for Access by Giving Democrats $300,000, N.Y. Times,* Sept. 19. 1997, at A1; Marc Lacey and Robert Jackson, *Financier Says Donations Opened White House Doors, L.A. Times,* Sept. 19, 1997, at A1.

27. The Annenberg Public Policy Center estimates that the Democratic National Committee spent $44 million and the Republican National Committee $24 million on so-called issue ads supporting President Clinton and Bob Dole in the last election. A significant portion of these expenditures came from the parties' soft money funds. See Deborah Beck et al., Annenberg Public Policy Ctr., *Issue Advocacy Advertising During the 1996 Campaign* 34, 55 (visited Apr. 27, 1998) ⟨http://www.asc.upenn.edu/appe/reports/rep16.pdf⟩; see also Abramson and Wayne, *supra* note 21.

28. See Brennan Center Letter, *supra* note 24.

process. Lawmakers solicit contributions by promising special access or threatening to cut off access. The great majority of the American people, unable to make large donations, are angry and frustrated at the belief they are being excluded from their own political system.[29] Voter turnout in the last presidential election hit its lowest level in seventy-two years.[30] We must not ignore these warning signs about the health of our democracy.

CONCLUSION

While it is not the only problem that reformers must address, soft money is the hard core of the current campaign funding scandal. It is imperative that we work to limit the influence of money on the process of making public policy, and banning soft money is the first step.

Unfortunately, even taking this one simple step for reform has not been easy in the United States Senate. In late February, we were unable to muster the necessary sixty votes on the Senate floor to break a

29. Public opinion polls have consistently shown that the public wants reform of the current campaign finance system. For example, in a Gallup/*USA Today*/CNN poll conducted between October 3 and October 5, 1997, 77 percent of the respondents agreed with the statement, "Elected officials [are] influenced mostly by pressure from campaign contributors." Fifty-nine percent agreed with the statement, "Elections [are] for sale to whoever can raise the most money." Fifty-nine percent also said they believed that, no matter how the law reads, special interests will "always find a way to maintain power." Fifty-six percent said the most important goal of campaign finance reform is "protecting government from influence by contributors." See Tom Squiteri, *Thompson Challenges President, Calls on Clinton to 'Step Up to the Plate,'* USA Today, Oct. 8, 1997, at A6.

In a *Los Angeles Times* poll conducted between September 6 and September 9, 1997, 63 percent of the respondents said the campaign finance system needs either "a fundamental overhaul" or "major improvements." Seventy-three percent believed both major political parties were guilty of fund-raising abuses. Seventy-nine percent believed that limiting the role of soft money should be a goal of reform. See Jonathan Peterson, *The Times Poll: Clinton Retains High Job Rating: Gore Image Hurt,* L.A. Times, Sept. 12, 1997, at A1.

30. See Curtis Gans, *Voter Malaise Hobbles the Nation,* Newsday, Nov. 11, 1996, at A33 (reporting the Committee for the Study of the American Electorate's finding that voter turnout dropped in the 1996 elections to 48.8 percent of eligible voters). See generally Federal Election Commission, *About Elections and Voting* (visited Apr. 14, 1998) ⟨http://www.fec.gov/pages/electpg.htm⟩ (indexing FEC voter turnout information).

threatened filibuster, so, despite having majority support, McCain-Feingold did not pass.[31] But a minority cannot prevail indefinitely. In the end, the American people will decide if they want a representative democracy or a corporate democracy, and the Congress will heed their wish. I am confident they will choose the right course.

31. A motion to invoke cloture and end debate on McCain-Feingold, which required 60 "aye" votes, failed by a margin of 51–48. See 144 *Cong. Rec.* S1045 (daily ed. Feb 26, 1998).

# Index